POSTCARD HISTORY SERIES

Conshohocken in Vintage Postcards

This book is dedicated to our parents, Dorothy Welsh,
John Welsh, and Anthony and Marie DeSantis;
our siblings, Jack Welsh, Kathy and Michael Taggart,
Janet Leflar, Doreen DeSantis, Deborah and Kenneth Gavin,
Anthony DeSantis, and Mark and Tina DeSantis;
and our nephews and nieces, Scott Leflar, Jim Taggart,
Kenneth, Christopher, Alex, and Kelsey Gavin, and
Mark, Anthony, Dominic, and Angela DeSantis.

POSTCARD HISTORY SERIES

Conshohocken

IN VINTAGE POSTCARDS

Phillip and Sharon Welsh

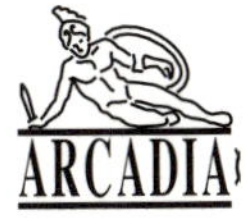

ISBN 0-7385-0987-6

First printed in 2002.

Published by Arcadia Publishing,
an imprint of Tempus Publishing, Inc.
2A Cumberland Street
Charleston, SC 29401

Printed in Great Britain.

Library of Congress Catalog Card Number: 2001098516

For all general information contact Arcadia Publishing at:
Telephone 843-853-2070
Fax 843-853-0044
E-Mail sales@arcadiapublishing.com

For customer service and orders:
Toll-Free 1-888-313-2665

Visit us on the internet at http://www.arcadiapublishing.com

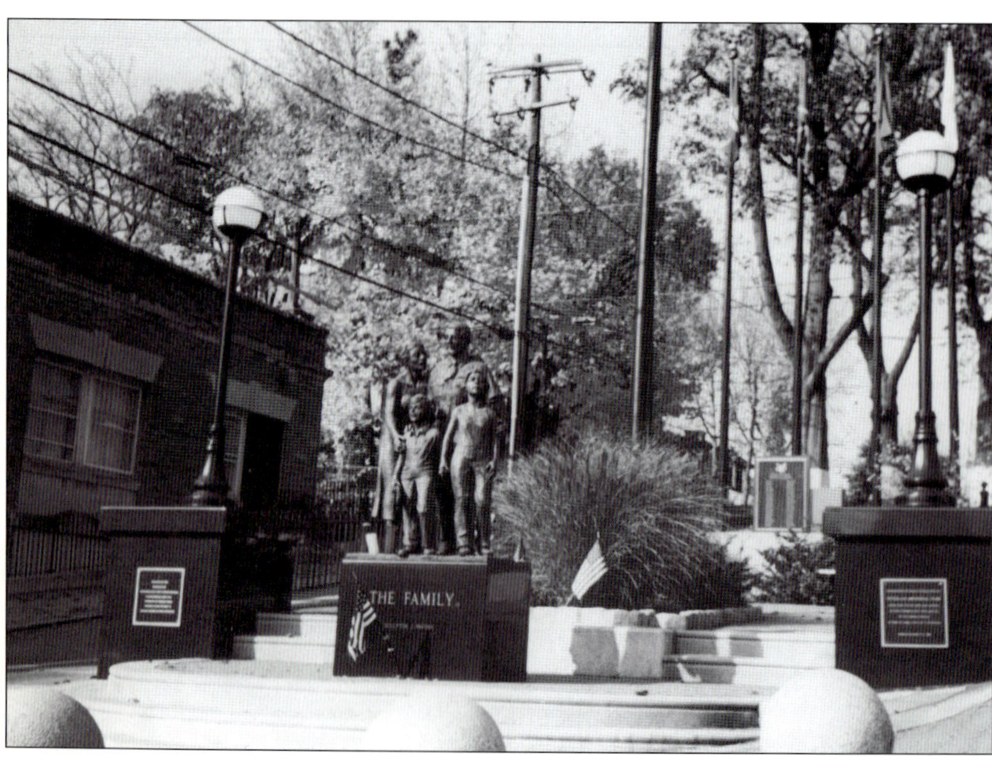

Conshohocken is a close-knit community that has sacrificed many sons and daughters over the years to defend the freedom of this country. This is a view of Monument Square on Second Avenue and Fayette Street. The monument pays tribute to the courage and honor of our veterans and the love and strength of our families.

Contents

Acknowledgments 6

Bibliography 6

Introduction 7

1. Bird's-Eye Views 9

2. Railways and Waterways 15

3. Fayette Street and the Avenues 27

4. Historic Landmarks 41

5. Business and Industry 51

6. Bravely Serving the Community 69

7. On the Field 81

8. Bubbling Springs 89

9. Faith and Wisdom 97

10. General Views 119

Acknowledgments

We are grateful for the assistance, expertise, and photographs from the following: the Conshohocken Historic Society; Joe Collins, president of the Conshohocken Historic Society; Jack Coll, Coll's Custom Framing, Conshohocken; postcard dealers John Klein, Klein Postcards, Adamstown; Gordon McKenzie, York; and Jim Luty, Dillsburg; postcard photographers and publishers American News Company, New York; Art Glo Postcard Company, Philadelphia; Art View Card Distributors, New Jersey; Bill Bennett, Philadelphia and Pennsburg; O.S. Bunnell, Bussa, Norristown; Clearview Studio Inc., Lafayette Hill; Colorcraft Studio, New York; Color Picture Publishers, Massachusetts and Connecticut; Art Colortone Postcard; Custom Studios, New Jersey; Gillam Photographer, Norristown; Graham & Johnson, Conshohocken; McCoy's Drug Store, Conshohocken; Mercantile Studio, Philadelphia; E. Moebius Photographtype, New Jersey; W.M. Neville; Picto-Cards; Kaeser & Blair Inc., Ohio; Postcard Distribution Company; P.S.C. Company; Recorder Publishing Company, Conshohocken; Roberts Company, Wayland, Massachusetts; Rotograph Company, New York; Phillip Sander, Philadelphia; William H. Sliker, Philadelphia; Tuck's PostCard, New York; World Post Card Company, Philadelphia; Wyco Products, Jenkintown; and D.M. Yost & Company, Norristown.

Bibliography

Alderfer, Gordon E. *The Montgomery County Story*. Norristown, Pennsylvania: Commissioner of Montgomery County, 1951.

Bean. *History of Montgomery County*. Vols. I–II. 1884.

Borough of Conshohocken. *Conshohocken Comprehensive Plan*. Conshohocken, Pennsylvania: 1964.

Collins, W.F. *Bicentennial Conshohocken: March to Valley Forge*. Conshohocken Bicentennial Committee, 1976.

Conshohocken Historical Society. *Conshohocken Historical Survey*. 1989.

Conshohocken Sesquicentennial Committee. *Vintage Scenes of Conshohocken, PA*. 1997, 1998, 1999, and 2000.

Historical Society of Montgomery County. *Historical Sketches*. Vols. I–V. Norristown, Pennsylvania: Herald Printing and Binding.

Kriebel, H.W. *A Brief History of Montgomery County Pennsylvania*. Norristown, Pennsylvania: Norristown Herald Printing and Publishing Company, 1923.

Smith, J.L. *Property Atlas of Montgomery County Pennsylvania*. Philadelphia, 1893.

Toll, Jean Barth, and Michael J. Schwager, eds. *Montgomery County: The Second Hundred Years*. Vols. I–II. Montgomery County Federation of Historical Societies, 1983.

INTRODUCTION

Conshohocken is a thriving suburb in Montgomery County, Pennsylvania, measuring approximately one square mile on the east bank of the Schuylkill River, 13 miles northwest of Philadelphia. "Conshy," as it is known to residents, was incorporated in 1850, but its colorful history had its beginnings as Native American territory until 1684, when William Penn purchased the land from Tammany, chief of the Lenni Lenape Nation.

Conshohocken's ideal location along the Schuylkill River near a newly constructed canal and railway system provided the transportation and power resources necessary for it to prosper. An abundance of local iron ore, marble, and limestone, along with the proximity of commercial markets in Philadelphia, provided the natural elements for the growth of industry.

With the establishment of the first mills in the area, Conshohocken was transformed from a pioneer settlement to a booming industrial community. The growth of local industry brought together wealthy Quaker entrepreneurs and immigrant laborers from Ireland, Poland, Italy, and other European countries. This wealth and diversity shaped the commercial, residential, civic, and religious community.

Over the last 150 years, Conshohocken has evolved dramatically. There are now large professional office buildings where rolling hills and textile mills once stood along Washington Street. The elaborate train stations are gone, and the lower Fayette Street commercial area below First Avenue has been demolished to make way for parking lots and more professional buildings. Along the upper avenues of Fayette Street, mansions and grand homes that belonged to Conshohocken's industrialists were replaced by gas stations, convenience stores, banks, and the post office.

This book brings to life some of the town's colorful characters and history with pictorial postcard views of Conshohocken from the early 20th century to today. Before the telephone, radio, television, and computer, postcards were a major means of communication. Pictorial views of small towns were very popular, for keeping in touch with family and friends and documenting special occasions. There are more than 30 postcard photographers and publishers that produced views of the Conshohocken area, but the most prolific detailed images of the town were done by William H. Sliker of Philadelphia and Graham and Johnson of Conshohocken. These photographers and publishers captured and portrayed the beauty of Conshohocken in its heyday on vivid postcards for generations to enjoy. Without their efforts, this book and our collection would not have been possible.

It has taken more than 12 years to collect the postcards that are reproduced in this book. The purpose of this book is to share our passion for the collection and our hometown with others. We hope that you enjoy our collection as much as we do. The citizens of Conshohocken are proud of their heritage—of the shared past that has brought them together and gives their community identity and purpose. In fact, many families have lived here for several generations; the great-grandchildren of Conshohocken's founding father still live here today.

One
Bird's-Eye Views

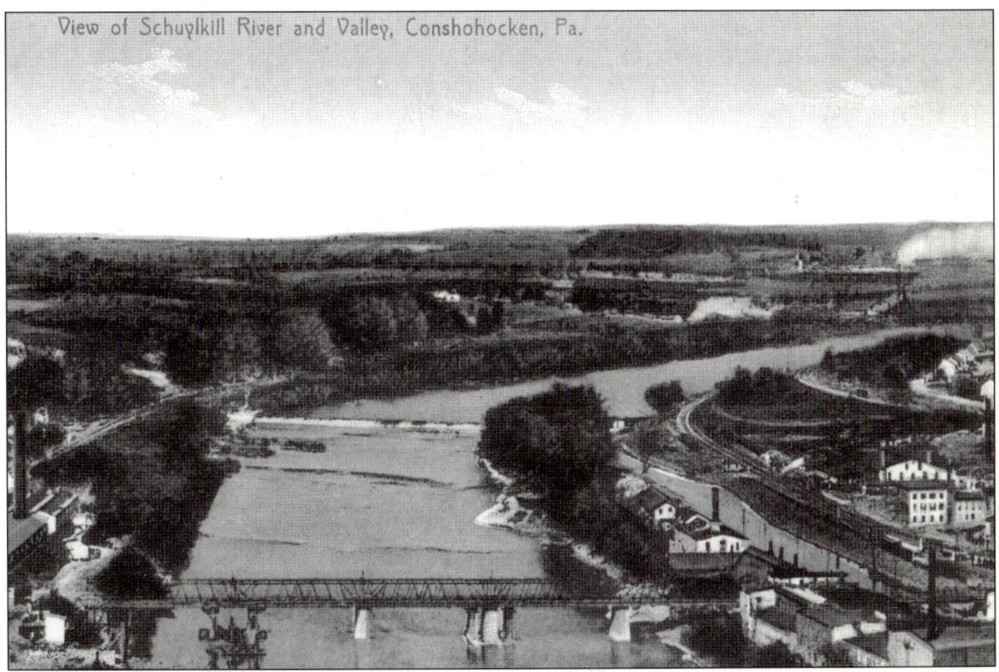

Conshohocken borders the east bank of the Schuylkill River about 13 miles northwest of Philadelphia. In its infancy, Conshohocken's ideal location near a newly constructed Schuylkill canal and railroad depot provided the transportation and power resources necessary to grow as an industrial community. The rich abundance of local iron ore, marble, and limestone provided the key elements for those industries.

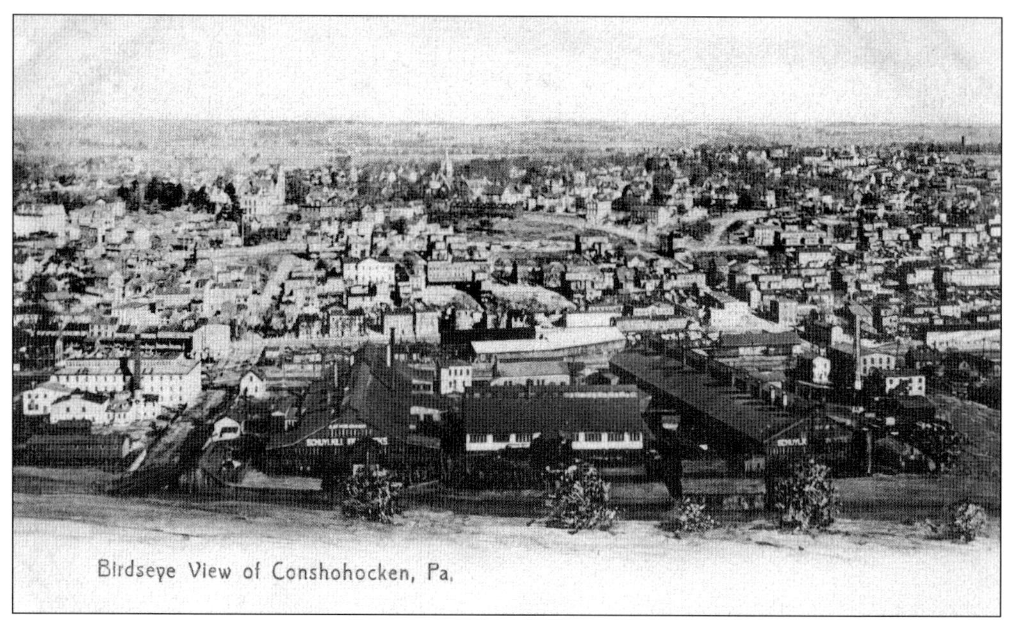

By the time Conshohocken was incorporated in 1850, it was already at the center of the iron industry and was living up to its nickname, Iron-borough. The three major buildings in the front along the canal all make up the Alan Wood Schuylkill Iron Works, owned by Alan Wood and Lewis Lukens. Alan was the son of ironmaster James Wood, who was a founding father of the borough.

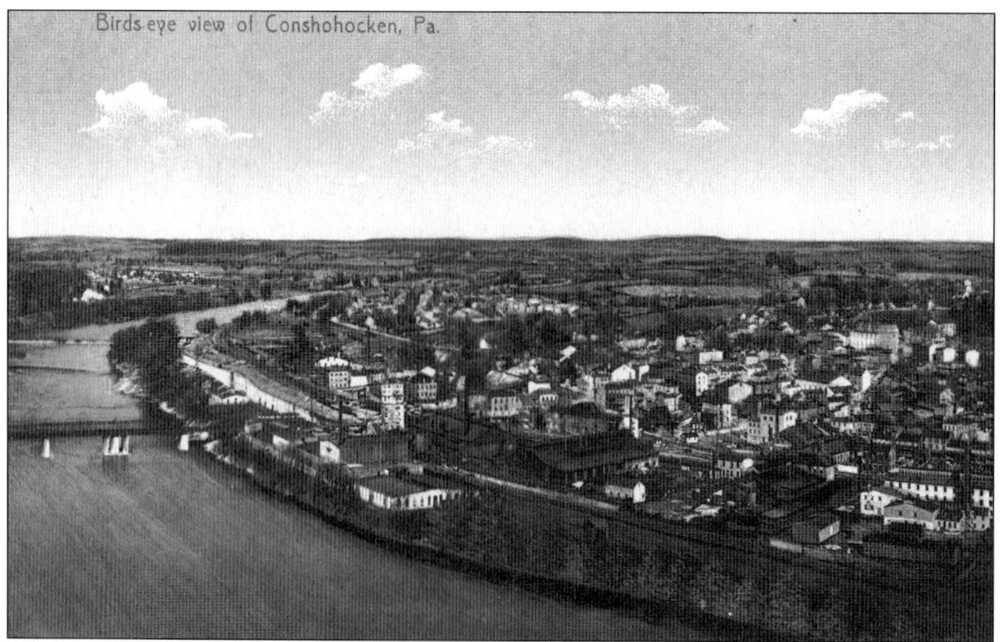

This is a 1906 view of Conshohocken. The buildings near the bridge belonged to Albiun Print Works. Jonas Eberhardt, a West Conshohocken resident, owned the old print works. The property later became the John Wood Manufacturing Company until it was devastated by fire in 1878. Other companies along the river include the S. Lees Cotton Mills, the John Wood Boiler Company, and the Alan Wood Schuylkill Iron Works.

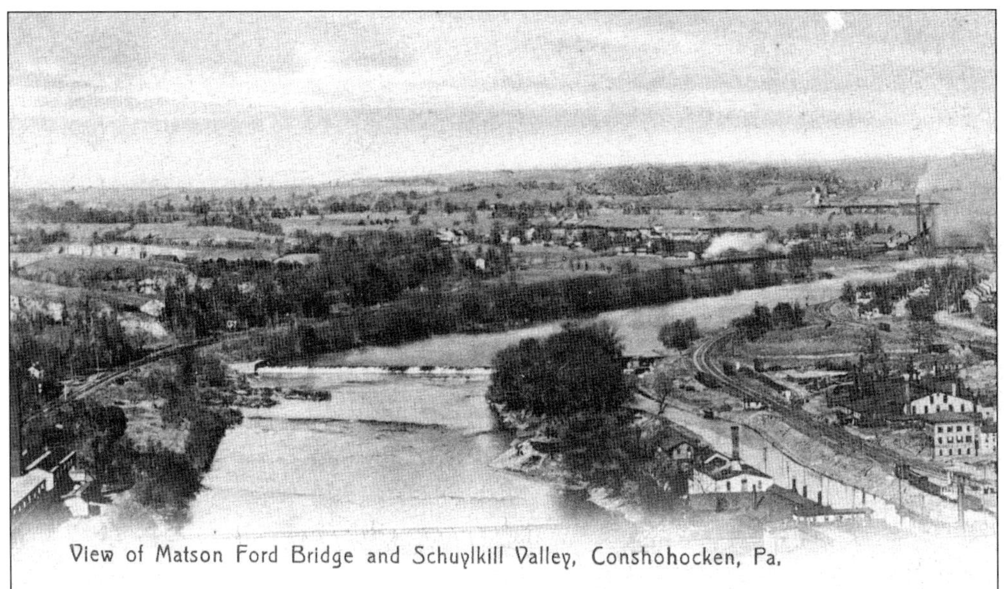

The bridge is not visible in this 1906 view, but the card does portray the natural ford that was used before the bridge. Notice the ripple in the water near the clump of trees on the right. This was Matson's Ford, named after Peter Matson, who owned the land on the south side of the river in 1741. Matson's Ford acquired special historic significance during the Revolutionary War, when General Lafayette led 2,000 troops across it in a dramatic escape from the British on May 19, 1778.

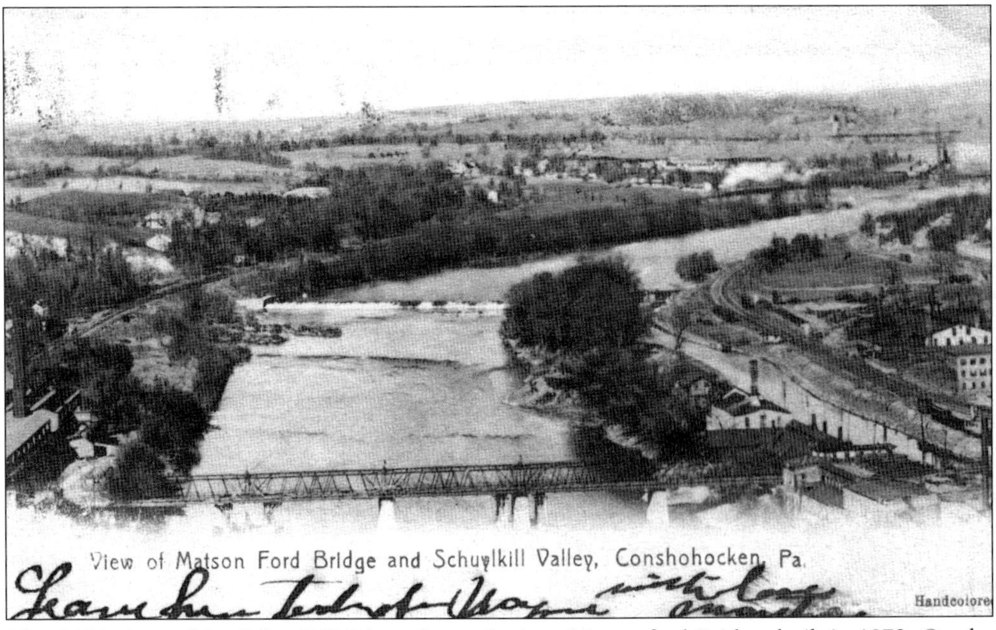

This 1906 view of the Schuylkill River shows the iron Matsonford Bridge, built in 1872. On the West Conshohocken side is the Conshohocken Worsted Mill, once owned by George Bullock. Over the years, several companies occupied this building before its demolition, such as the Merion Worsted Mill and the George W. Hepworth & Company. Even Milton Shapp owned the plant before running for governor. Today, a high-rise office building occupies the area.

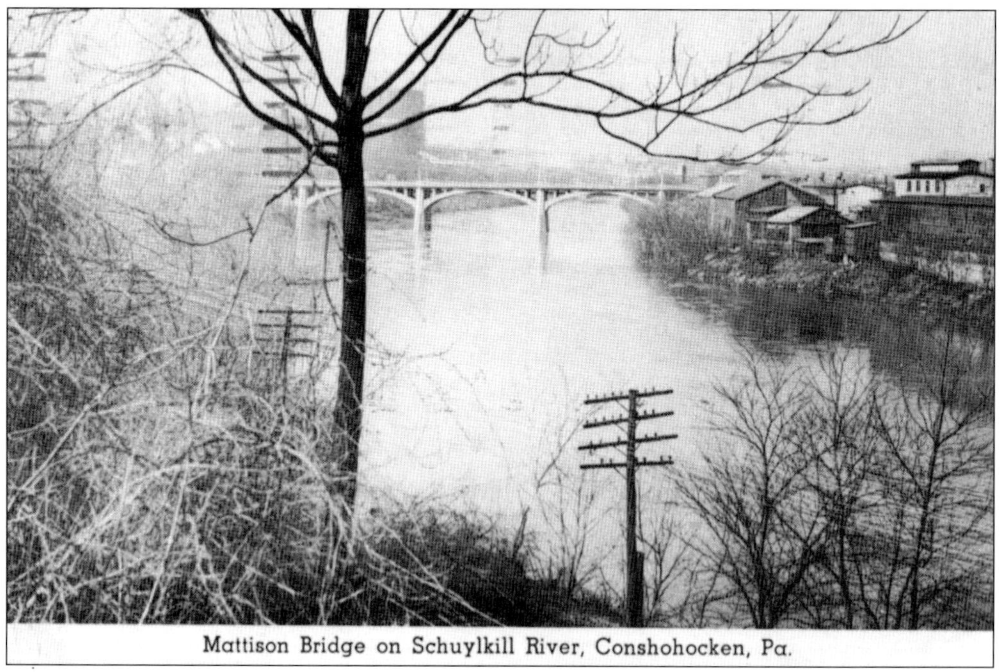
Mattison Bridge on Schuylkill River, Conshohocken, Pa.

The name of the Matsonford Bridge is misspelled on this 1950 postcard, which shows the bridge from the West Conshohocken riverbank. The concrete bridge was built in 1921 and was hailed a modern marvel of its time.

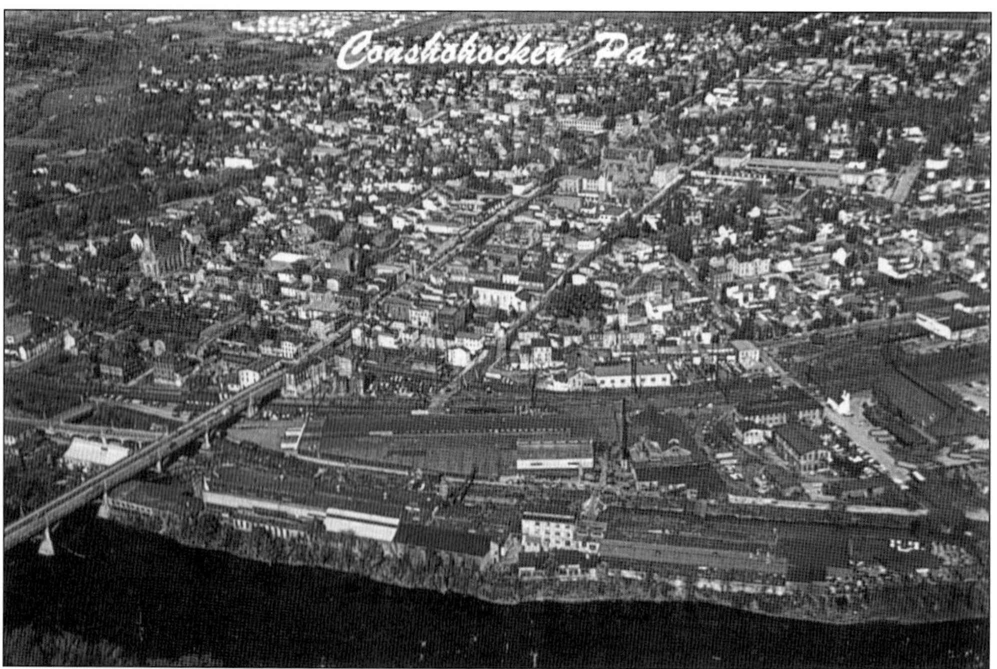

This 1960s view of Conshohocken shows the industrial centers along the river then in operation. Today, the riverfront looks very different, with high-rise office buildings and hotels. This view also shows the lower end of Fayette Street before urban revitalization.

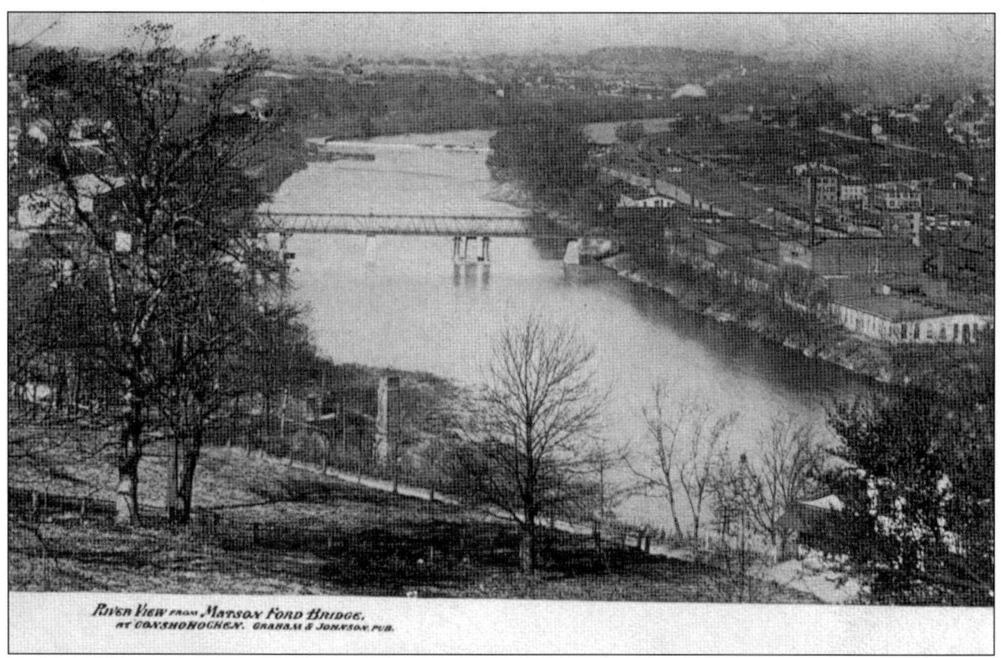

These two 1910 views were taken from the West Conshohocken side of the river. The above view shows the iron Matsonford Bridge and the Old Print Works plant. Below, several homes still exist along the west bank of the river on River Road. Today, only a few homes are left in this area; most were demolished for the Schuylkill Expressway.

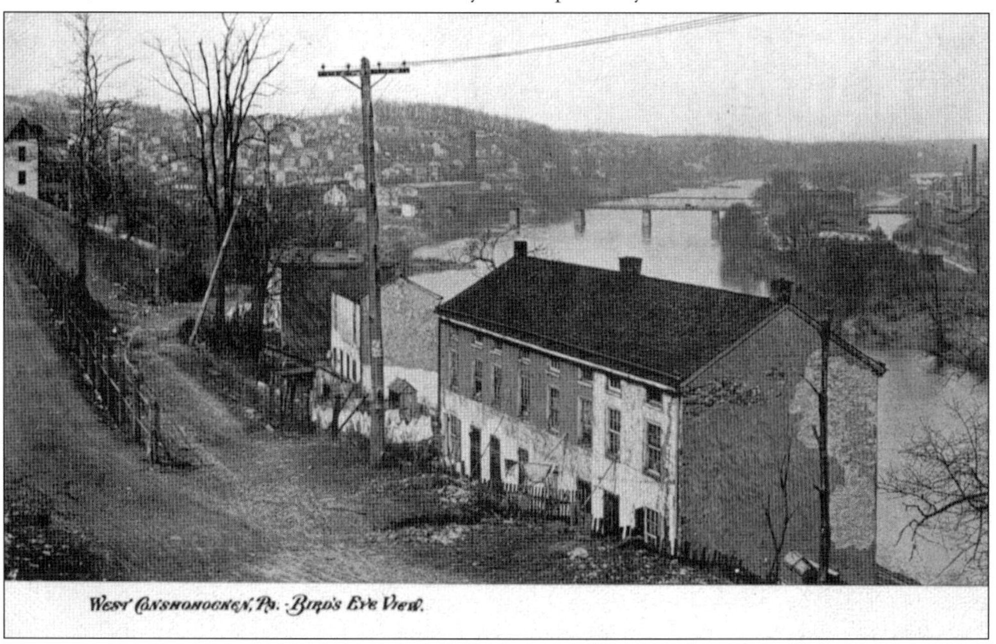

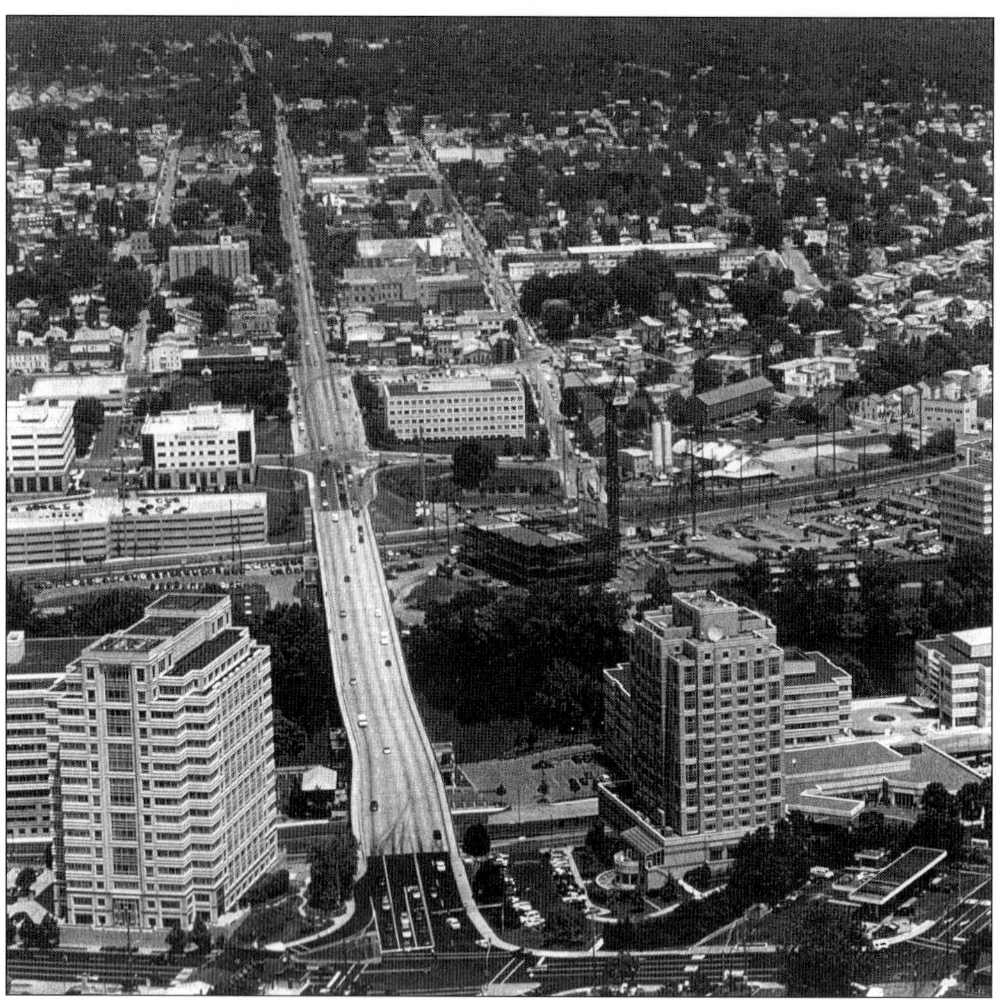

This is Conshohocken today. This generation of the Matsonford Bridge was built in 1987. The professional buildings on either side of the bridge and river foretell the future of Conshohocken. The town has changed from an industrial community to one of professional businesses. In the course of this transition, some historic town landmarks have been sacrificed.

Two
Railways and Waterways

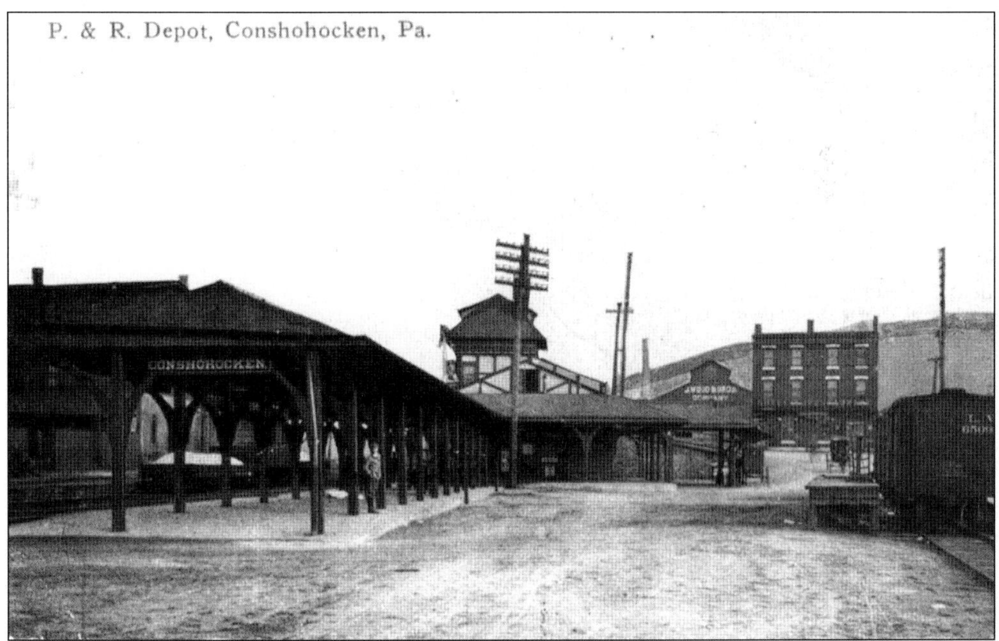

The Philadelphia & Reading Railroad (later the Reading Railroad) opened for business from Norristown to Philadelphia in 1836. One of the stops was Conshohocken. This photograph shows the Conshohocken station on Washington Street. The two buildings in the background are the J. Wood Brothers Company and the Ford Hotel.

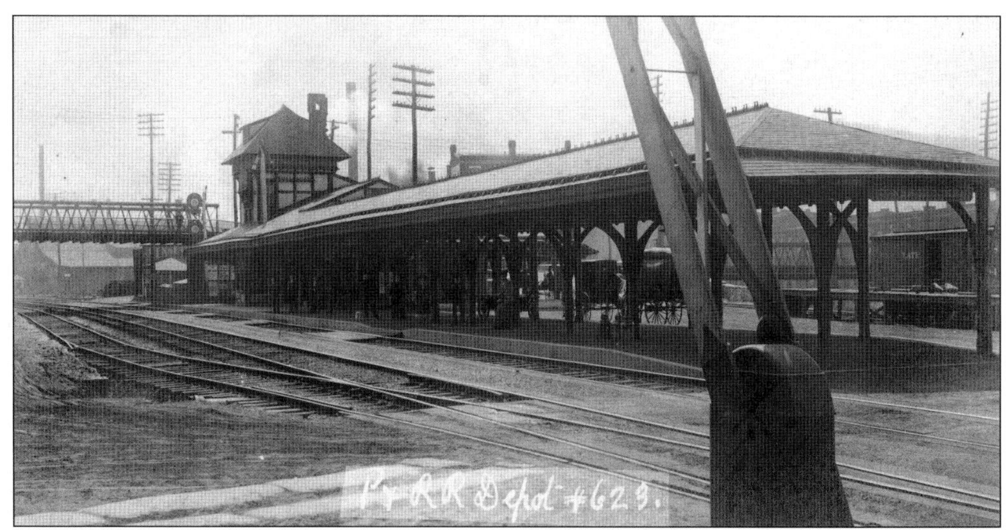

Passengers wait for a train at Conshohocken's Philadelphia & Reading station *c.* 1906. Originally, the rail lines were intended for transport of coal, stone, lumber, and other freight. The addition of passenger cars gave people the freedom to work outside of their hometown, and this freedom stimulated the growth of new towns. Passengers' horse-drawn carriages are parked to the right of the station. To the left is the bridge over the tracks, and someone is standing on the bridge, looking for the train.

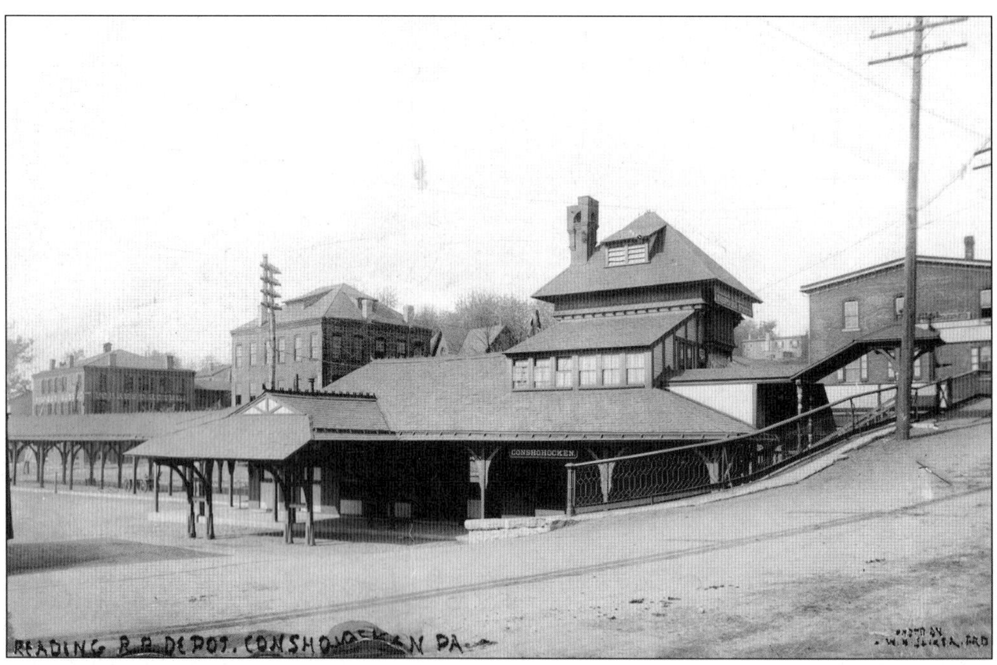

At the beginning of the 20th century, the Pennsylvania and Reading Railroads (each with stations in Conshohocken) made marginal investments in branch lines, luxury trains, and elaborate stations for suburban passenger service. This view of the Reading station in Conshohocken shows an example of one of those elaborate stations. In the background on the far left is the Forrest Hotel.

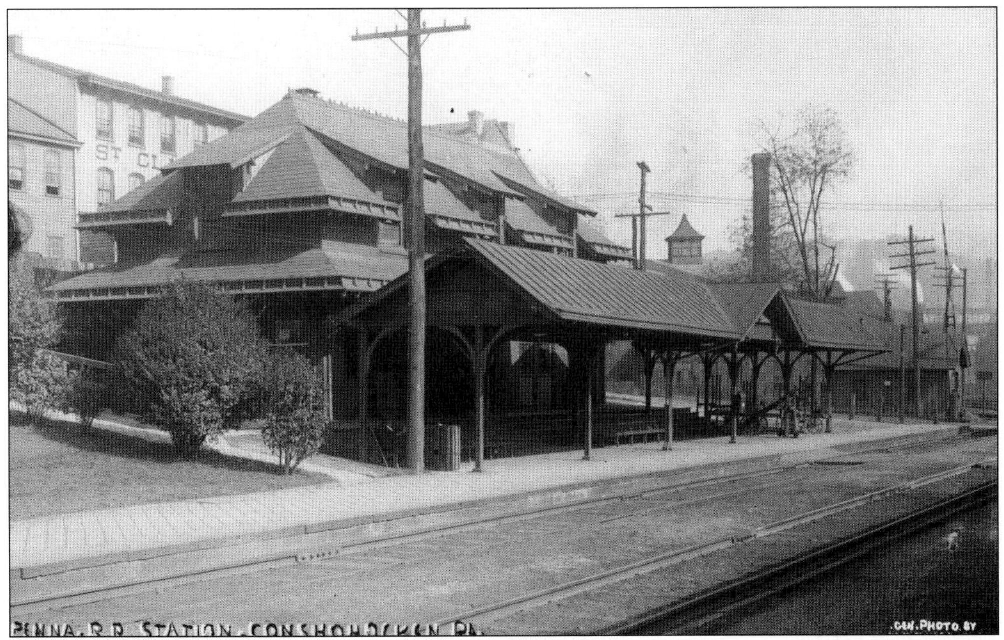

The Pennsylvania Railroad elected to duplicate the Reading's main line in the Schuylkill Valley. By 1884, it had completed a line from West Philadelphia to Norristown with a station in Conshohocken. This 1908 photograph shows the Conshohocken station at the foot of Harry Street on Washington Street. The building behind the station is the St. Clairs Hotel. Today, the train station is an antique store called the Outbound Station, owned by Joseph and Barbara Collins.

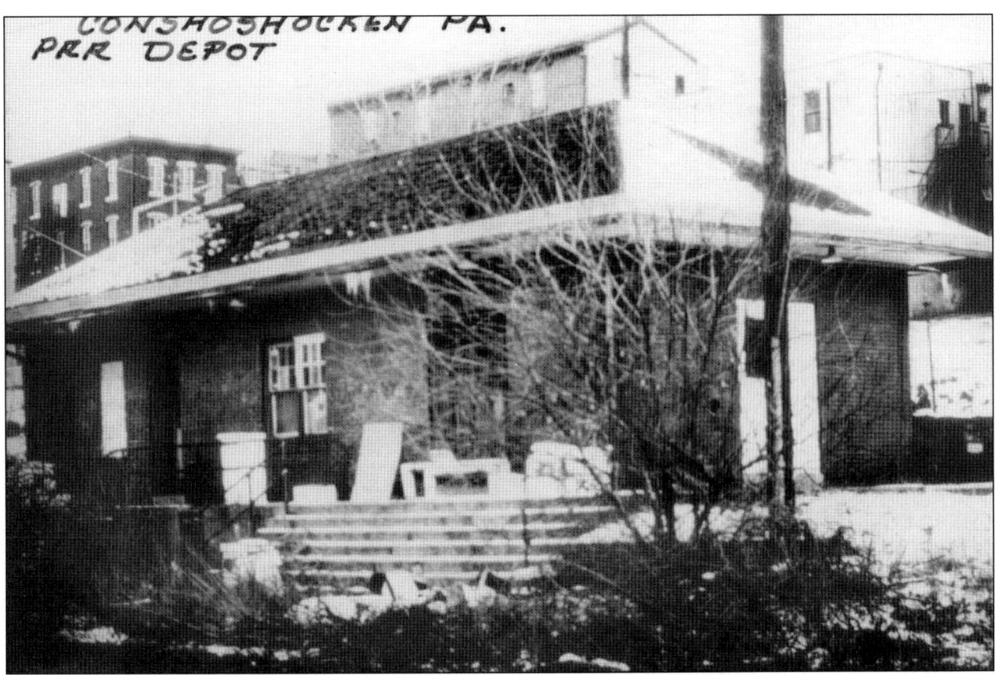

By the 1970s, Conshohocken's grand elaborate train stations fell into disrepair. This is the Outbound Station before it was refurnished by Joseph and Barbara Collins.

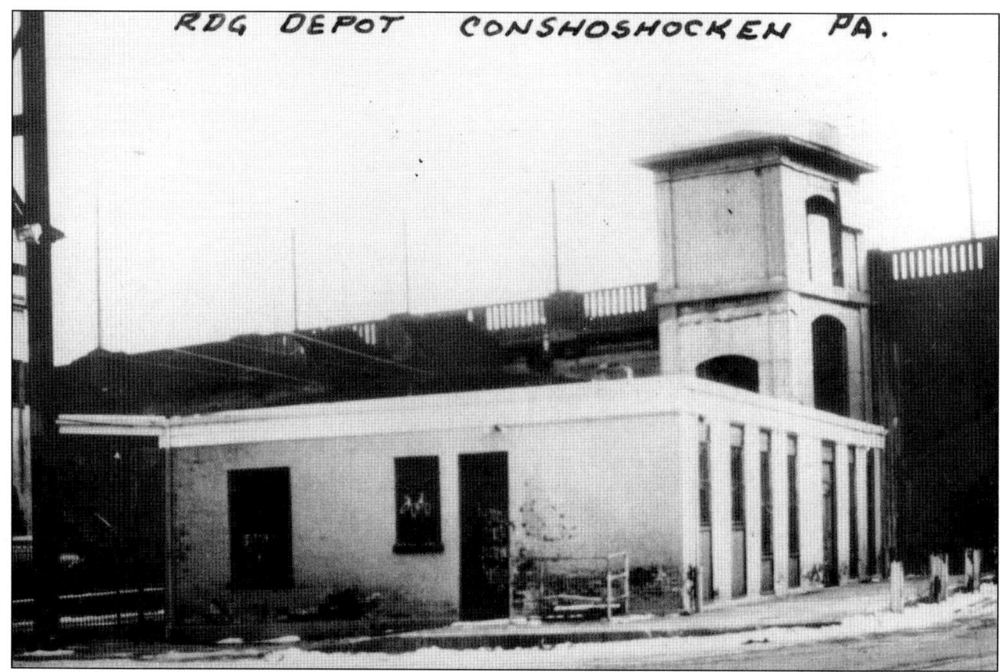

The Reading Railroad's Conshohocken station sat alongside the Matsonford Bridge but no longer exists. The tower was a staircase from the bridge walkway to the station. When the railroad began selling tickets on the train, suburban station houses became obsolete.

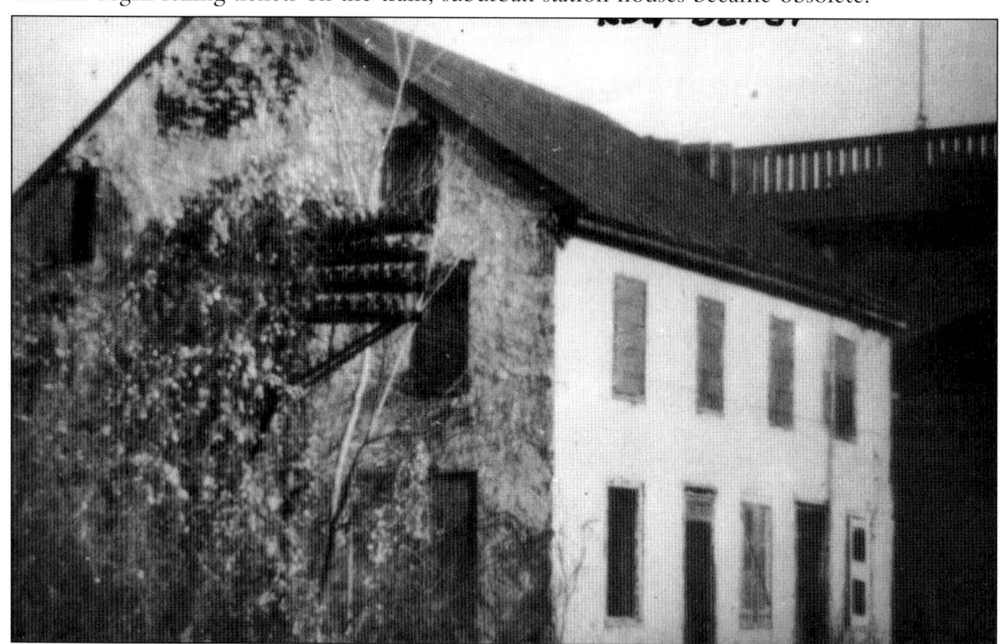

The Reading Railroad built a train system on the west bank of the Schuylkill River. By 1839, service reached West Conshohocken. The tracks fanned out to four parallel tracks through West Conshohocken because of the heavy traffic occasioned by the industrial plants along the river. A passenger station stood on the east side of the Matsonford Bridge from Conshohocken into West Conshohocken. Service was discontinued *c.* 1950 because of diminished use.

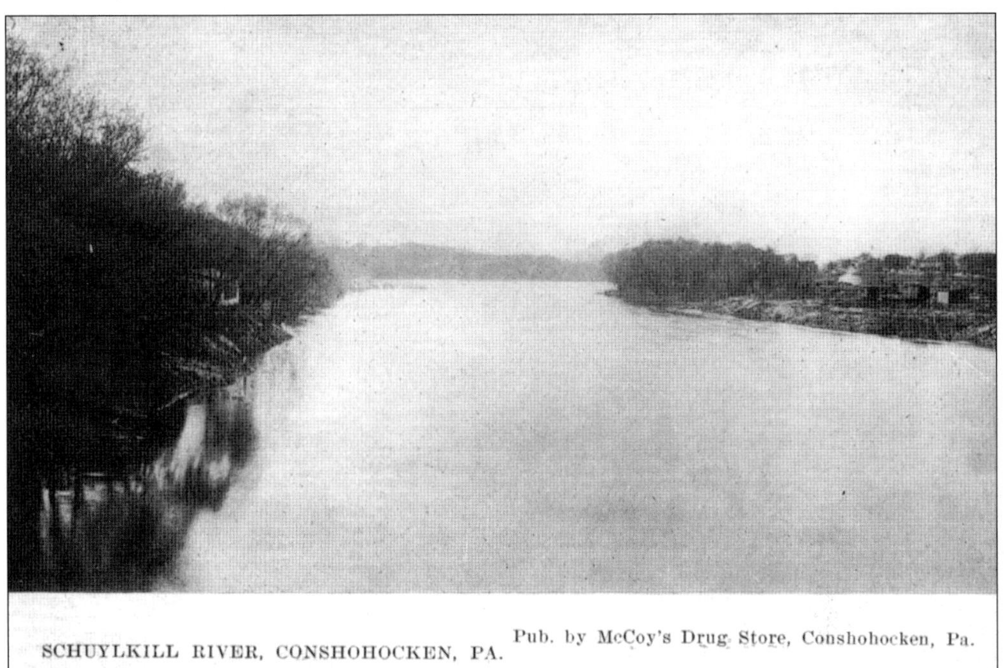

SCHUYLKILL RIVER, CONSHOHOCKEN, PA. Pub. by McCoy's Drug Store, Conshohocken, Pa.

The most important event in the early development of Conshohocken was the building of the Schuylkill Canal. Begun at Philadelphia in 1816, the canal reached Conshohocken in 1818. It not only provided a transportation route along the unnavigable Schuylkill River, it also brought the waterpower, which spurred the development of the first mills in the area.

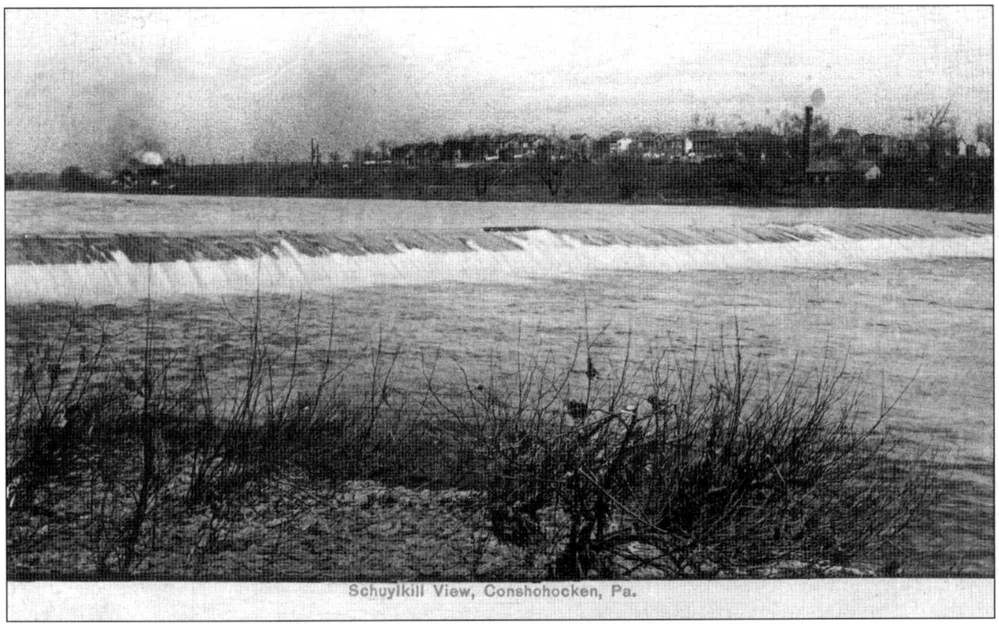

Schuylkill View, Conshohocken, Pa.

The Plymouth Dam on the Schuylkill River just north of Conshohocken was built to back up long pools of water deep enough for canal boats. Headwater coal wastes and agricultural sediments gradually filled the pools behind these dams and, by the late 19th century, canal traffic had virtually come to a halt.

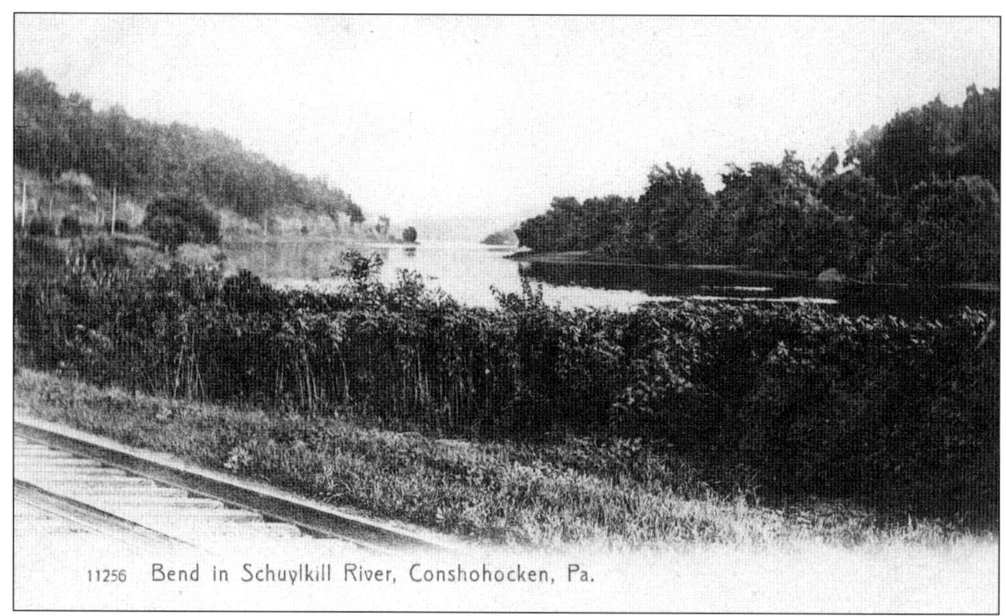

In addition to the Schuylkill Canal, transportation in Conshohocken was enhanced in the 1830s when tracks were laid for the rail system that ran from Philadelphia to Reading. This is a 1906 view of the tracks running along the river.

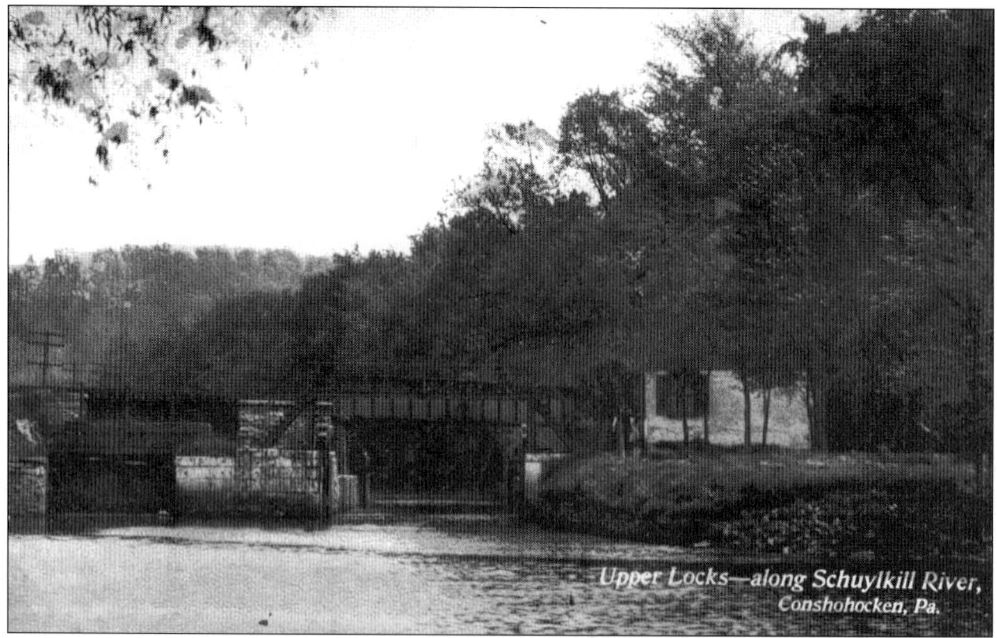

This 1907 postcard shows a rare view of the Upper Locks and Lock House on the Schuylkill Canal at Conshohocken. Horses were used to pull the canal boats through the locks. Navigation of the canal took a lot of skill. In 1827, S. Alspach published a manual for navigators to assist them safely through the points, rocks, and bars. These were his directions for the Plymouth Dam area: "Descending—Take on the horse at the locks—direct to the first wharf and keep down to the second. Land the horse and keep off about 20 feet at the point in particular, and continue to keep out about 20 feet till you arrive at the locks."

This rare 1935 photo postcard depicts the dredging operation of the Upper Lock's chamber. The operator on the platform was called a "dipper tender." In the foreground is a dump scow, which could hold about 40 tons.

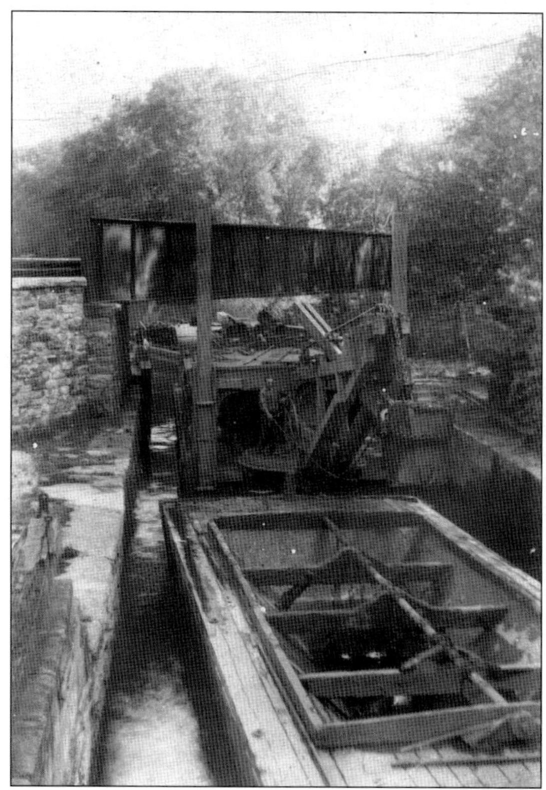

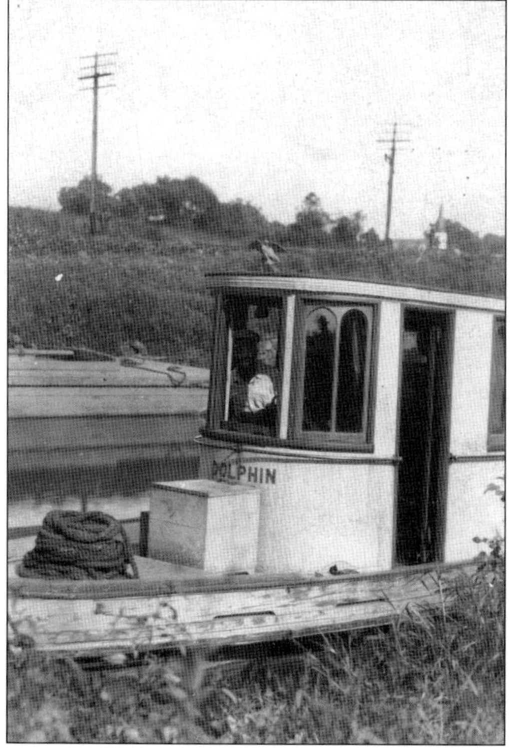

The *Dolphin*, a tugboat on the canal, is shown in this 1935 real photo postcard. By this time, tugboats had replaced horses along the canal. Alongside the tugboat is a dump scow. In the background on the right is a church steeple, probably that of St. Mary's.

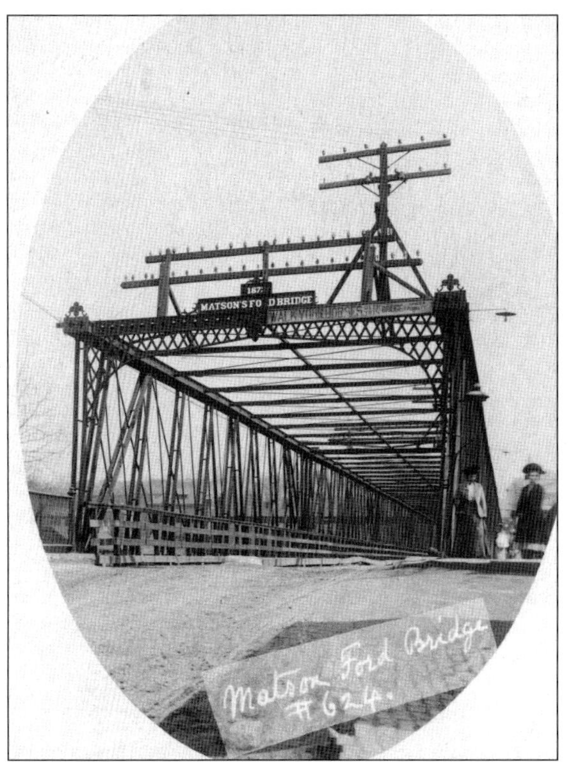

The Matsonford Bridge, built in 1872, spanned the Schuylkill River, connecting Conshohocken to West Conshohocken. To the right are two women on the walk path. The sign above the bridge reads, "Walk your horses over this bridge under penalty."

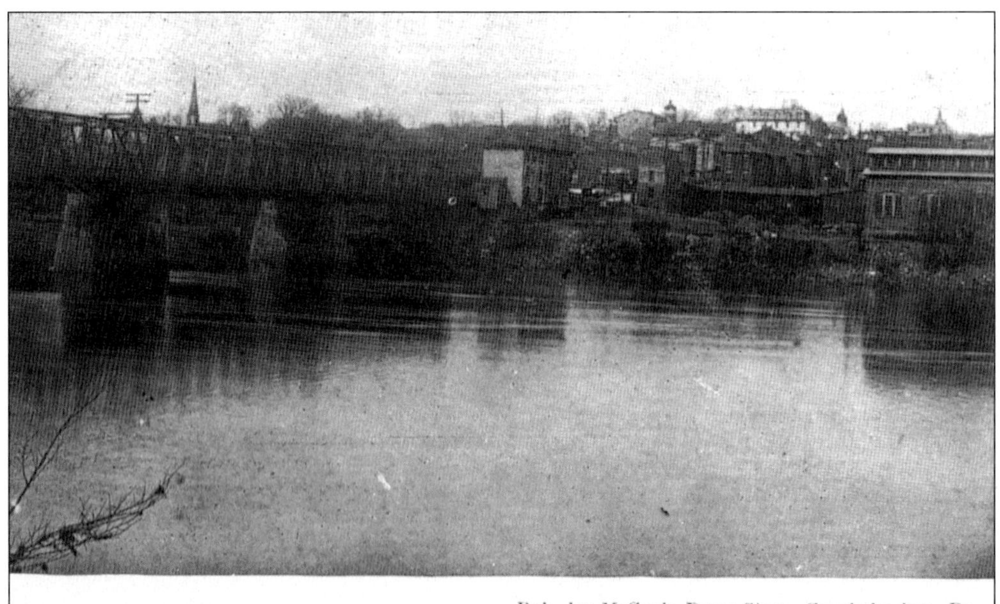

Over the last 165 years, there have been several Matsonford Bridges. The first, a wooden covered bridge, was built in 1836. In 1850, the bridge was destroyed by a severe flood. The second bridge was built in 1850–1851. By 1870, there was a need for a much sturdier bridge. Construction started on the iron bridge in 1870 and was completed in 1872. It was a toll bridge until 1886, when Montgomery Country purchased the property from the Matson family.

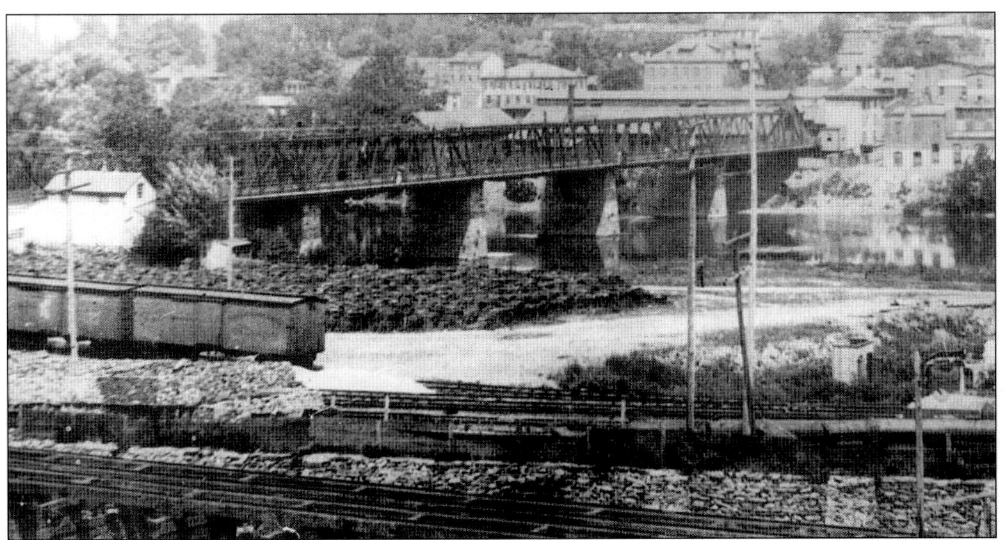

It took about two years to complete the construction of the iron bridge. In 1919, just 47 years after its construction, the bridge was demolished and replaced with a concrete 10-arch-span bridge. (Courtesy of Jack Coll.)

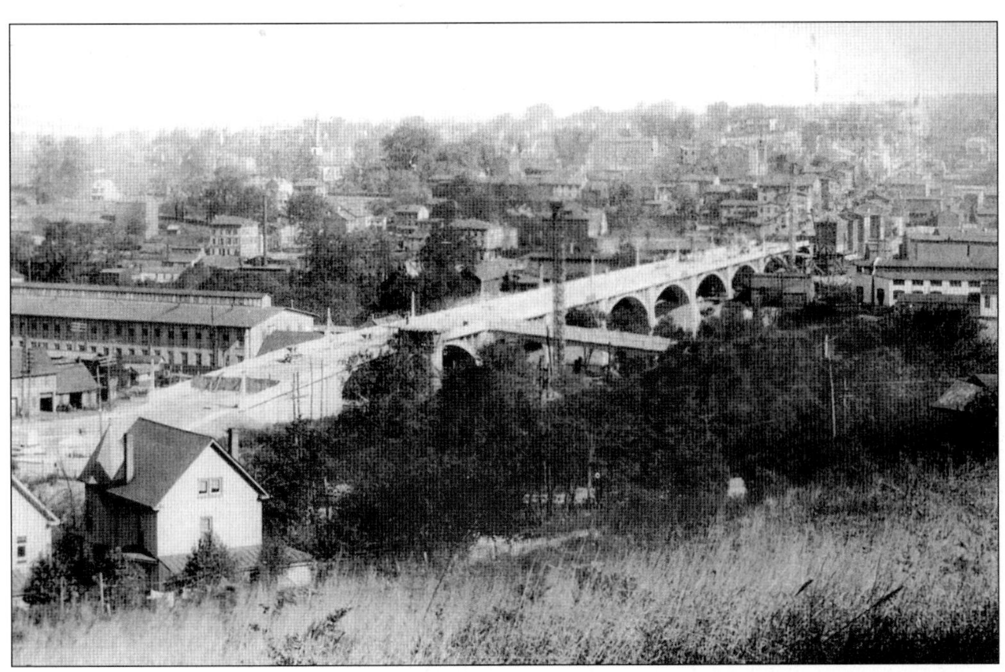

Considered an architectural marvel of the 20th century, the 10-arch-span concrete bridge in Conshohocken opened on Friday, November 11, 1921. It was the first bridge of its kind in Pennsylvania to span across a river, two roadways, and three sets of railroad tracks. Total cost of construction was $500,000. (Courtesy of Jack Coll.)

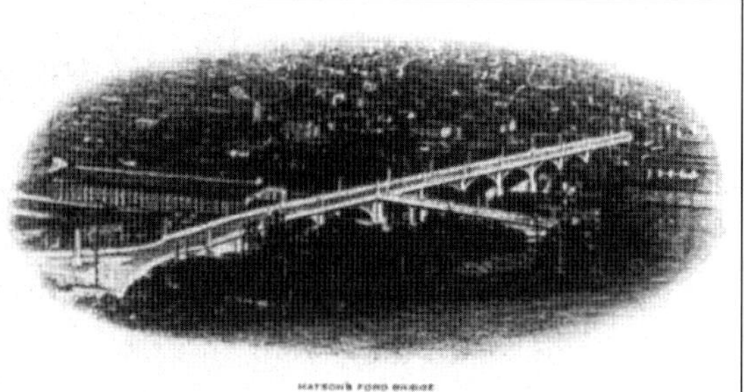

MATSON'S FORD BRIDGE

The Matson's Ford Bridge
Citizens Committee of
Conshohocken and West Conshohocken
cordially invite you to attend the ceremonies
in connection with the dedication of the
New Bridge
spanning the Schuylkill River
at Conshohocken, Montgomery County
on Friday, November the eleventh
nineteen hundred and twenty-one
at one thirty o'clock P. M.

This is an invitation to the dedication ceremony for the 1921 Matsonford Bridge. The engineer and designer for the bridge was B.H. Davis, and the contractor was Seeds & Derham. Members of the Citizens Committee, which was in charge of construction promotion, were Horace C. Jones, David Ross, Charles Heber Clark, S. Gordon Smyth, Henry W. Tracy, John Booth, Reese Davis, and Richard G. Wood.

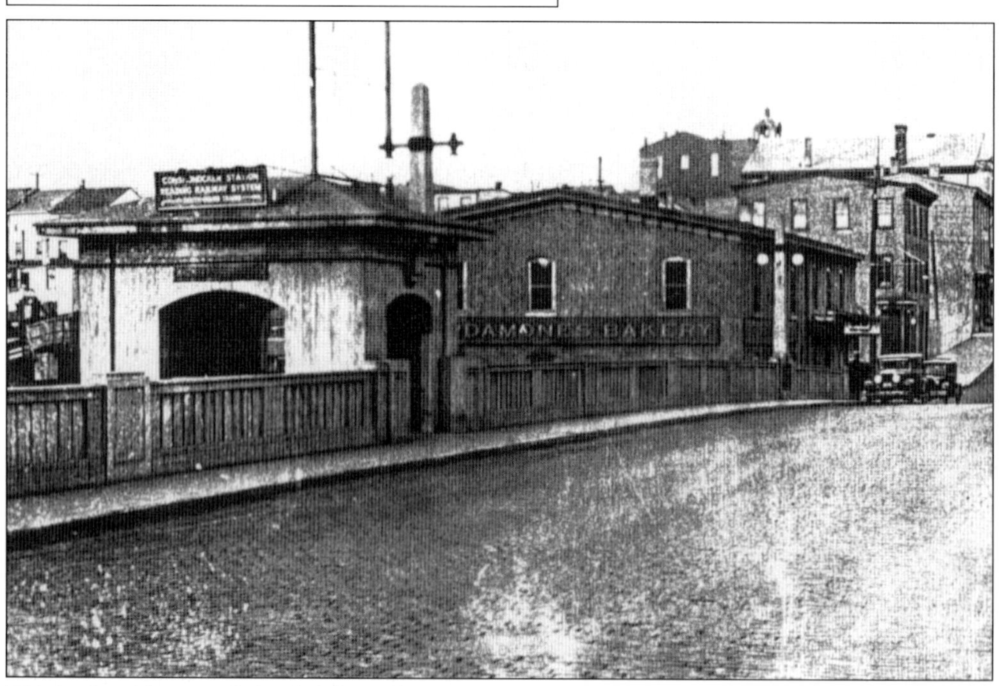

This is the old stairwell that led from the top of the Matsonford Bridge to the Reading Railroad station below. Although cars were becoming very popular in the 1920s, most people in town walked to the train station. (Courtesy of Jack Coll.)

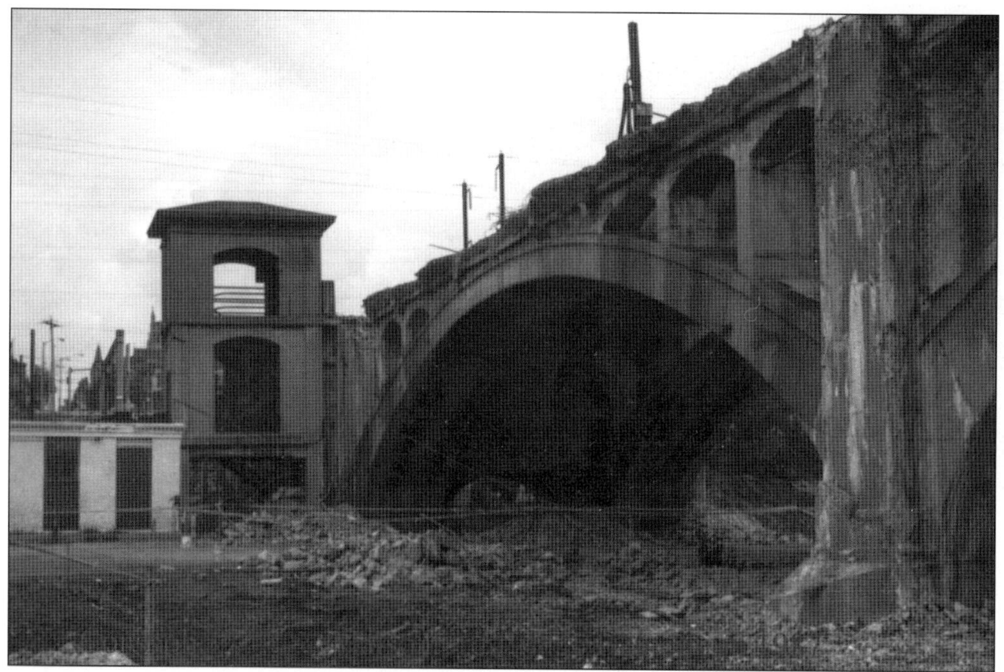

With the growth of business in Conshohocken and the increased traffic to and from the Schuylkill Expressway, it was time to tear down the old bridge and build a new one. This is a view of one of the arches from Washington Street near the old Reading train station. The bridge stairwell is being razed. (Courtesy of Doreen DeSantis.)

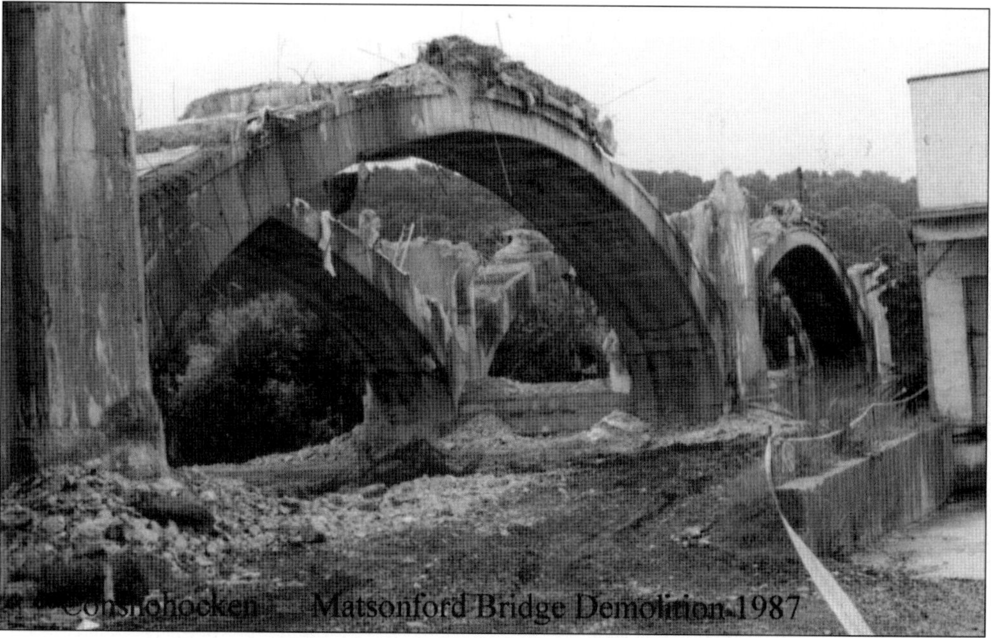

These massive arches were hailed as a modern marvel in 1921, but the constant flow of traffic over the bridge soon left it irreparable. In 1987, the bridge was demolished and the next generation of the Matsonford Bridge was built. The current bridge connecting Conshohocken and West Conshohocken cost more than $12 million. (Courtesy of Doreen DeSantis.)

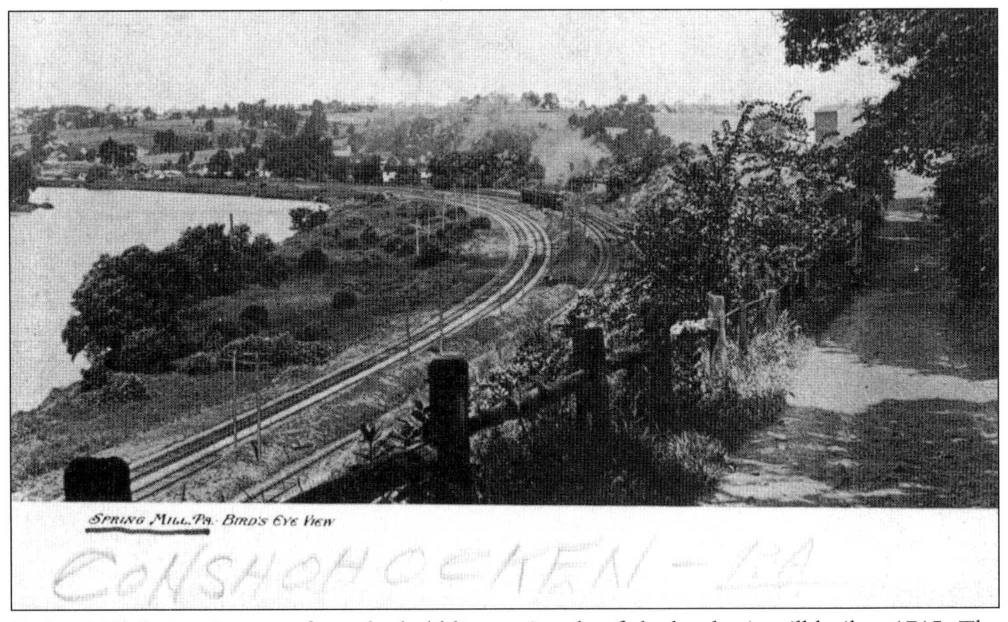

Spring Mill derives its name from the bubbling spring that fed a local gristmill built *c.* 1715. The village was ideally situated along the Schuylkill River for water and rail transportation and was a vital shipping area for the marble industry in the Whitemarsh area in the early 1800s. General Lafayette marched his 2,000 soldiers through Spring Mill along the river to the Matson's Ford to escape the British.

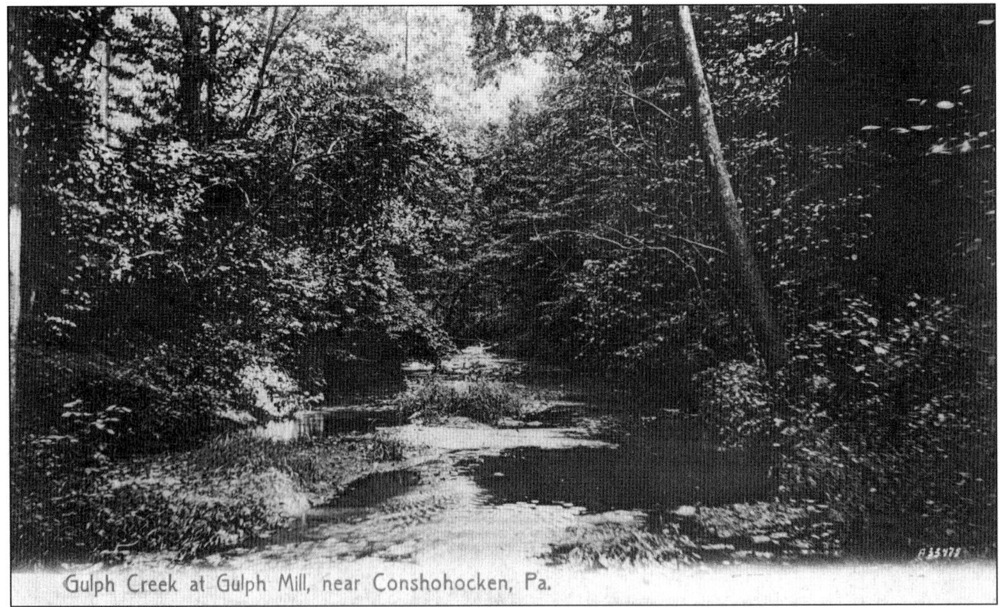

Gulph Creek supported many of the industries that lined its banks from Gulph Mills to West Conshohocken at the beginning of the 20th century. Some of these businesses were the Gulph Woolen Mills on Gulph Road, Conshohocken Woolen Company on the upper part of Balligomingo Road, the Ice Factory and Brewery on Balligomingo Road near the bridge, and Conshohocken Woolen Company–Balligomingo Mills in West Conshohocken. The creek empties into the Schuylkill River.

Three

Fayette Street and the Avenues

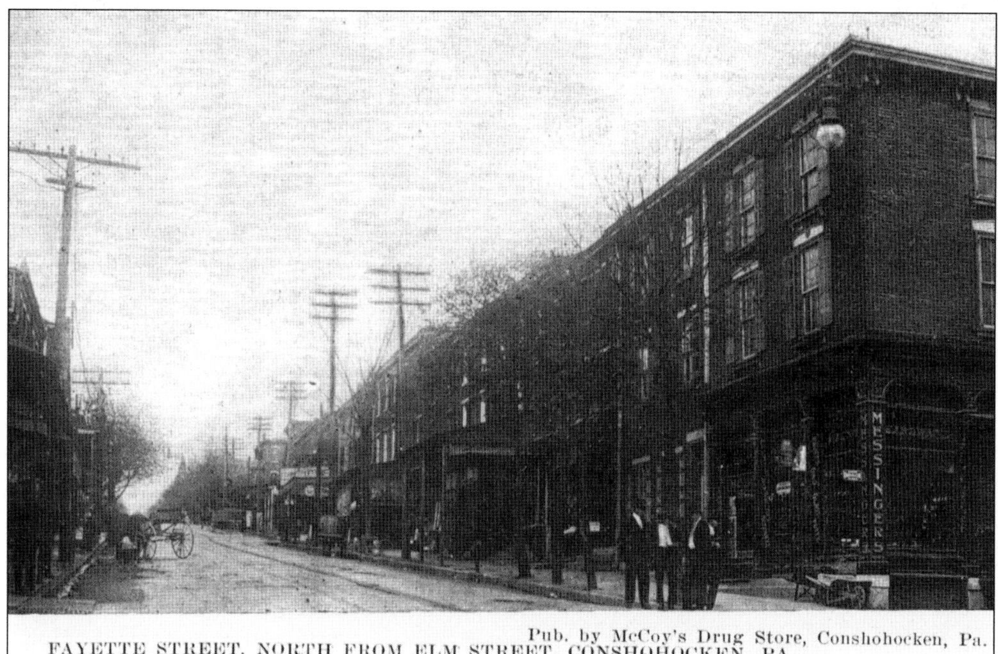

Although Conshohocken was growing into an industrial center along Washington Street where the railroad was built, retail businesses favored Fayette Street. Looking north *c.* 1906, this view shows the lower area of Fayette Street. On the right is Harry Messenger's hardware store.

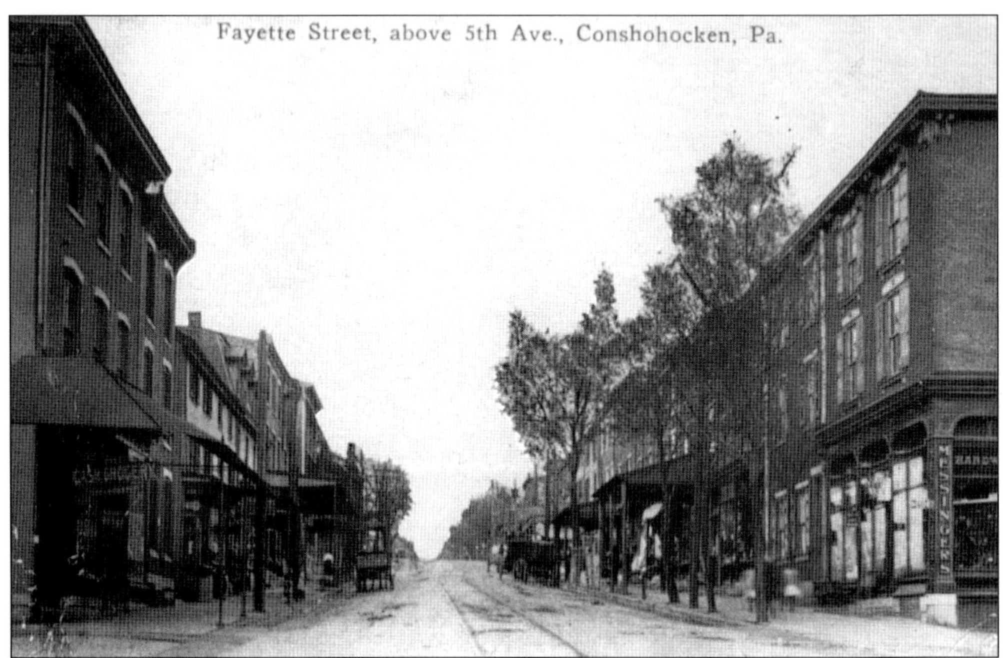

This Fayette Street postcard is mislabeled. The view, looking north from Elm Street, shows lower Fayette Street. Harry Messenger's hardware store is on the right, and a grocery store is on the left. Horse-drawn wagons on Fayette Street were a very common sight in town *c.* 1907.

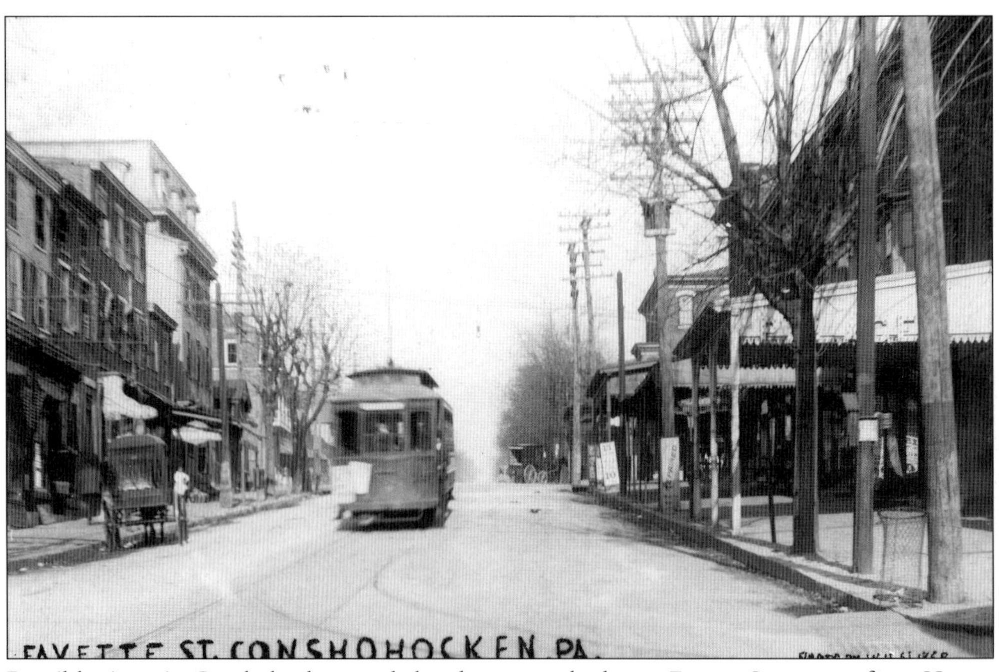

Retail business in Conshohocken tended to locate on the lower Fayette Street area from Hector Street to Second Avenue. This 1906 view of Fayette Street looks north from First to Second Avenues. Featured are the typical modes of transportation for the period—the trolley and the horse-drawn wagon.

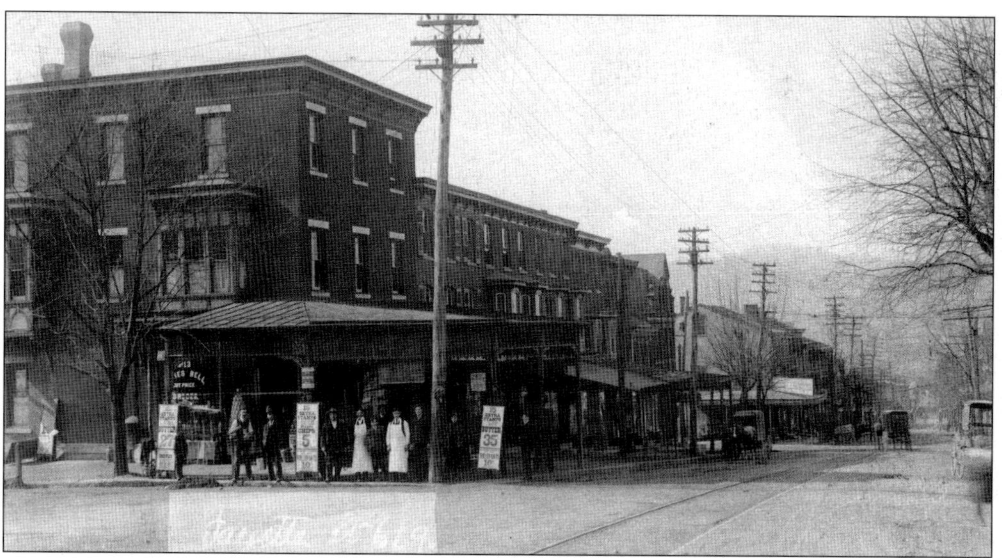

This view is looking south on Fayette Street toward the Matsonford Bridge. The staff at James Bell's grocery store can be seen outside on East Second Avenue and Fayette Street. Down the street on the left, at the corner of First and Fayette Street, is the Tradesmen's National Bank.

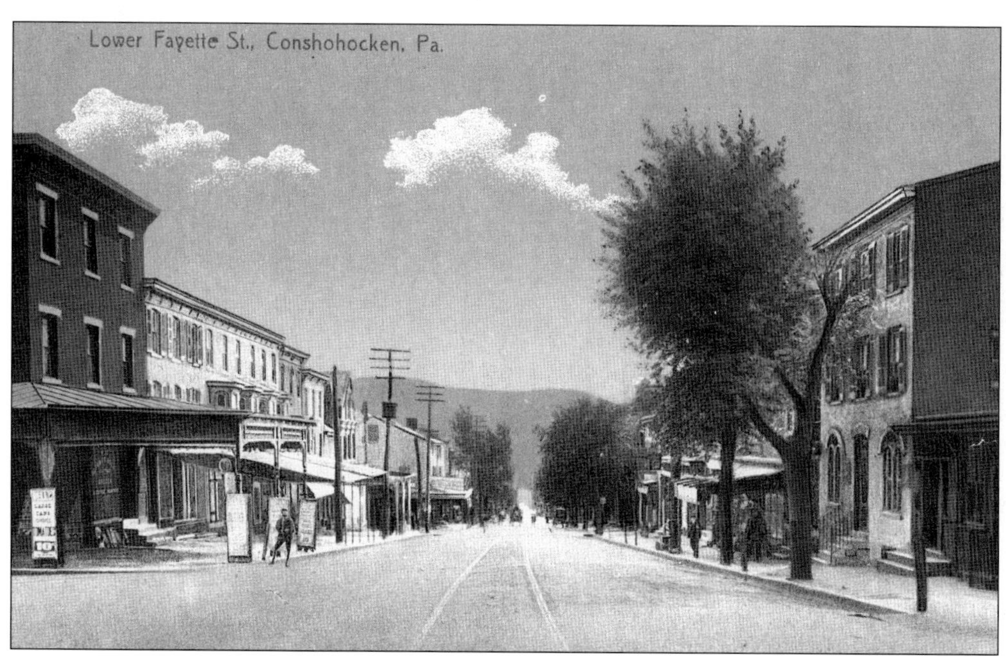

An artist's version of Fayette Street, looking south from Second Avenue in 1908, shows many buildings that are now retail stores, bars, and eateries. The street is rarely deserted anymore.

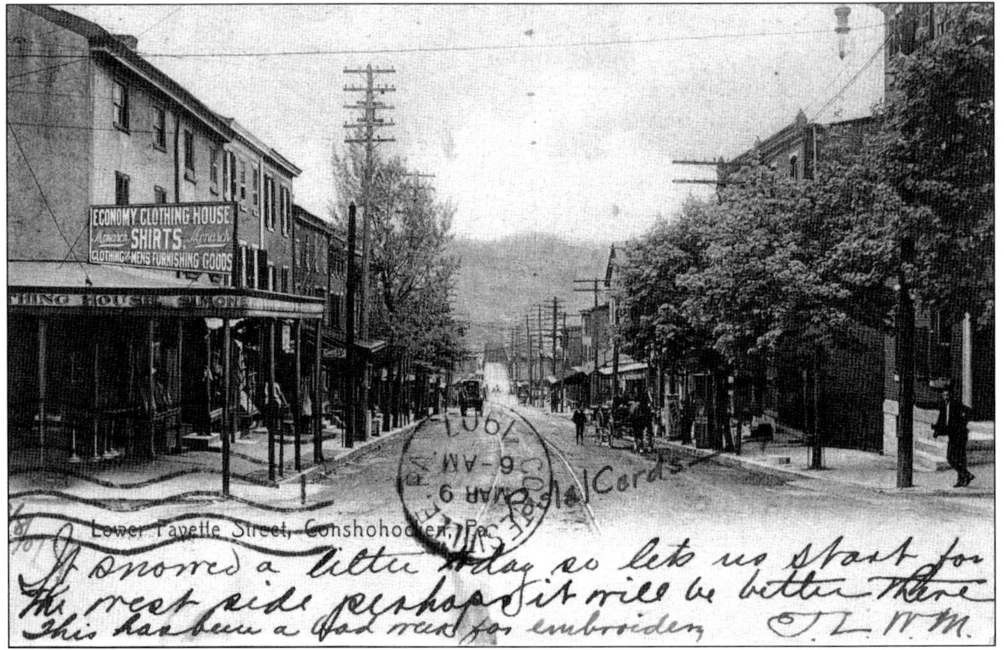

This view, taken from First Avenue, looks south on Fayette Street toward the Matsonford Bridge. On the right is a man outside the First National Bank of Conshohocken. Just below the horse-drawn wagon is a laundry. On the left is the Economy Clothing Store. According to the 1930 census, Conshohocken had 230 retail shops in the borough, most of which were located on Fayette Street.

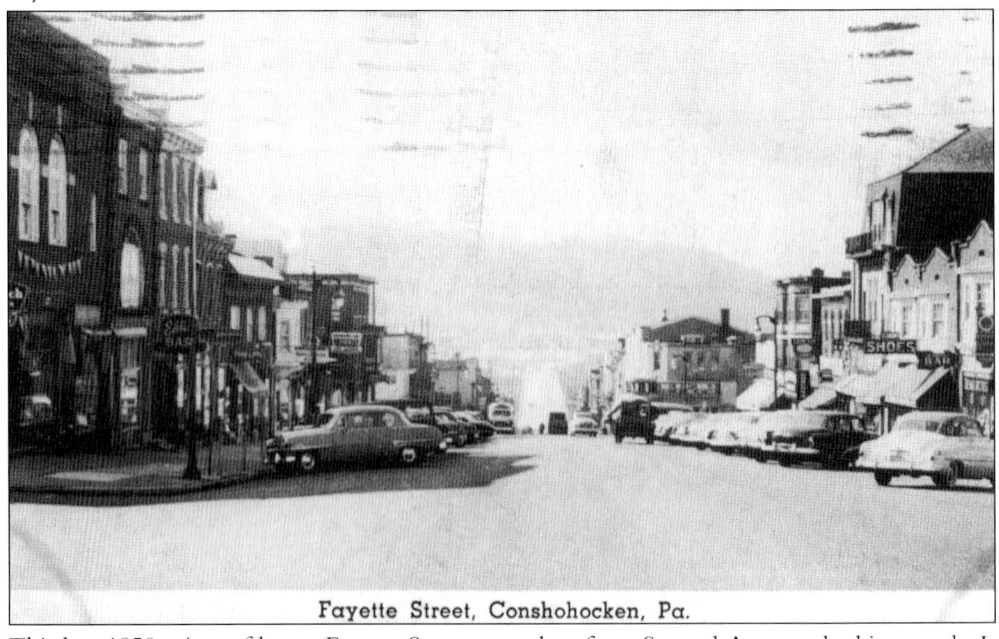

This late-1950s view of lower Fayette Street was taken from Second Avenue, looking south. It is clear that business was booming. Shops below First Avenue no longer exist, such as the Riant Theater on the lower right. In the background on the left is an Auch bus traveling north on Fayette Street. Bus transit in Conshohocken started in 1933.

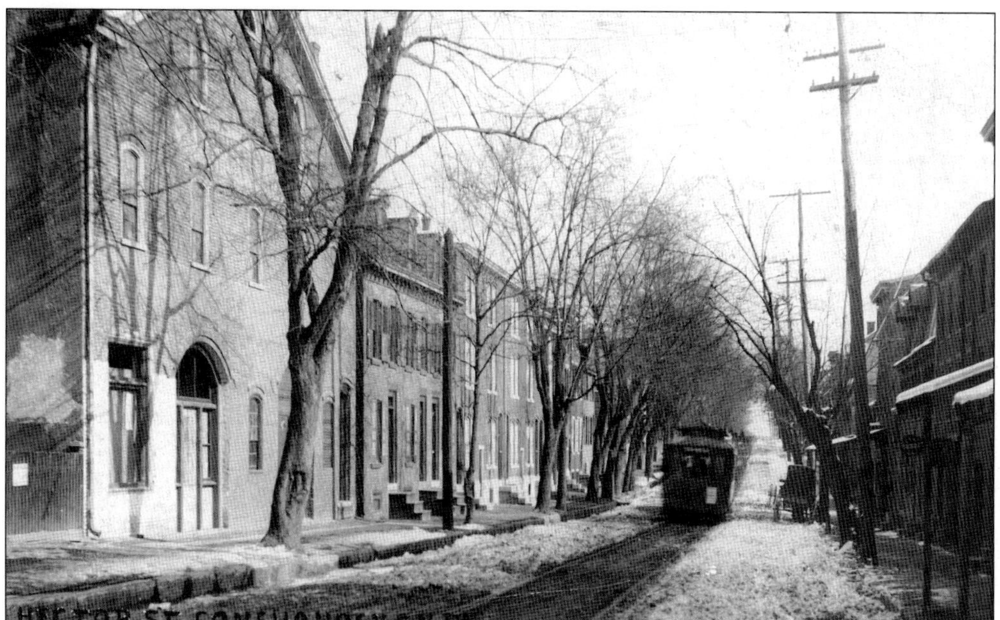

A trolley rocks along East Hector Street *c.* 1907. Residents would use the trolley to ride to Fayette Street to shop. Taken from Poplar Street, the photograph shows a horse and wagon in front of Zadroga's Market on the right and Moser's Glassworks on the left. The Moser's Glassworks building, on Poplar and Hector Streets, was the site of Conshohocken's first professional basketball game.

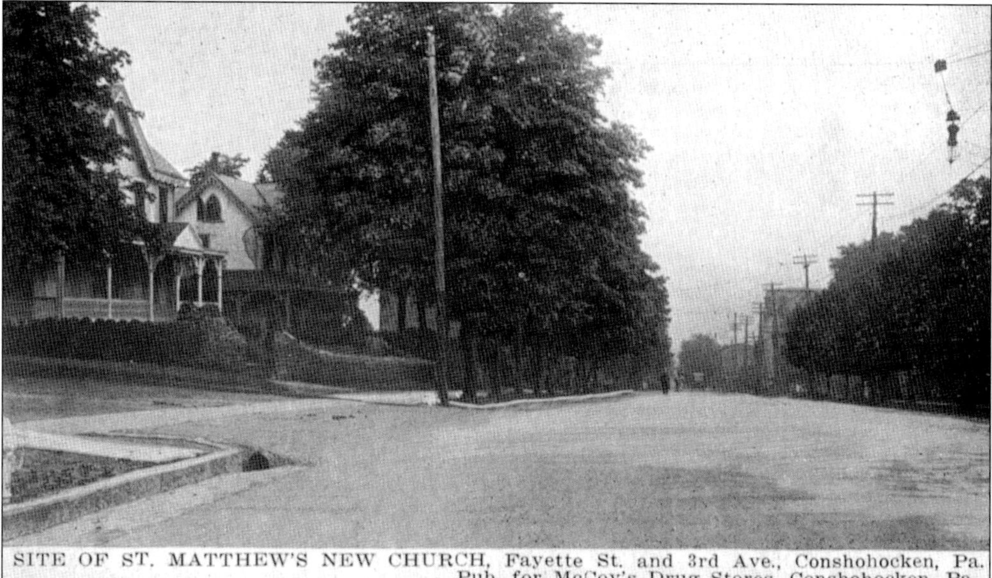

This property on Third Avenue and Fayette Street later became the site of St. Matthews Church. The last owner before the church was John F. Bowker. A previous owner, in 1893, was Stanley Lees, who also owned a cotton mill on Ash and Washington Streets. The home was moved to the corner of Third Avenue and Harry Street and was converted to St. Matthews Convent. The second home in this view belonged to the S. Pugh estate. It was demolished for the construction of the church.

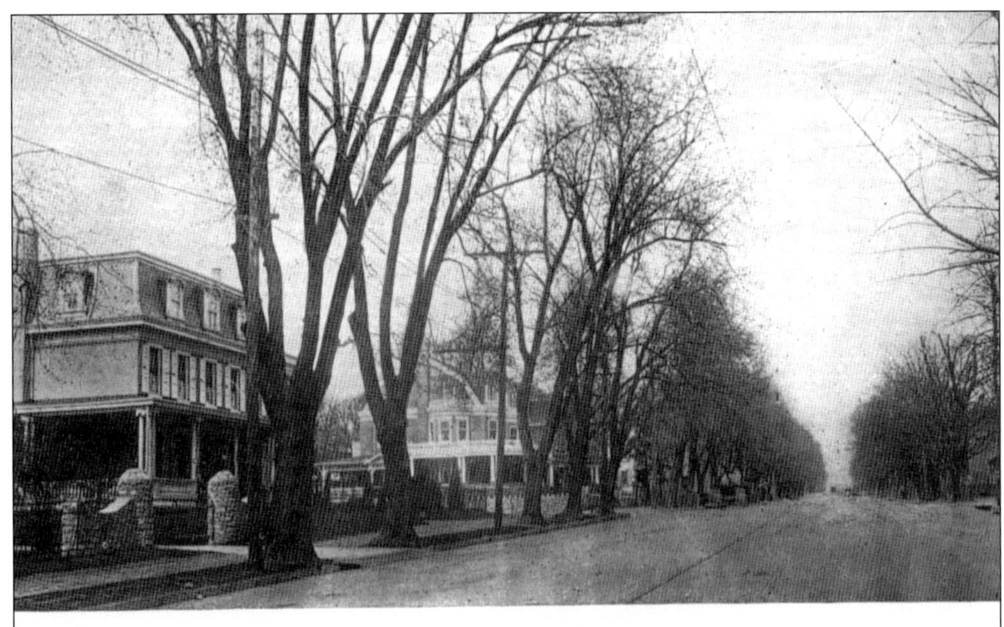

The home on the left was part of the David L. Wood estate in 1893. It was located on Fayette Street south of Fifth Avenue. Today it is the site of a bank. The next home, almost in the center of the postcard, originally belonged to J. Wood Jr. but more recently had been home to the Katz family. A doctor's office and a dentist's office were located in the front part of the house. Today the home is under new ownership and renovation.

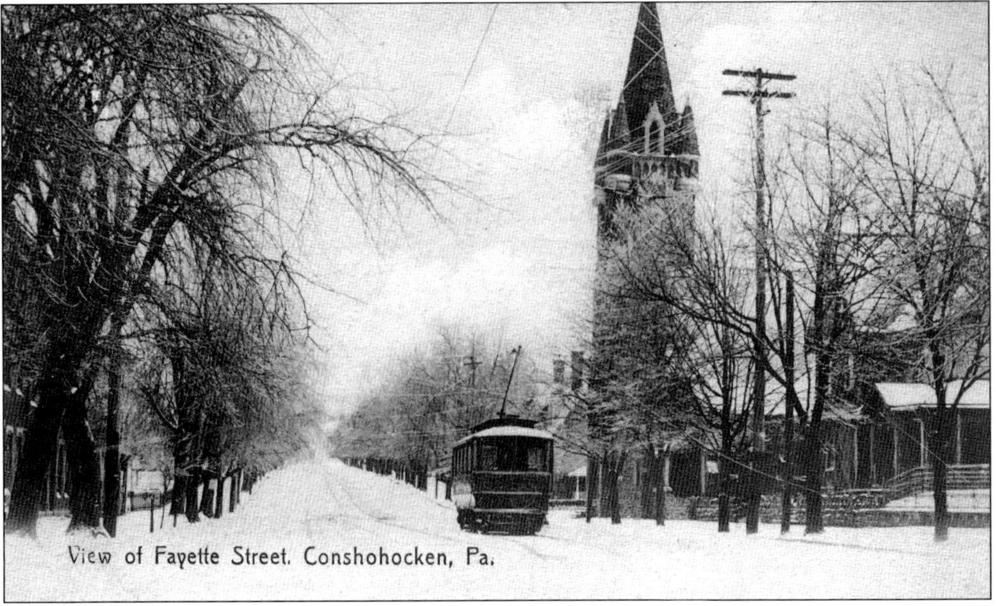

A trolley travels north on snow-covered Fayette Street past the Episcopal church on Fourth Avenue. Trolleys were a very popular mode of transportation in Conshohocken for 40 years. In the winter, it was a cold way to travel, but it was better than walking. Trolley transportation in town ended in 1933.

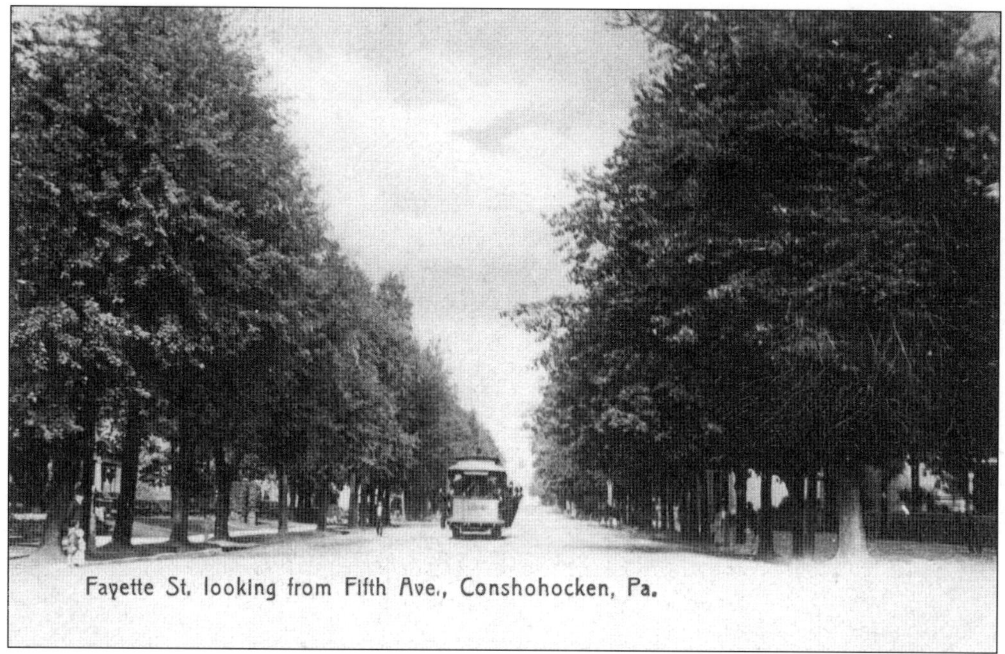

This is an early-1900s view of a trolley traveling tree-lined Fayette Street. In 1893–1894, the Conshohocken Passenger Railway Company built a trolley line, which connected Norristown, Plymouth Meeting, and Conshohocken. Originally, the line only carried passengers as far as Twelfth Avenue. Within a year, track was laid the length of Fayette Street to Marble Street.

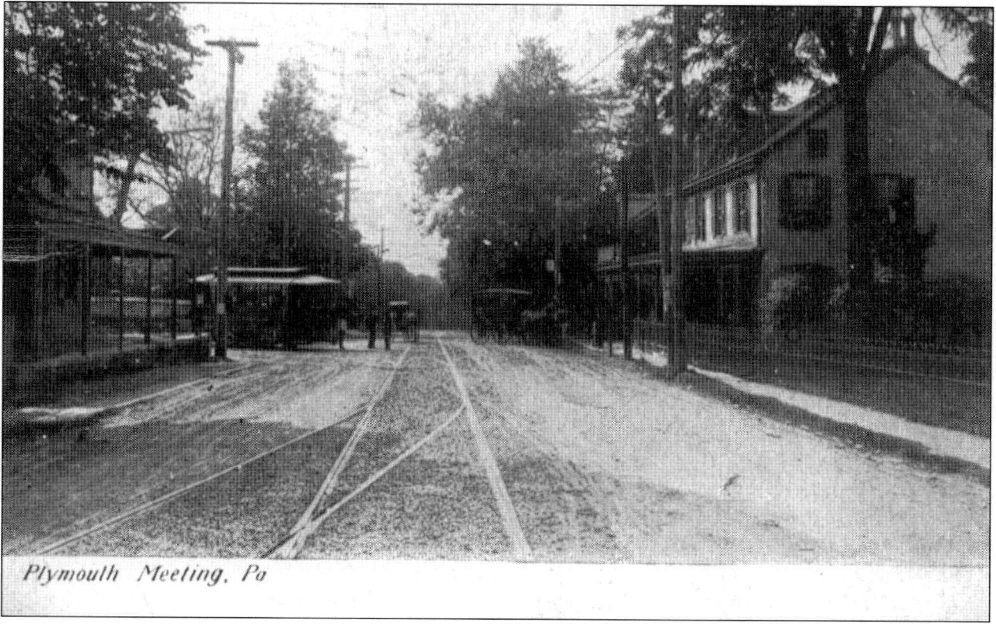

A trolley heads to Conshohocken from Plymouth Meeting. This trolley is at the intersection of Butler and Germantown Pikes. This intersection is actually the earliest village of Plymouth Township. On the right stands a general store and post office. Today the road is paved, the trolley no longer rocks along the street, the buildings on the right and left are offices, and the horse-drawn wagons are long gone.

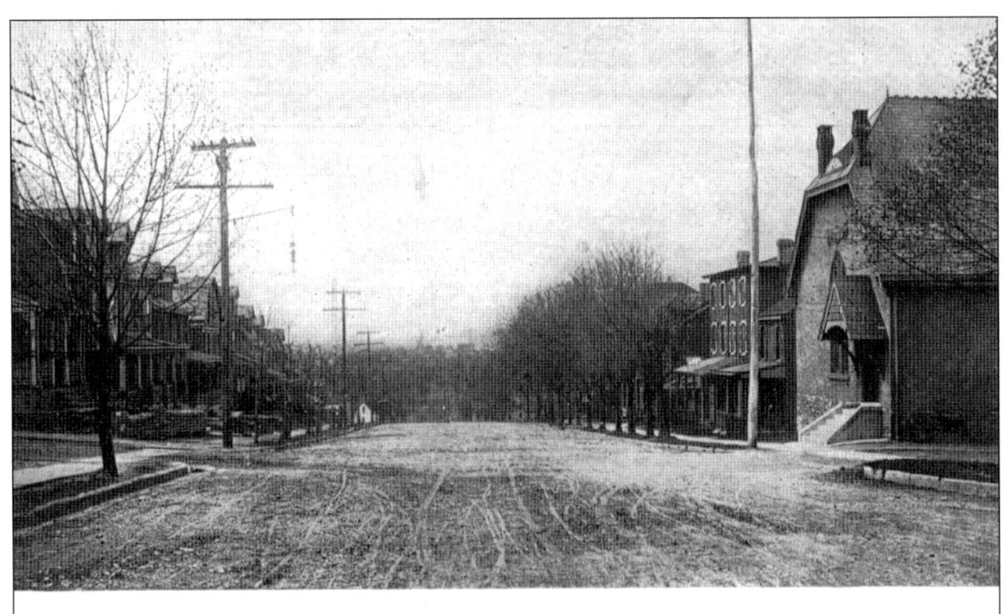

Pub. by McCoy's Drug Store, Conshohocken, Pa.
WEST THIRD AVENUE, CONSHOHOCKEN, PA.

This is a 1905 view of West Third Avenue. The building on the right was built by the Conshohocken branch of the Women's Christian Temperance Union in 1890. This hall housed a series of civic and religious organizations, such as St. Mark's Lutheran Church, the Knights of Columbus, the Grand Army of the Republic, and the Coptic Orthodox Church.

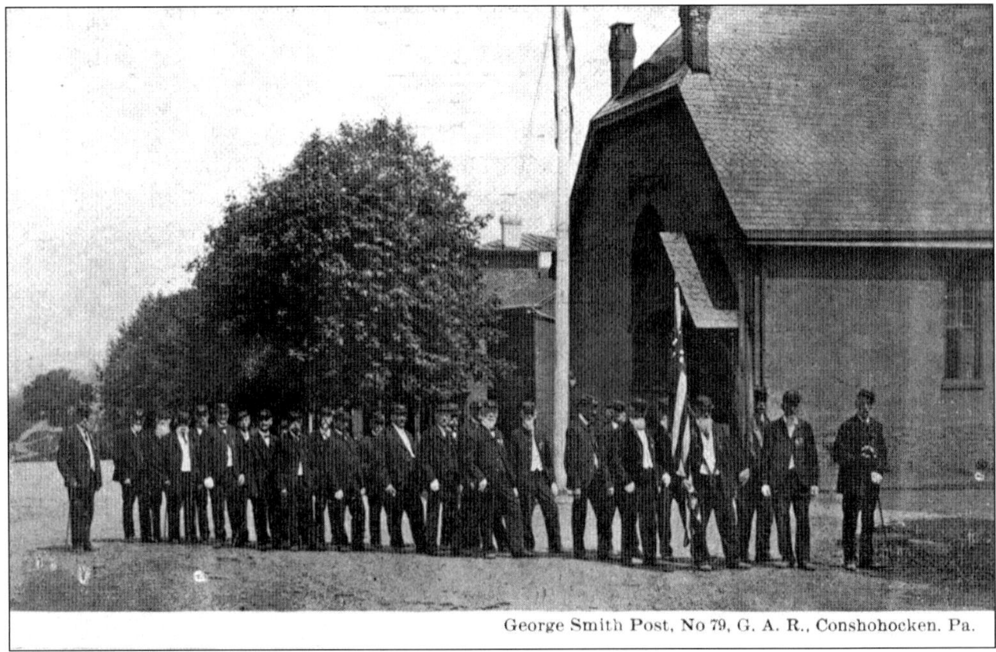

George Smith Post, No 79, G. A. R., Conshohocken. Pa.

This photograph of the George Smith Post, No. 79, Grand Army of the Republic, was taken on July 4, 1907, outside its headquarters on West Third Avenue and Forrest Street. Made up of Civil War veterans, the was organized in 1867. It was named after the first borough resident killed in the Civil War.

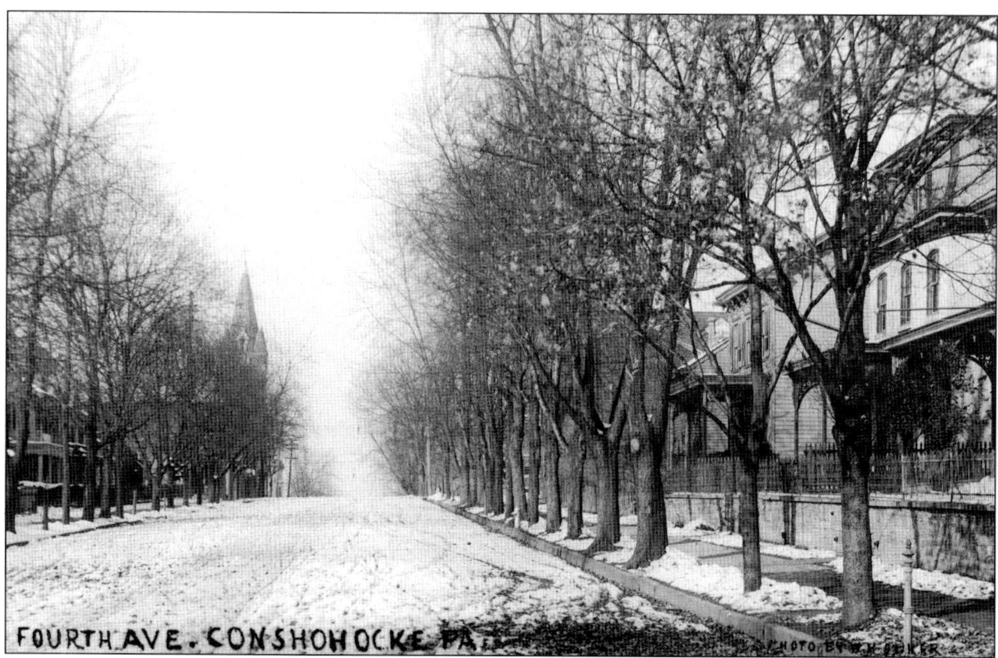

Snow-covered East Fourth Avenue is shown in a view looking west toward Fayette Street. In the distance on the left is the Calvary Episcopal Church.

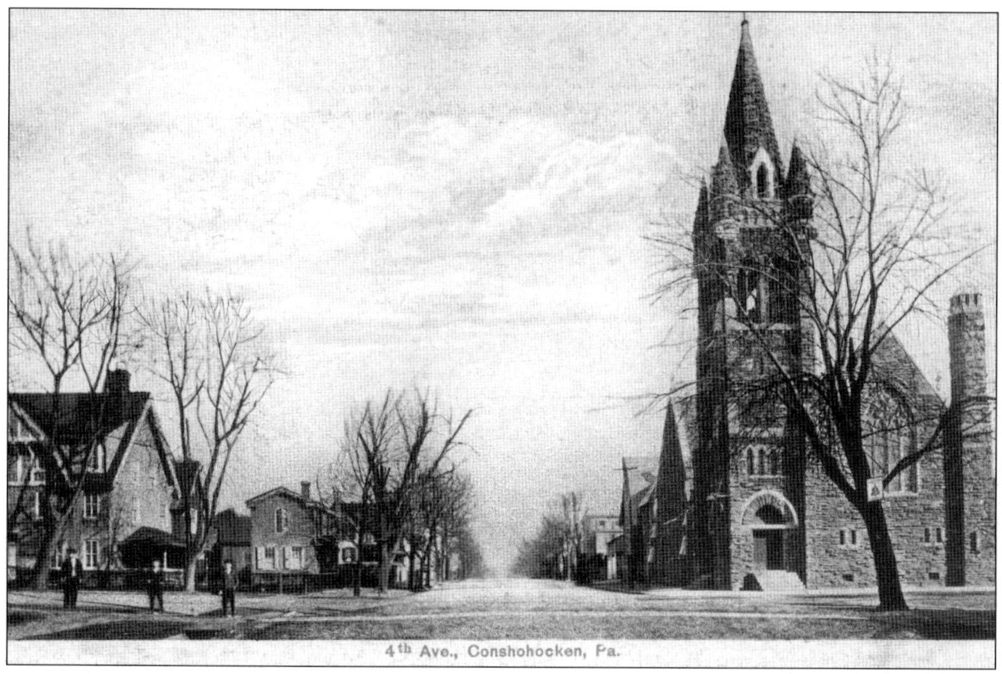

This is a view looking east on Fourth Avenue from Fayette Street. On the right is the Calvary Episcopal Church and on the left is the current site of the 401 Diner. The house on the left in the foreground is where the Progress Bank stands today.

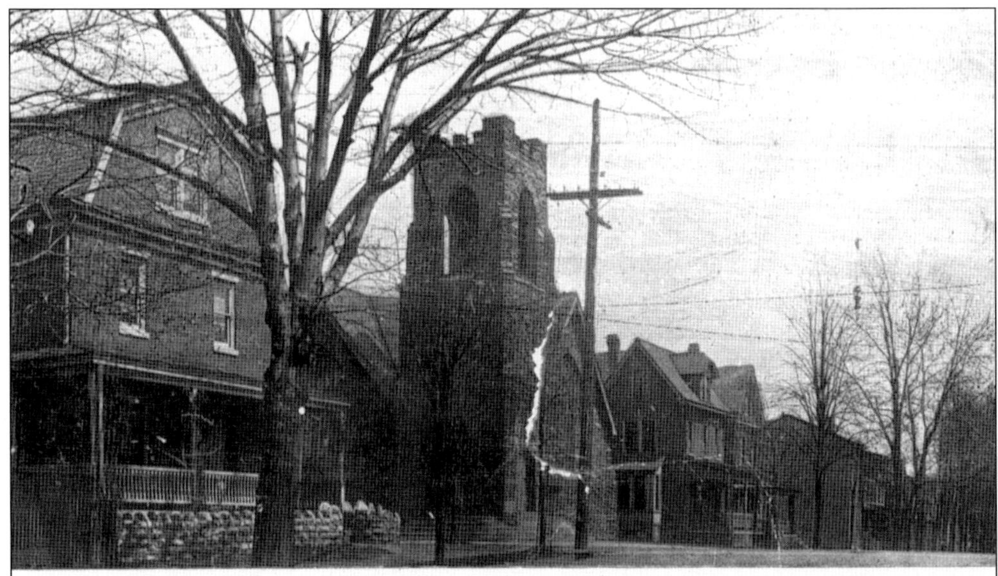

This Fourth Avenue view shows the First Baptist Church, on the corner of Harry Street. According to the Smith atlas of Montgomery County (1893), the end house on the left belonged to the Charles Lukens estate.

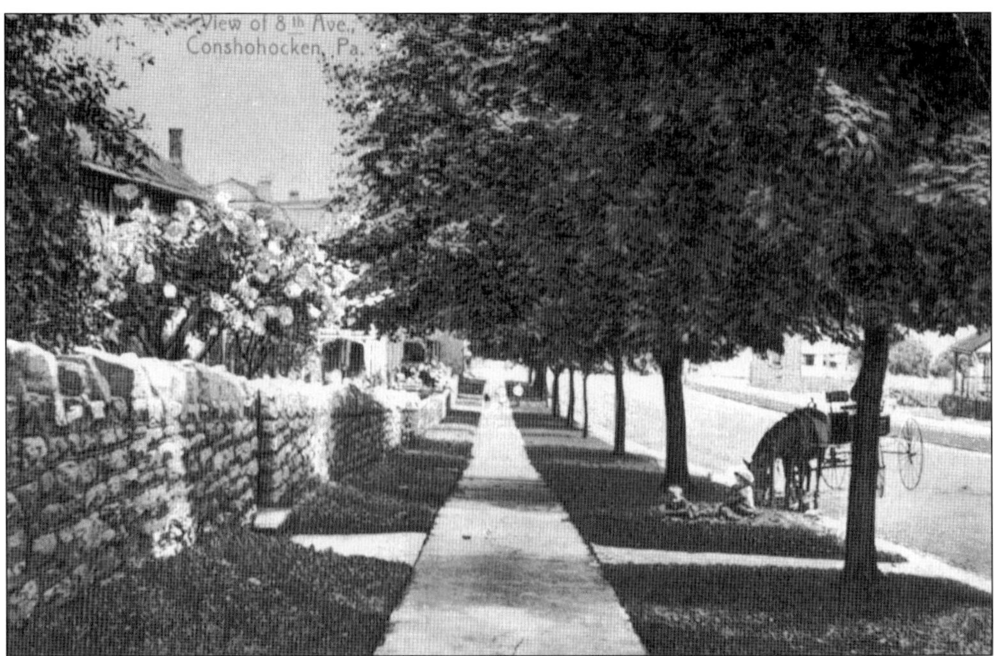

Children play on the front lawn near a hitching post with a horse and wagon. Today, portions of the stone wall on this block of East Eighth Avenue still exist, and automobiles have replaced all of the horse-drawn wagons.

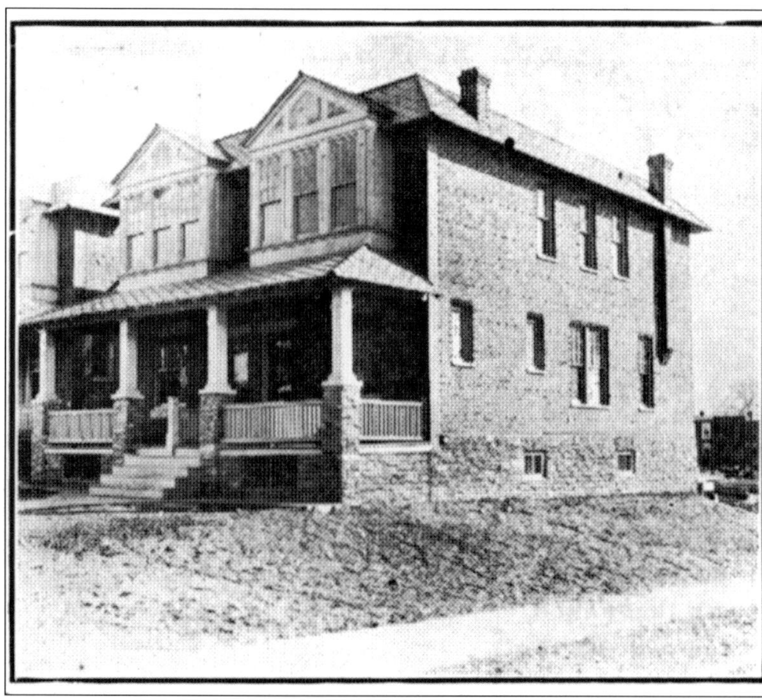

An advertising postcard from the George Light Real Estate and Insurance Company shows the newly built homes on West Eighth Avenue and Maple Street. These homes were built *c.* 1915.

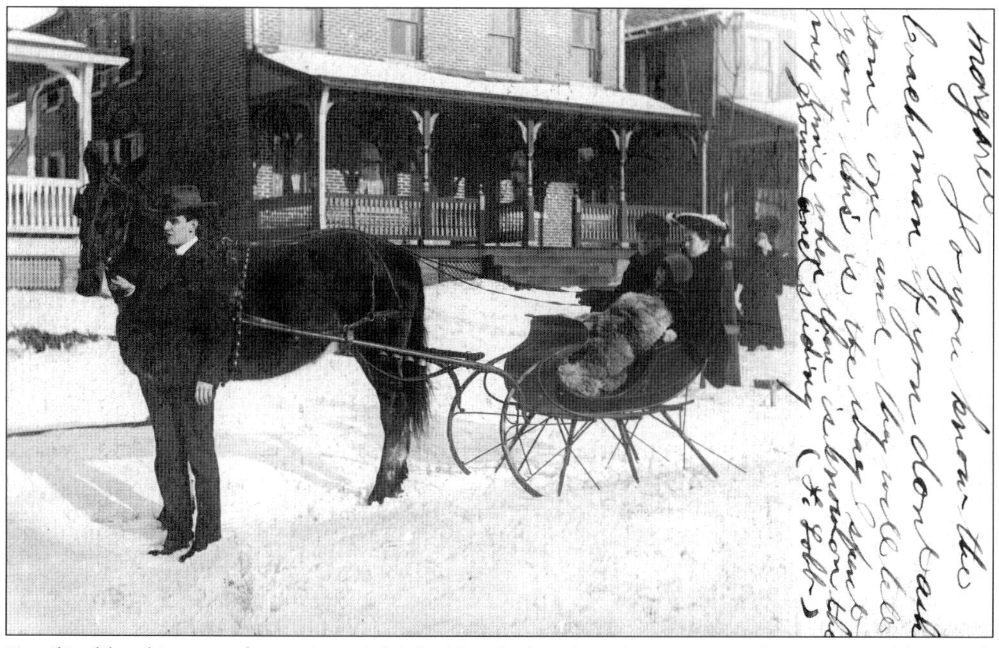

Families like this one often enjoyed sleigh rides during the winter, even when it was cold enough to require a fur blanket. This postcard dates from the early 1900s.

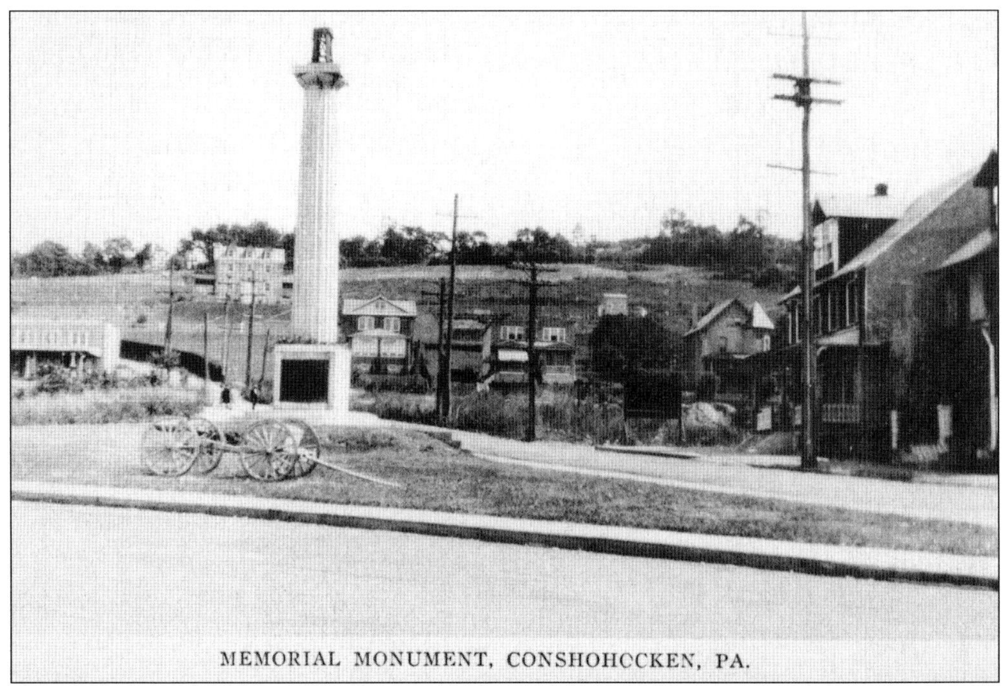

This is a view of the intersection of Route 23 and Matson Ford Road, which connects Conshohocken and West Conshohocken, prior to the construction of the Schuylkill Expressway. The war memorial monument was constructed in 1921 on a triangular island in the middle of the intersection. The monument honors those who served in World War I. It was designed by S. Gordon Smyth Jr. and cost $6,000. It was demolished in the early 1950s to make way for the Schuylkill Expressway.

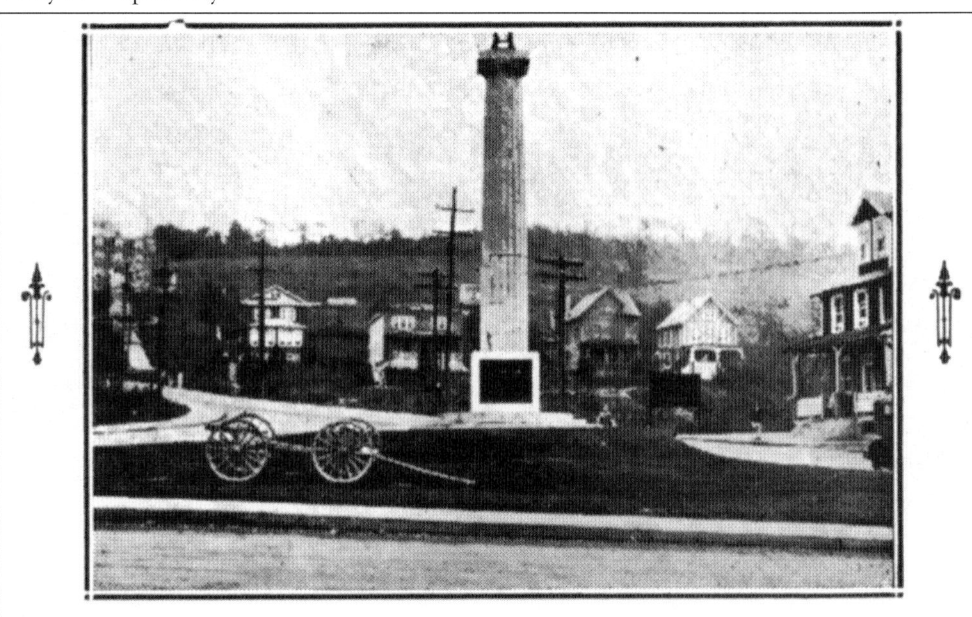

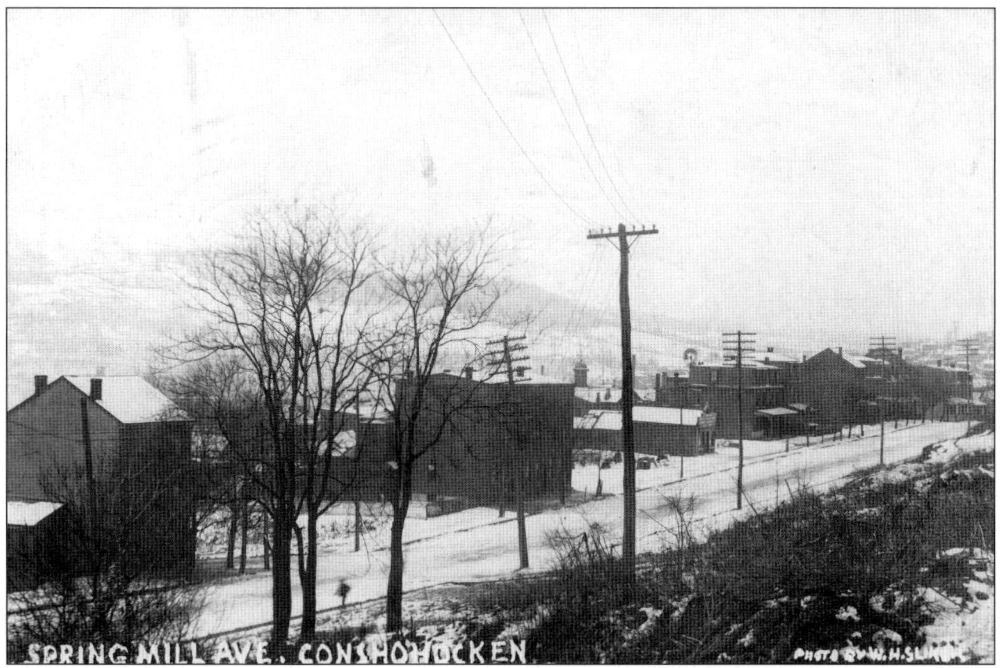

Here is another wintry scene in Conshohocken of Spring Mill Avenue, possibly of the section between Ash and Poplar Streets. In the center background is a dome tower that belongs to the old St. Matthews School.

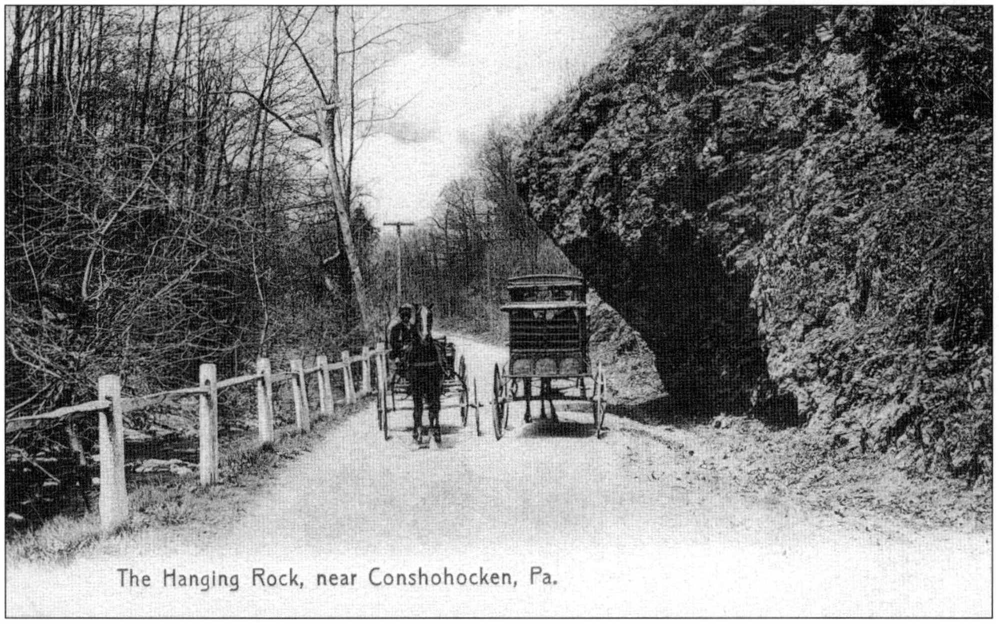

Washington's army encamped in this area in 1777, and local lore is that Washington took shelter under this rock during a storm. Gulph Road was very narrow at the rock overhang. Over the years, the site has come under threat of destruction several times to widen the roadway. In 1980, the Valley Forge Historic Society, which owns the site, agreed to cut the rock back from the road.

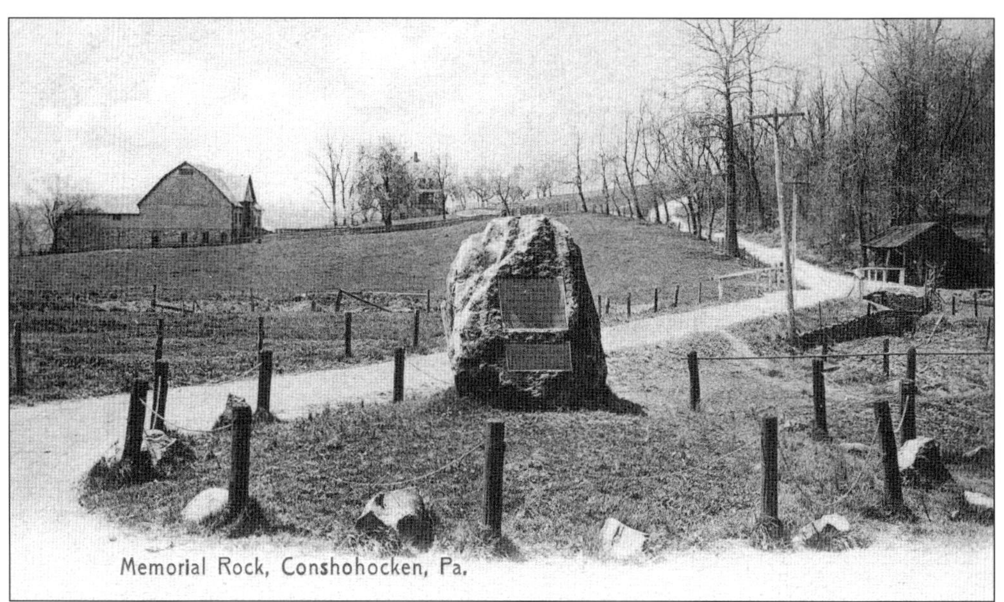

To commemorate Washington's encampment in Gulph Mills on his journey to Valley Forge, a monument, Memorial Rock, was erected at the intersection of Gulph and Matson Ford Roads. In the early 1900s, tourists would visit Hanging Rock and Memorial Rock on their way to Valley Forge.

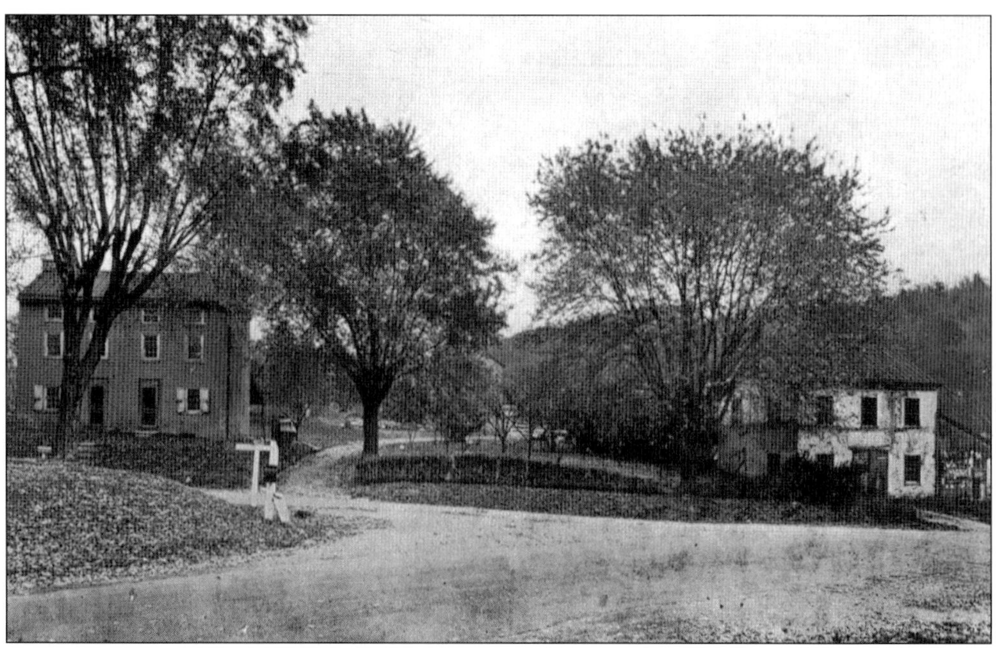

This 1920 view is of an area called Bird in Hand. It is actually a section of Gulph Mills below the Gulph train station. These homes are still standing. The caption on the back of the card refers to it as Gulph, Conshohocken, which was a typical description of the area in postcards from the early 1900s.

Four
HISTORIC LANDMARKS

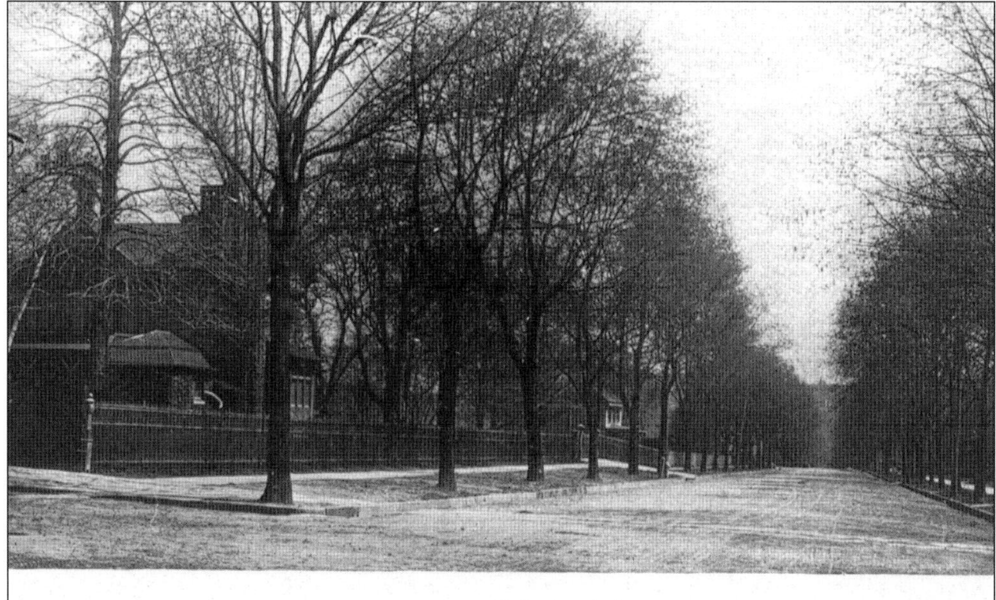

EAST FIFTH AVENUE, CONSHOHOCKEN, PA. Pub. by McCoy's Drug Store, Conshohocken, Pa.

The original Alan Wood Jr. estate was on Fifth Avenue. Fifth and Sixth Avenues and Harry and Hallowell Streets surrounded the estate. The main house was set back from the avenue by a circular drive connecting to a carriage house on Harry Street. Alan Wood Jr. and his wife, Mary, occupied this house from 1861 until 1892, when his mansion Woodmont, in Gladwyne, was completed. After her husband's death in 1902, Mary Wood returned to live at this house until her death in 1918.

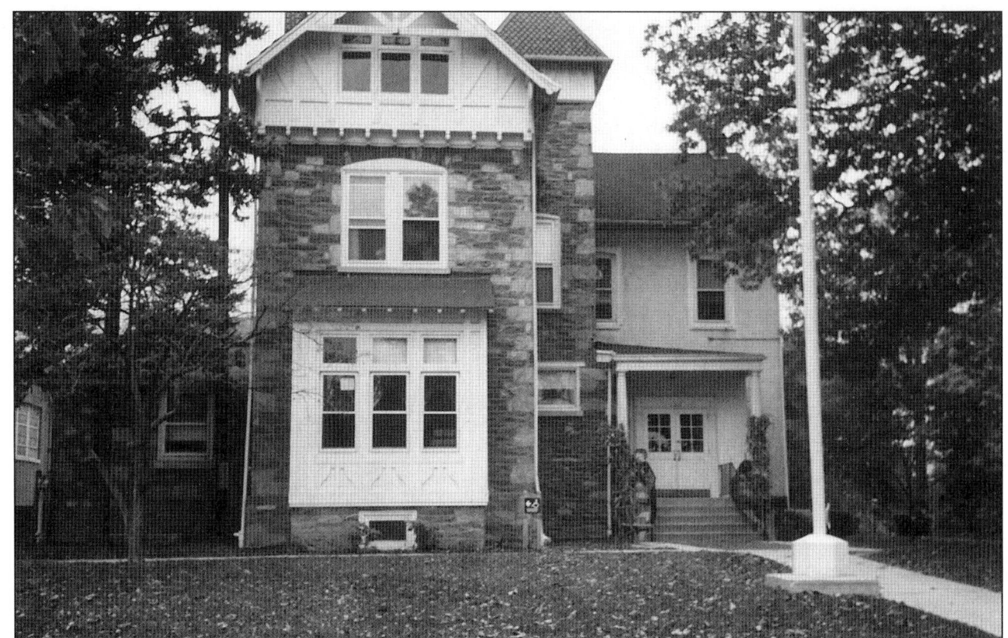

In 1918, Mary Wood bequeathed the original Alan Wood Jr. estate to the borough of Conshohocken. The Mary Wood Park House is currently used by several civic organizations. It is also home to the Conshohocken Historic Society, which was founded in the back room of George Rafferty's drugstore on lower Fayette Street. The official incorporation was held on February 26, 1963. Its first president was William F. Collins.

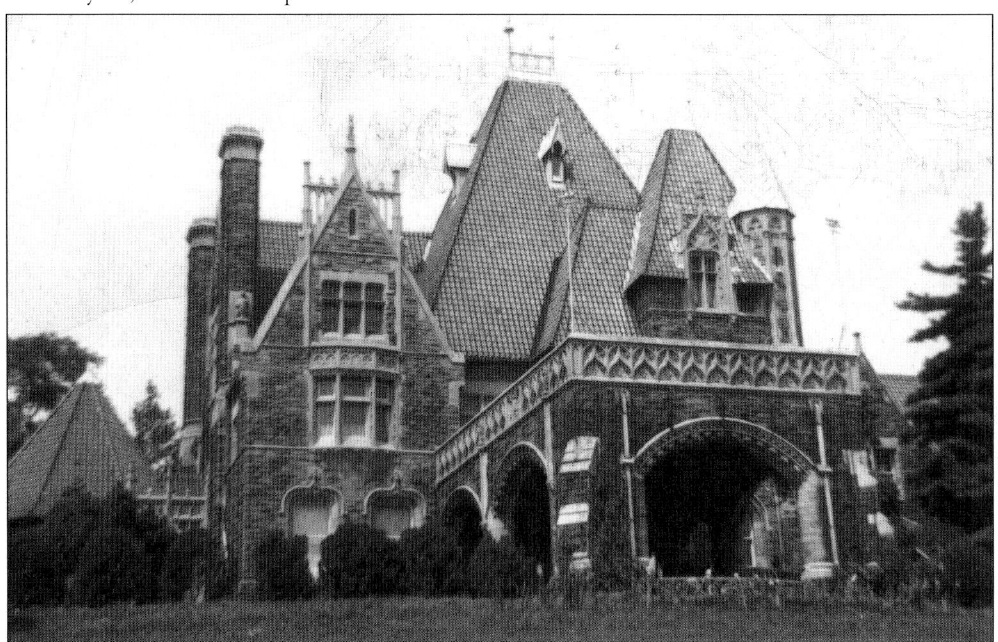

Alan Wood Jr.'s beloved Woodmont was a 32-room castlelike mansion built in 1892 at the estimated cost of $1 million. The home is in the French Gothic style and has a steel structure on solid rock. Its picturesque 73 acres overlook the bend in the Schuylkill River. Today it is known as the Father Divine Estate.

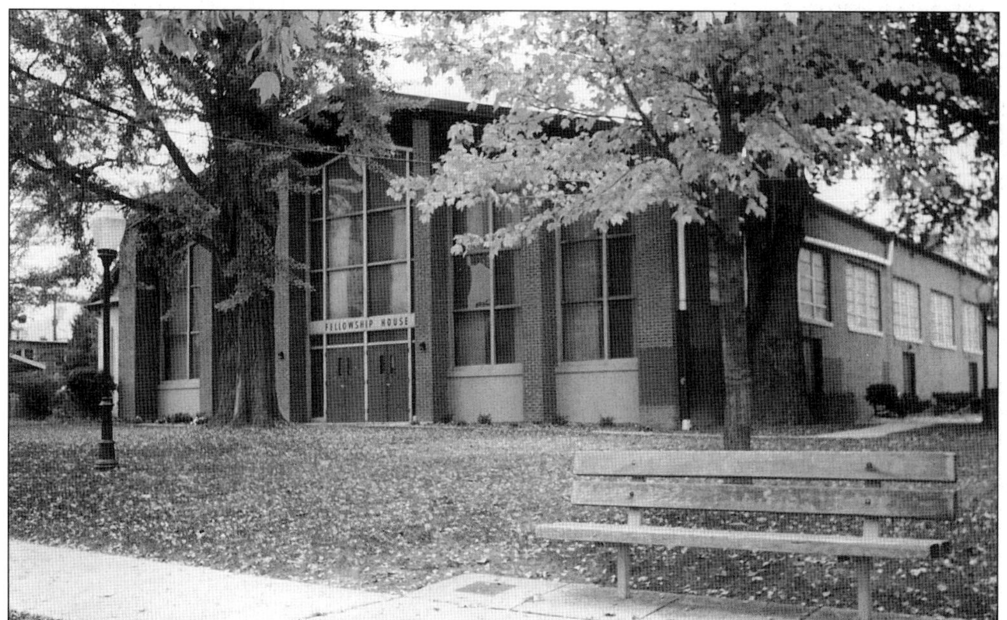

The Conshohocken Fellowship House, located on Harry Street between Fifth and Sixth Avenues, was built on the grounds of the original Alan Wood Jr. estate. The community center was constructed in 1953. Many of the area's schools have used the facility for sporting events.

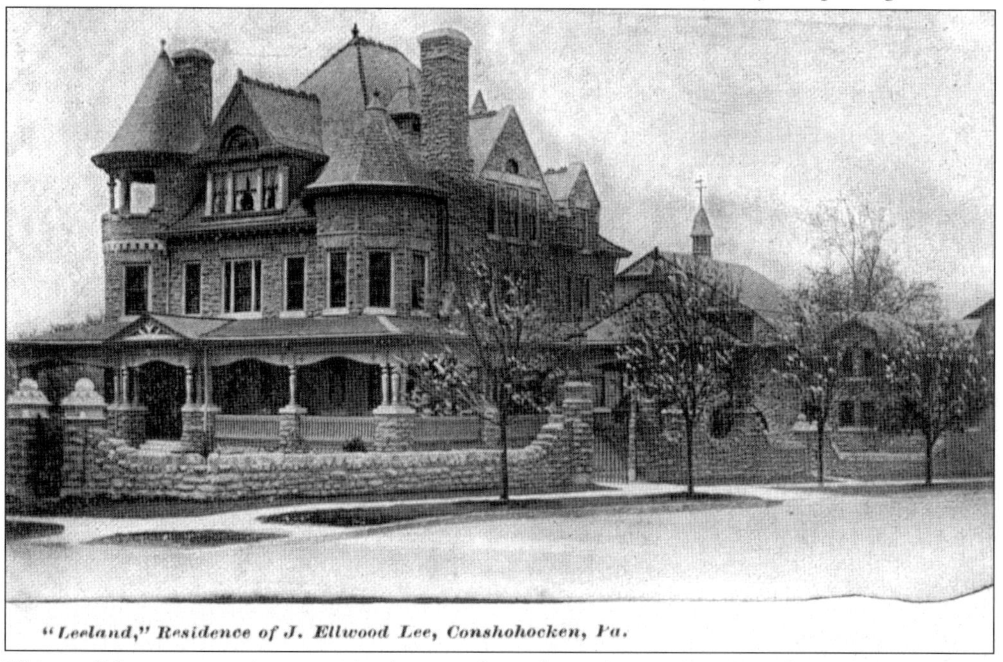

This well-known mansion was the home of J. Ellwood Lee, founder of JELCO, a surgical supplies company, and of Lee Tires of Conshohocken. Following the trend of other successful Conshohocken industrialist, Lee built Leeland in 1898. The three-story, 23-room mansion is located on Eighth Avenue and Fayette Street and is currently home to Conshohocken's borough hall. West of his house, between Eighth and Twelfth Avenues from Colwell Lane to Maple Street, Lee built a golf course.

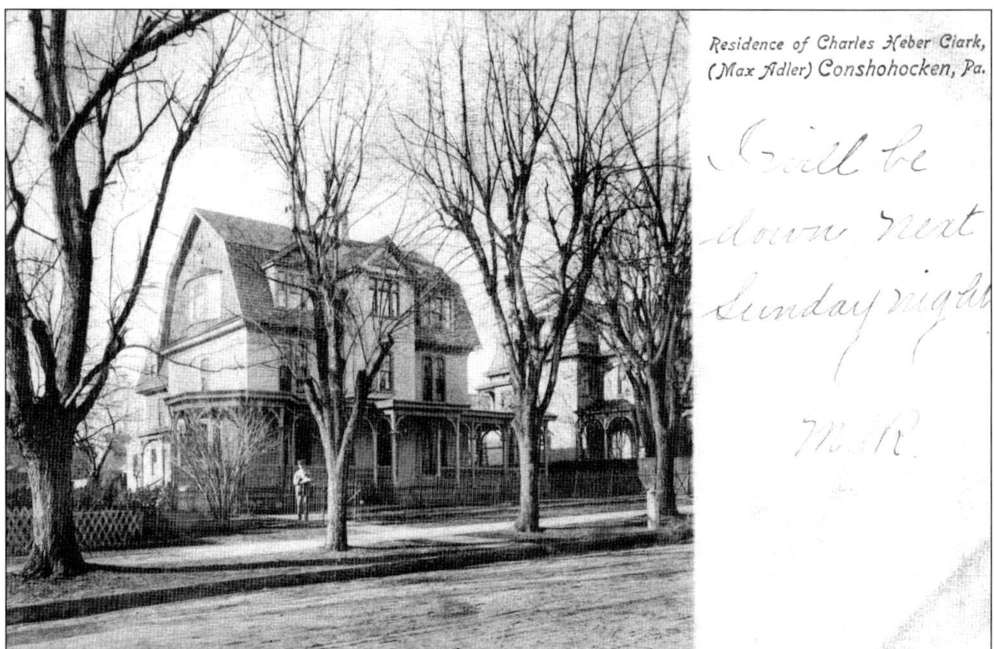

The Clark residence was located at 123 East Fifth Avenue and still stands today. At the beginning of the 20th century, Clark was an editor for the *Philadelphia Evening Bulletin*. He was also a well-known author who wrote under the name Max Adeler. Of the many books written by him, *The Quakeress* (1905) depicted life in a community called Connock. Connock is believed to be an area of Conshohocken. There are photographs in the book of the Calvary church and parsonage (on Fayette Street), Plymouth Meetinghouse (on Butler Pike), and Gulph Church. Charles Heber Clark was also a benefactor to J. Ellwood Lee, loaning him the necessary funds to start his surgical supply company.

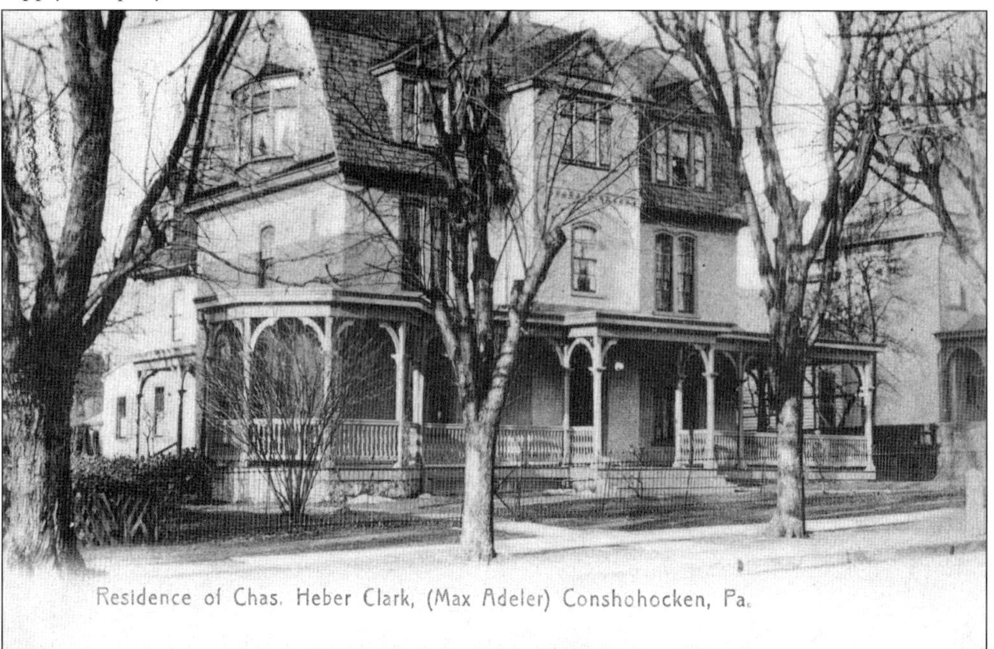

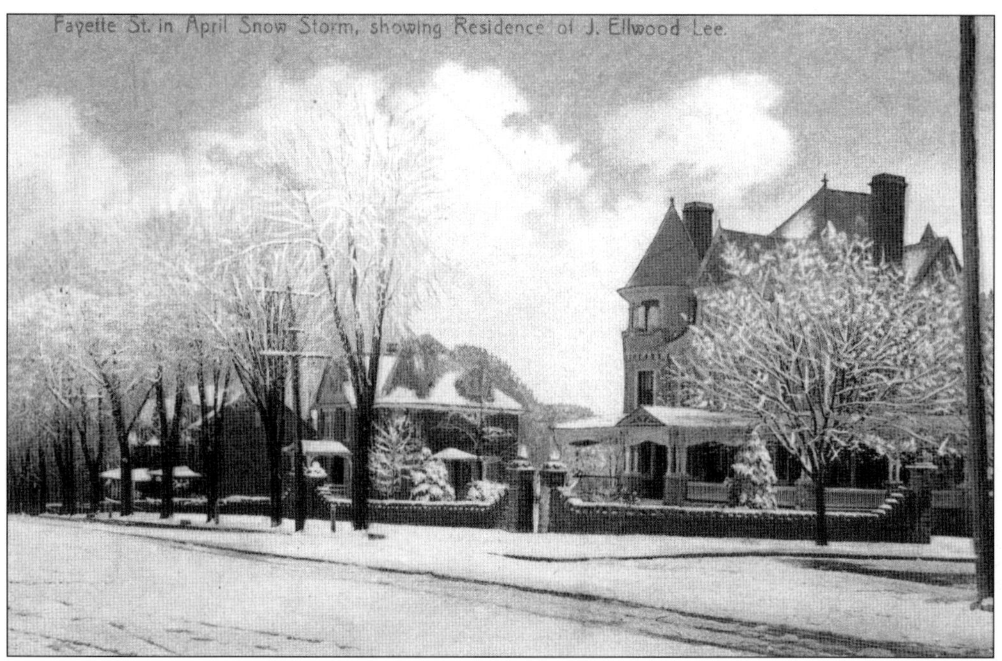

On the right of this view of Fayette Street between West Seventh and Eighth Avenues is Leeland, home to J. Ellwood Lee. According to the Smith atlas, the next home belonged to the Hewitt family and then became Mrs. McCall's home.

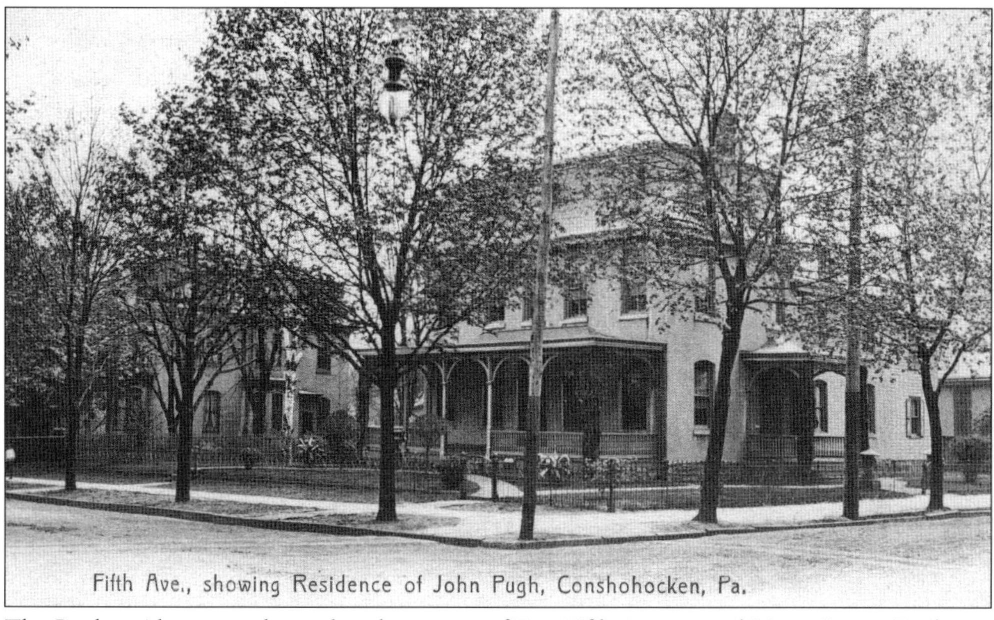

The Pugh residence was located at the corner of East Fifth Avenue and Harry Street. Pugh was a Revolutionary War veteran and owned a feed store at the foot of the Matsonford Bridge in the 1850s and 1860s. His home is the current site of the office of Dr. James J. Nicholson.

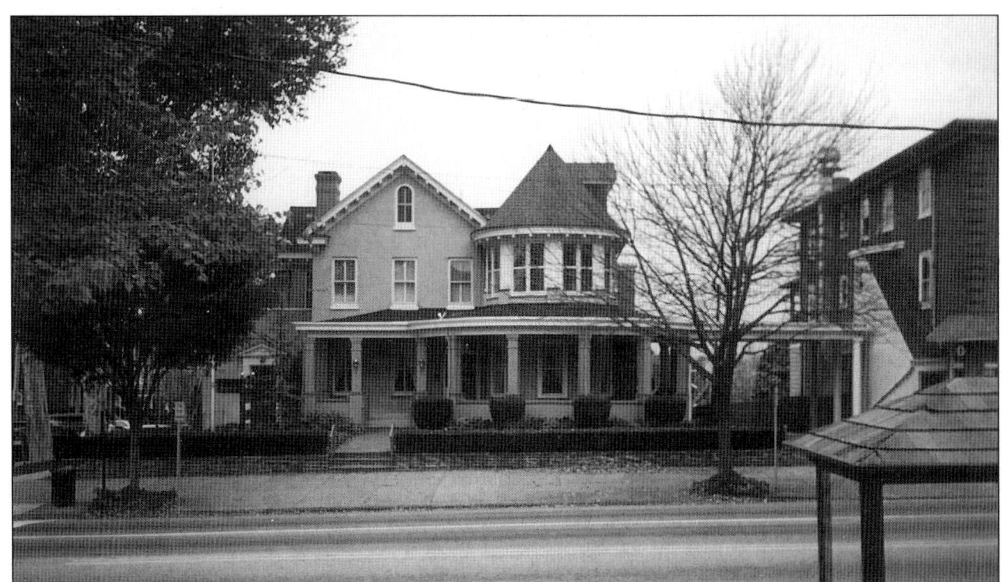

This is another grand home on Fayette Street and Third Avenue. The home has long served the town as a funeral home. In the 1930s, it was the Paul Miller Mortuary and then Ardels Funeral Home. Today, it is the Moore & Snear Funeral Home.

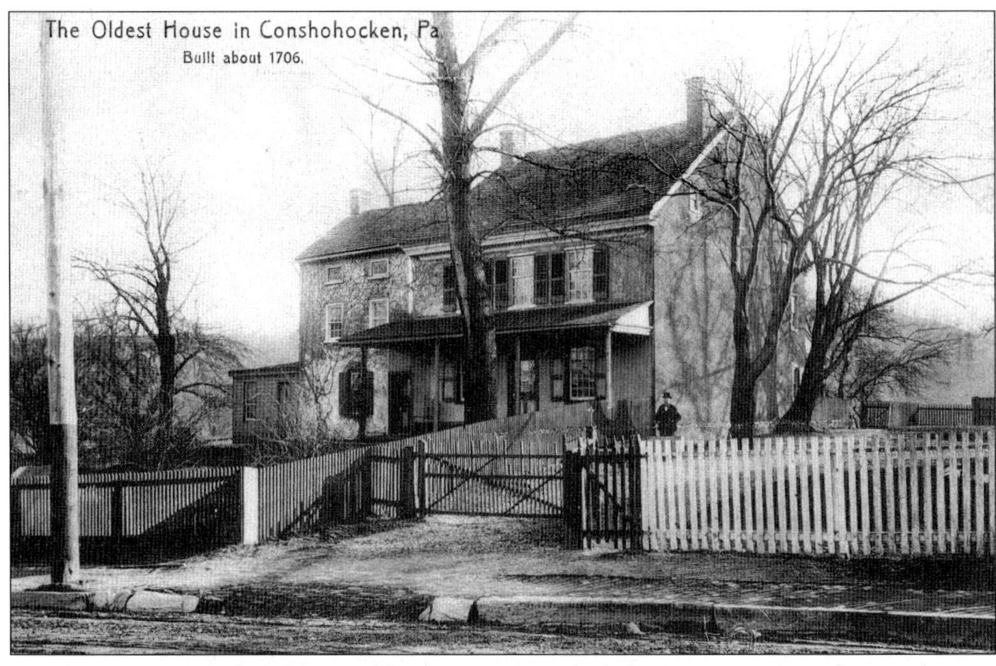

David Harry's original purchase of land in 1700 marked the starting point of more than six generations of the Harry family in Conshohocken. David Harry's two-story Mansion House, built in 1706 at what is now the intersection of Apple and Hector Streets, was for more than 200 years the oldest building in town.

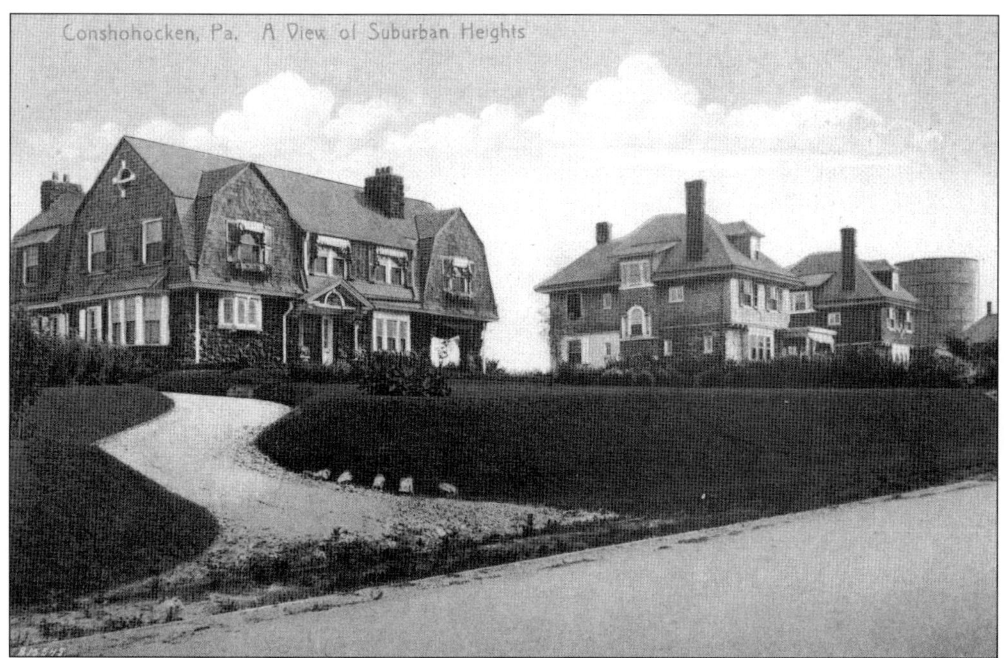

Grand homes lined either side of Fayette Street in the first half of the 20th century. Suburban Heights referred to an area on Fayette Street past Twelfth Avenue. This is the east side of Fayette just past Moore's Auto Dealership. The water tower in the background was located where a real estate and insurance company is today.

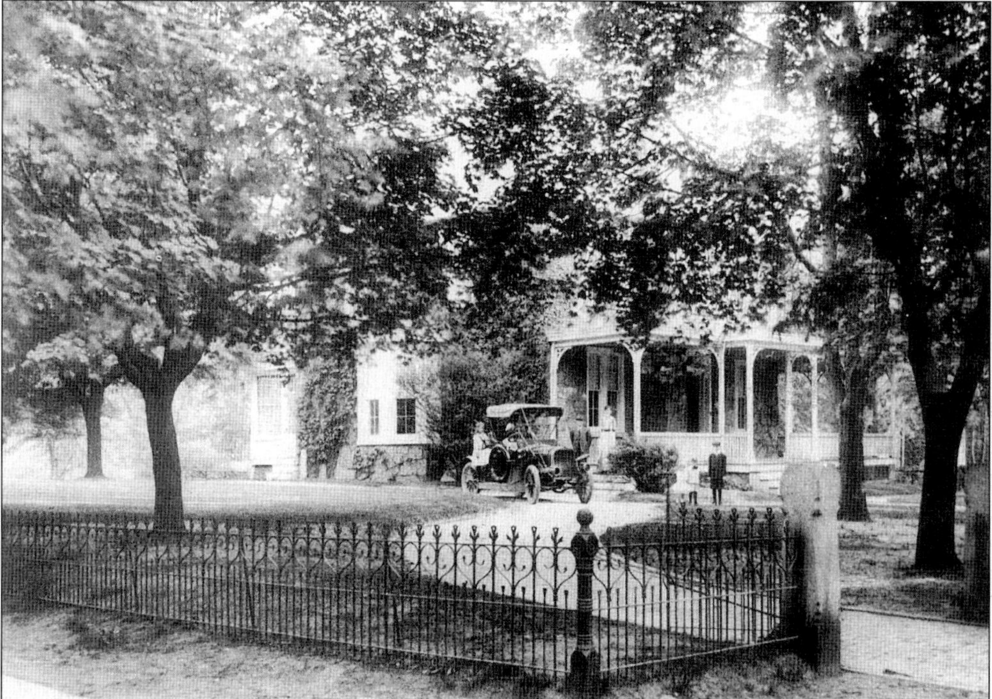

Pictured is Charles Lukens's house on East Fifth Avenue and Fayette Street. It was one of three Lukens family homes on Fayette and was demolished in 1939 to make way for the post office.

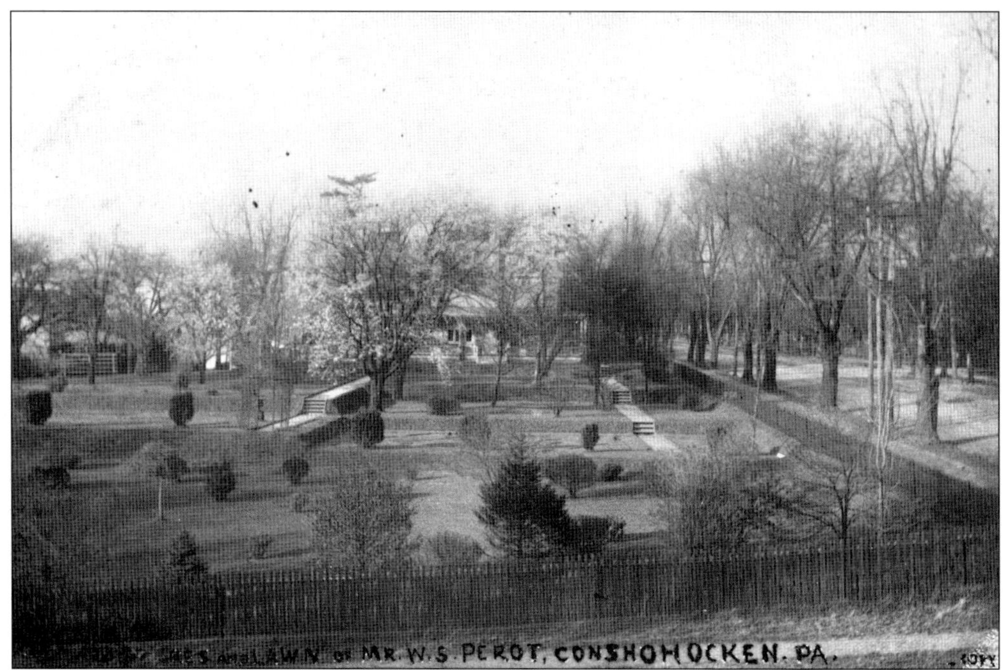

These are the beautiful gardens of the W.S. Perot residence, once located on West Fifth Avenue and Fayette Street. The estate stretched from Fourth to Fifth Avenue from Fayette to Forrest Street. The home was demolished to make way for a bank and a building that housed the Bell Telephone Company.

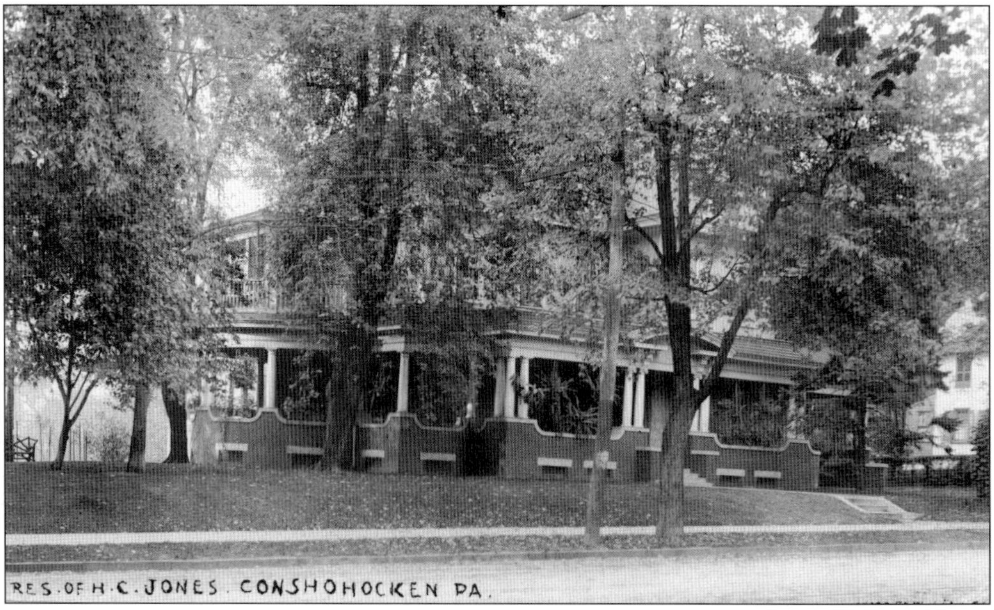

The lovely Horace C. Jones home was located on Fayette Street between Fifth and Sixth Avenues. Horace Jones—great-grandson of Isaac Jones, president of the Matsonford Bridge Company in 1837—followed his father's footsteps into the Jones Lumber Company and later partnered with Stanley Lees to form the H.C. Jones Company, a textile company. The home has belonged to the Ciavarelli family for about the last 50 years as a residence and funeral home.

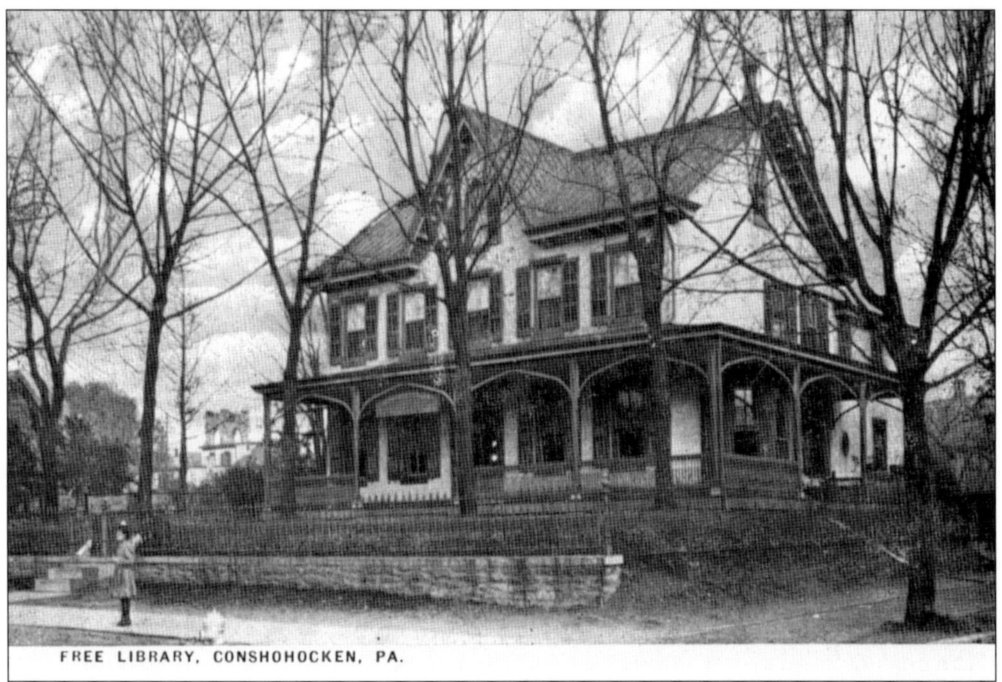
FREE LIBRARY, CONSHOHOCKEN, PA.

The Conshohocken Free Library, on the corner of Third Avenue and Fayette Street, is the former residence of Lewis Lukens. Of the three Lukens family homes on Fayette Street, this is the only one remaining. Lewis served as a burgess in 1859, 1860, and 1861. He was also director and president of the First National Bank of Conshohocken for 17 years.

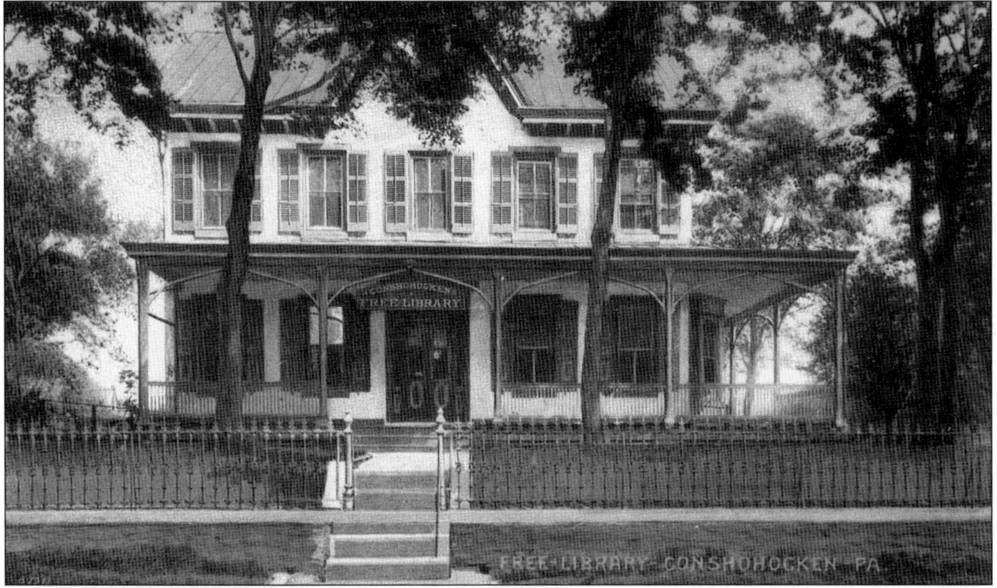

FREE LIBRARY CONSHOHOCKEN PA

The Conshohocken Free Library, founded in 1907, began in a room of the Harry School on Third Avenue. In 1909, the Lewis Lukens home, built in 1856, was rented to the borough by the grandchildren for the purpose of a town library, at a cost of $1 per year. Today the library is a branch of Montgomery County-Norristown Public Library and has recently undergone a remodeling to enlarge it.

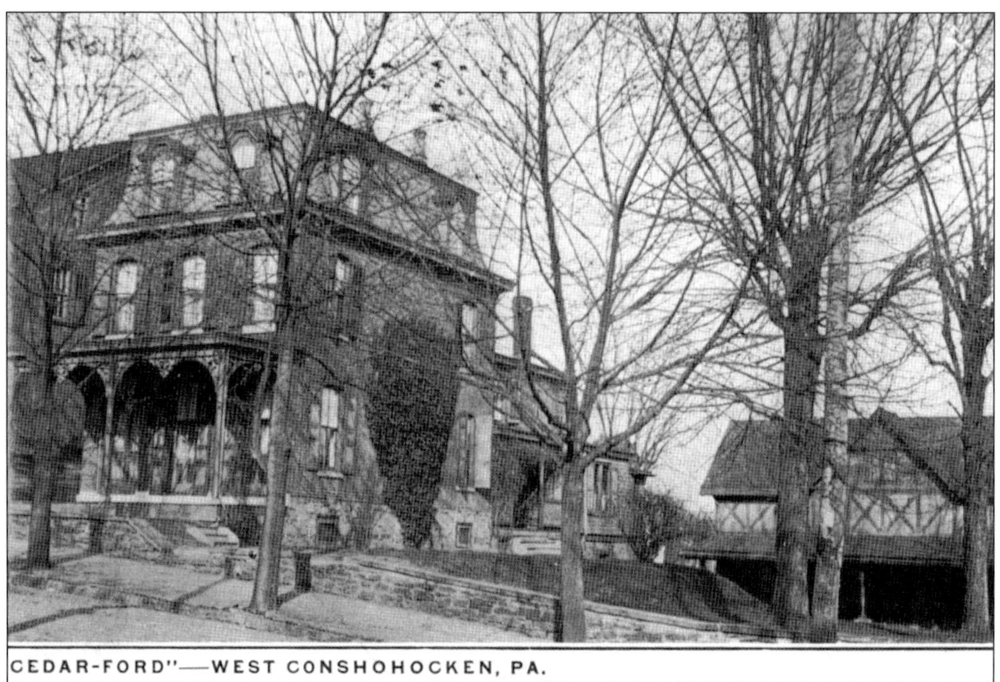

Still standing today, this home is located at the intersection of Cedar Avenue and Ford Street in West Conshohocken. The three-story home was built *c.* 1900.

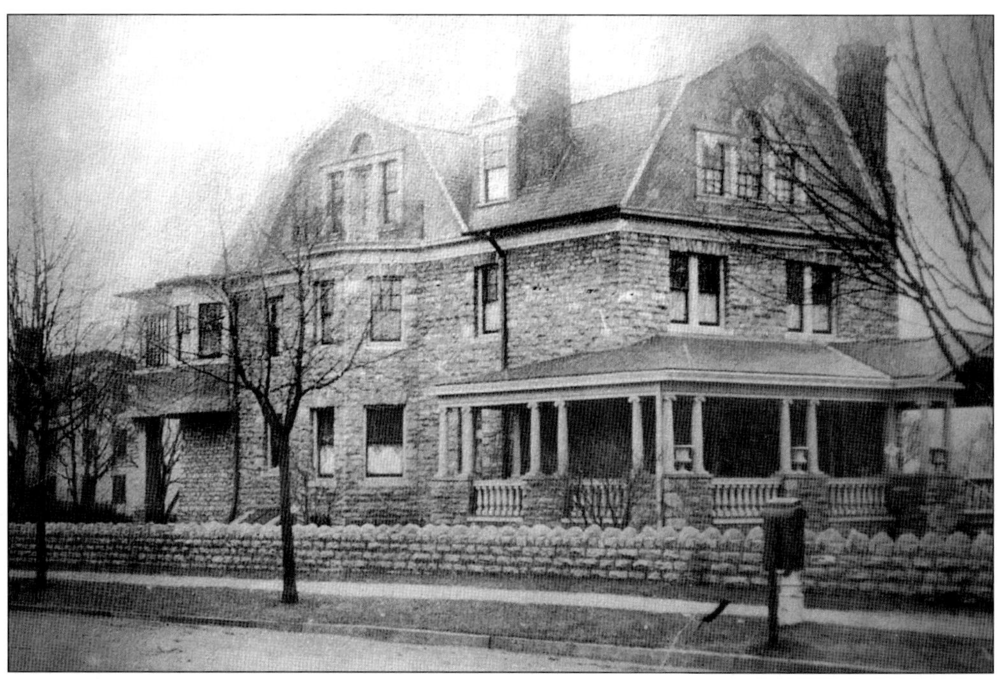

Nicknamed Indianola, this beautiful mansion, once owned by Henry Tracy, was located on the corner of East Eighth Avenue and Fayette Street. The home was typical of the mansions that lined Fayette Street at the beginning of the 20th century. Unfortunately, the home was demolished so that a gasoline station could be erected.

Five
BUSINESS AND INDUSTRY

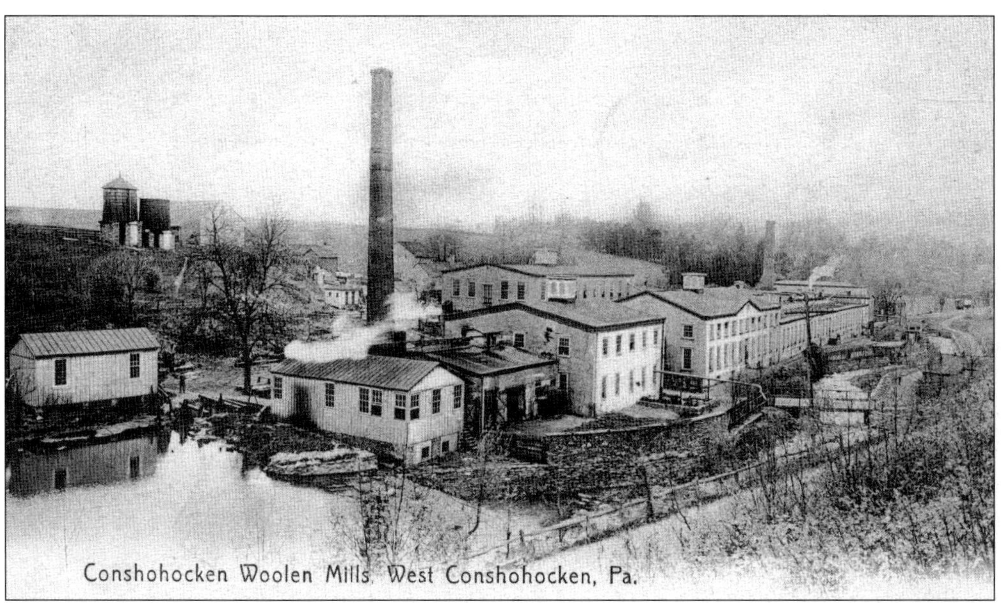

Numerous mills once lined the Gulph Creek in West Conshohocken. George Bullock, West Conshohocken's first burgess, operated two mills in the late 19th century. This view is of Bullock's Conshohocken Woolen Mill, on Balligomingo Road along Gulph Creek. This mill produced high-quality blue woolen cloth for the federal government for army uniforms. Still standing, this mill later housed the operations of Glassine Paper Company, the Westfield River Paper Company, and the West Conshohocken Paper Company. Today it is an industrial park.

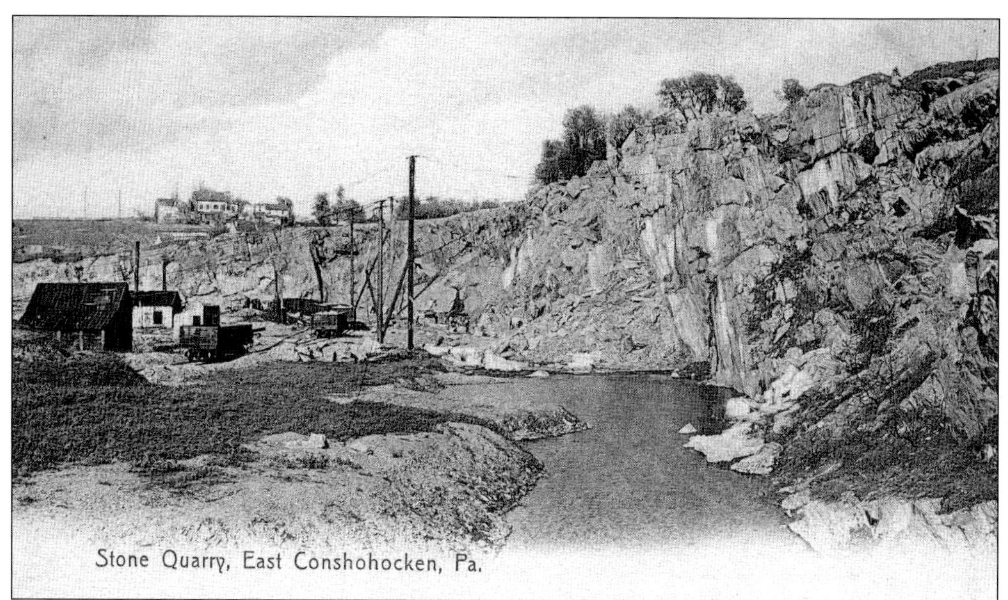

The East Conshohocken Stone Quarry was located along Colwell Lane in an area between Second and Fourth Avenues. The quarries in Conshohocken and West Conshohocken were very rich in fine stone and marble. The marble quarried in the area was shipped throughout the country for use in wealthy estate home and prominent public buildings.

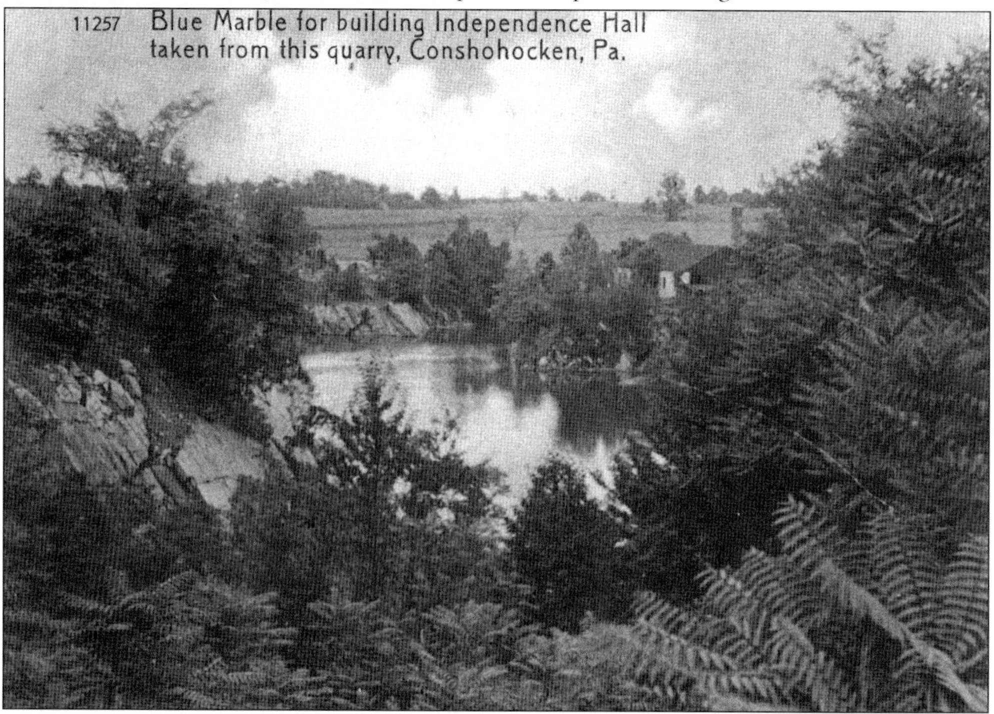

Potts quarry is located off Butler Pike behind Sherry Lake Apartments. Before 1900, blue marble was mined at the quarry and was used for Independence Hall and also to build the base of Philadelphia's city hall. Today, the marble can still be found in many of the historic buildings in and around Philadelphia.

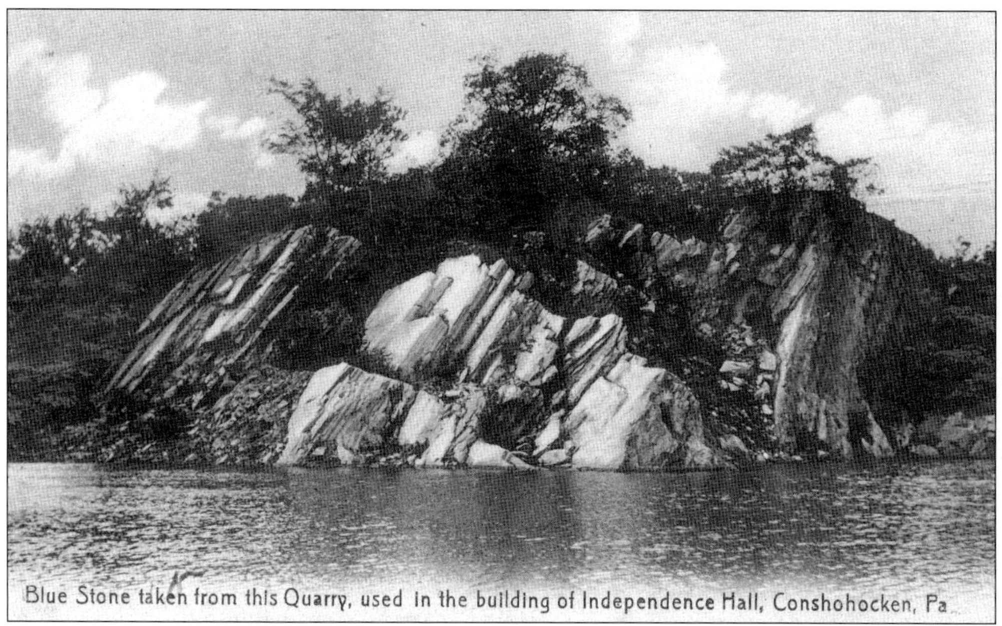

Famous for its beautiful bluestone marble, Potts quarry was also a very popular swimming hole for local residents. During the silent-film era, the quarry was used as a location for several movies. It was also popular because it was one of a few places in the country that a horse and rider could jump off a cliff into the water without injury.

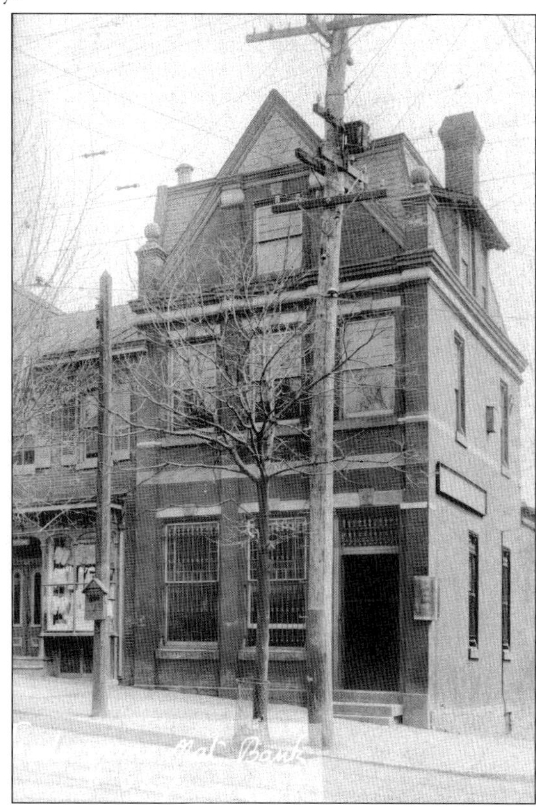

The Tradesmen's National Bank was founded in 1872 and had its one and only location at the corner of West Hector and Fayette Streets. It closed in 1943 and merged with the First National Bank of Conshohocken, located across the street.

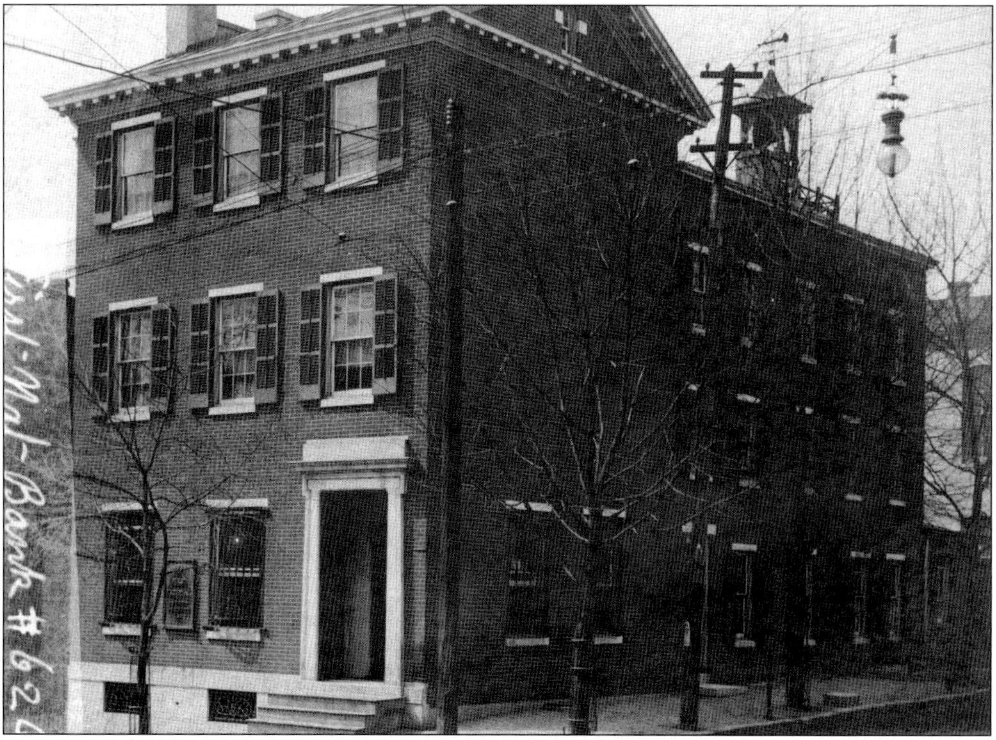

The First National Bank of Conshohocken was chartered on December 1, 1873. The first building was located on West Hector and Fayette Streets. Lewis Lukens was president of the bank for 17 years.

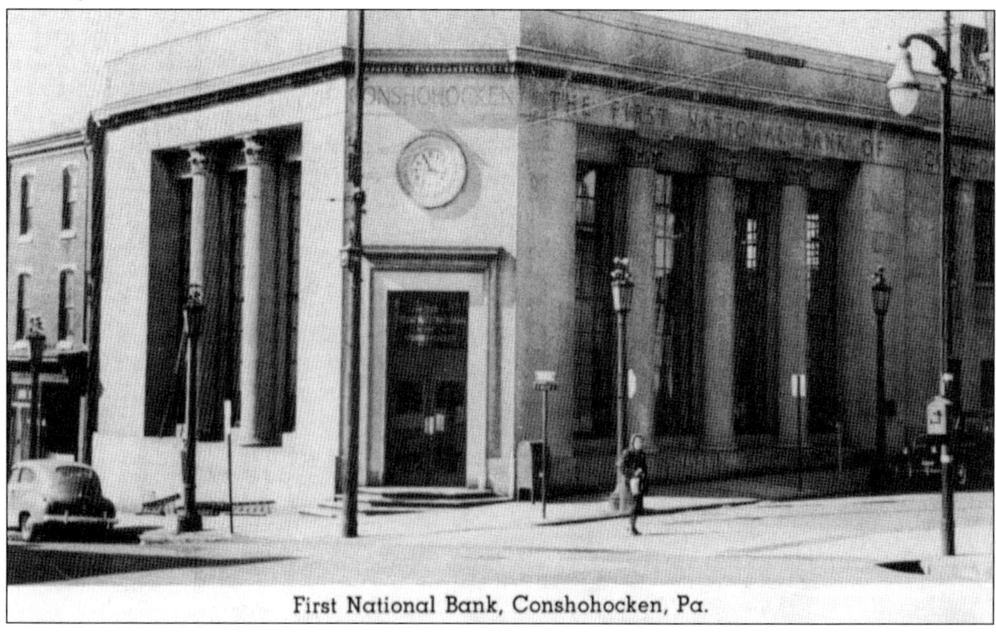

In the late 1920s, the First National Bank built a new structure on West Hector and Fayette Streets. The bank eventually merged with Philadelphia National Bank, and this building and many more on the lower end of Conshohocken were demolished for the revitalization project.

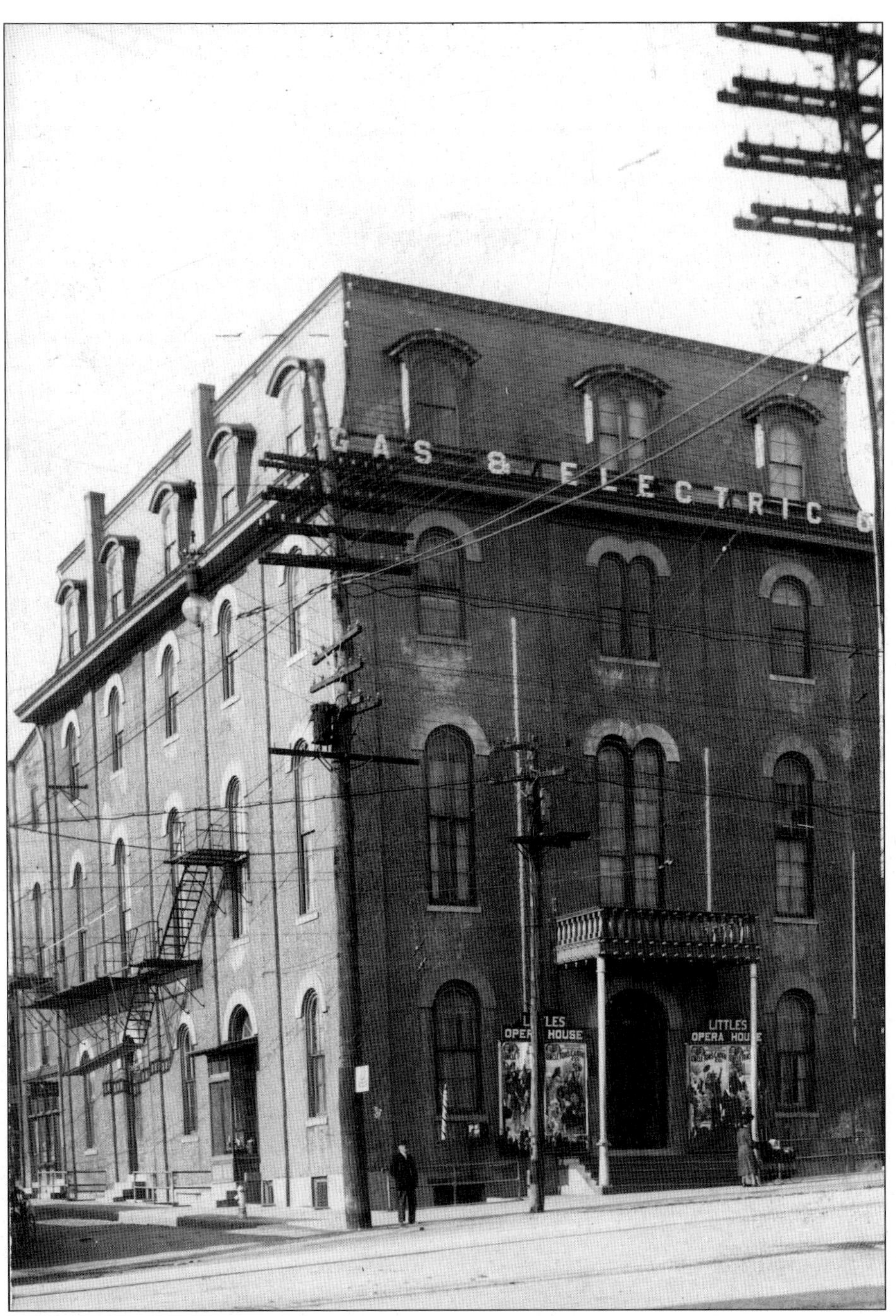

The Washita Hall was built in 1872 by the National Order of Red Men at the corner of West First Avenue and Fayette Street. Its second and third floors accommodated the candlelit Littles Opera House with red velvet plush seats and lined boxes for 500 patrons. Plays, minstrel shows, high school commencements, political rallies, and operas were staged there. Tom Thumb once performed there in 1888 with the Barnum & Bailey Circus. SS. Cosmas and Damian Church was founded in this building in 1911. The Counties Gas & Electric Company also had an office in the building. In 1928, the Washita Hall built a new home on the corner of Sixth Avenue and Harry Street.

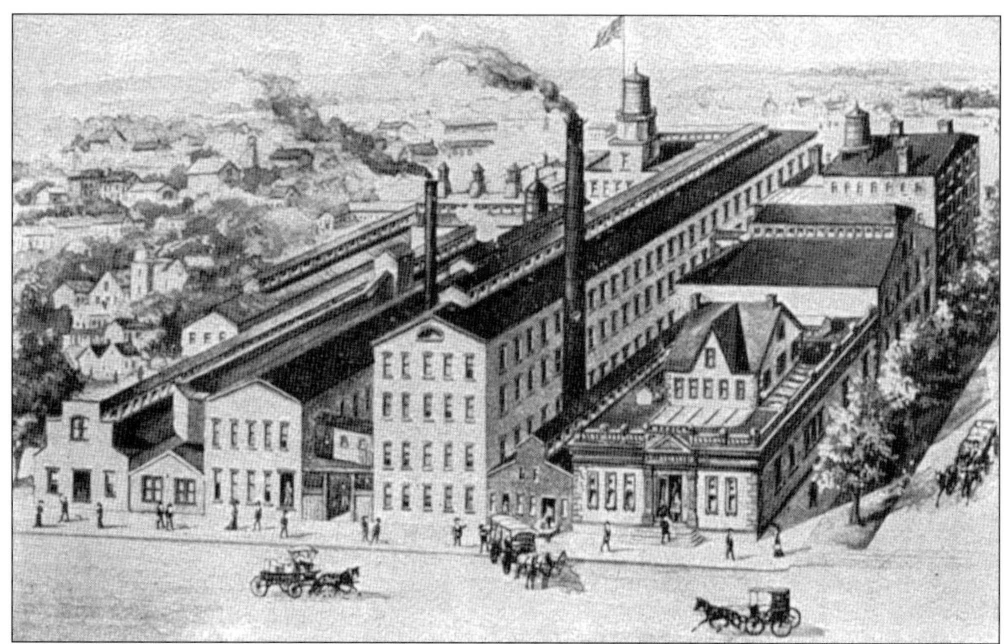

In 1883, J. Ellwood Lee was making surgical dressings on his mother's sewing machine. By 1887, his company, JELCO, had grown to produce a variety of medical products, and Lee built a three-story building on Eighth Avenue and Harry Streets. With 600 employees at the beginning of the 20th century, Lee's surgical supply company became the largest individual employer in Conshohocken. His factories at Eighth and Harry Streets expanded to a complex of 17 buildings in 1905. Lee merged operations with Johnson & Johnson in 1905, and production in Conshohocken continued until 1909.

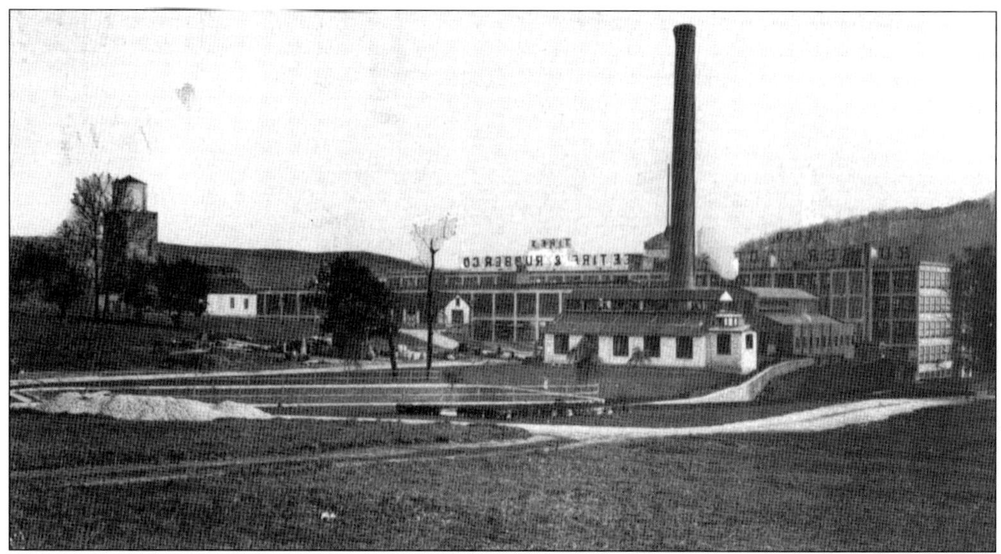

During the time that Lee's surgical supply company was being transferred, he was experimenting with retooling his rubber goods production. Lee foresaw the mass production of the automobile and corresponding markets in rubber tires. On May 1, 1912, the Lee Tire and Rubber Company opened its block-long, four-story modern factory on Hector Street and North Lane with 850 employees.

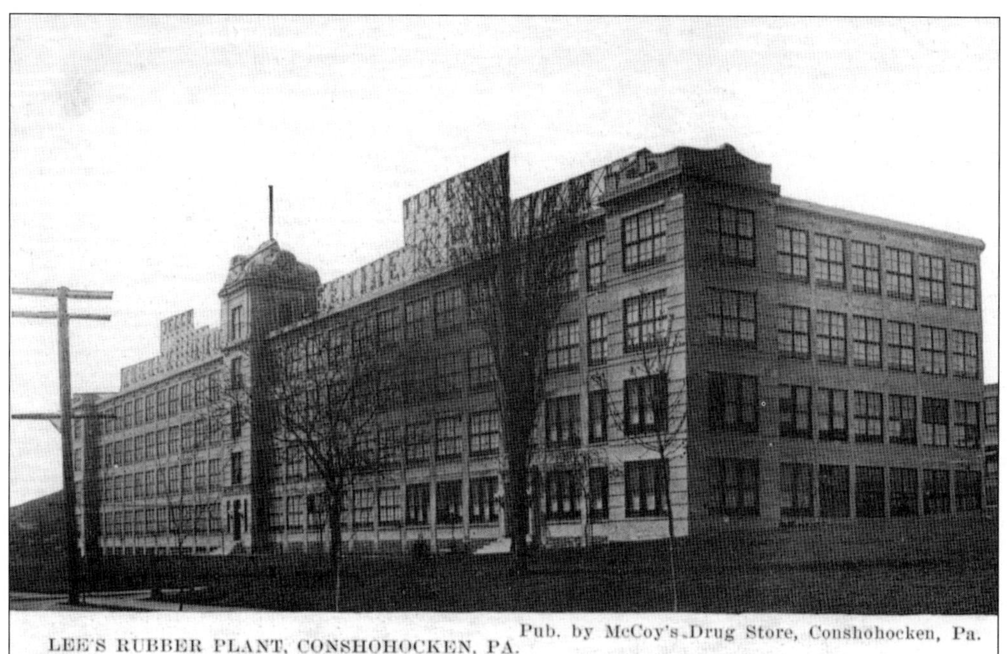

LEE'S RUBBER PLANT, CONSHOHOCKEN, PA. Pub. by McCoy's Drug Store, Conshohocken, Pa.

"Lee of Conshohocken," as it was known, was a prominent name around the globe for its puncture-proof tires. J. Ellwood Lee died in 1914, but the company continued to thrive long after his death. In 1936, the advent of balloon, or low-pressure, tires forced the company to cease making puncture-proof tires and turn to the manufacture of regular tires.

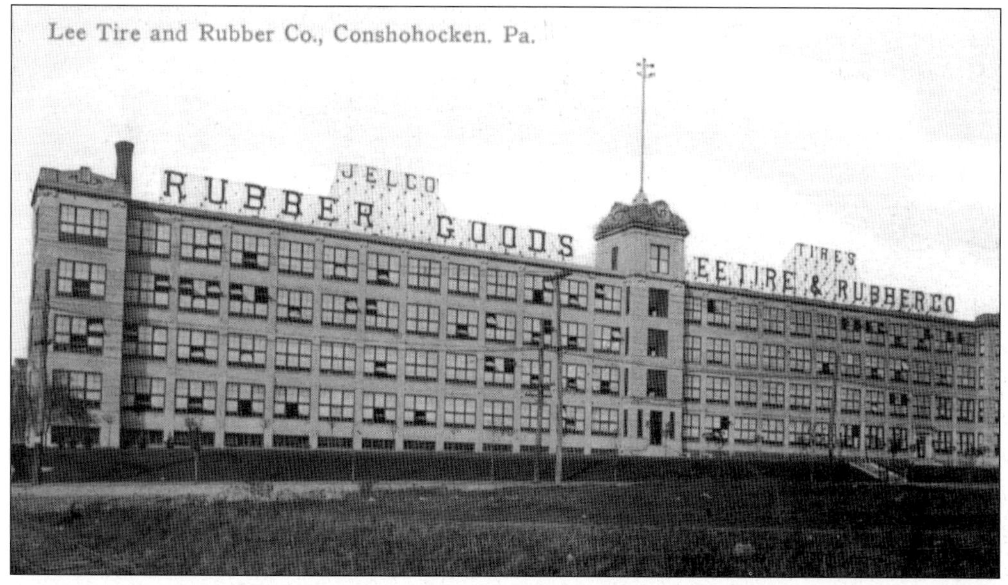

Lee Tire and Rubber Co., Conshohocken. Pa.

In 1962, the control of Lee's stock was taken over by raiders from a New York firm, and the company name was changed to Lee National Corporation. In 1965, Goodyear Tire and Rubber Company of Akron, Ohio, purchased the remains of the business and changed the name back to the Lee Tire and Rubber Company. By 1980, the radial tire had become popular, but the manufacturing plant in Conshohocken was not tooled to manufacturer this type of tire and was forced out of business. The site at Hector Street and North Lane is now an industrial park.

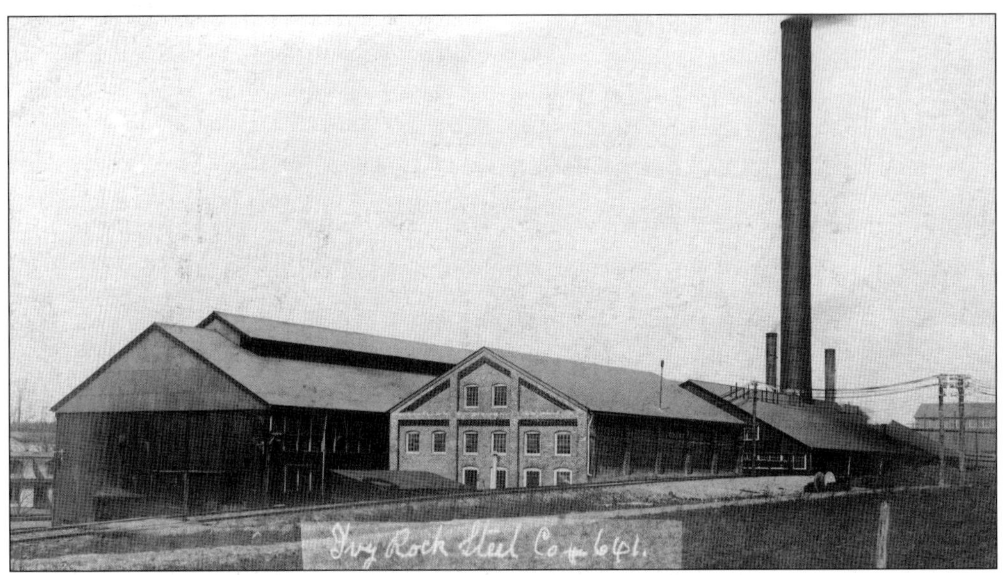

In 1901, the Alan Wood Steel Company needed its own means of steel production. The company purchased the Carey Farm along the Schuylkill River at Ivy Rock and built five 55-ton, open-hearth furnaces and a blooming mill. The company produced its first steel on June 1, 1903. This location became known as the Ivy Rock Steel Plant. In 1977, a petition for bankruptcy was filed and, after 145 years of history in the community, the Alan Wood Steel Company closed its doors.

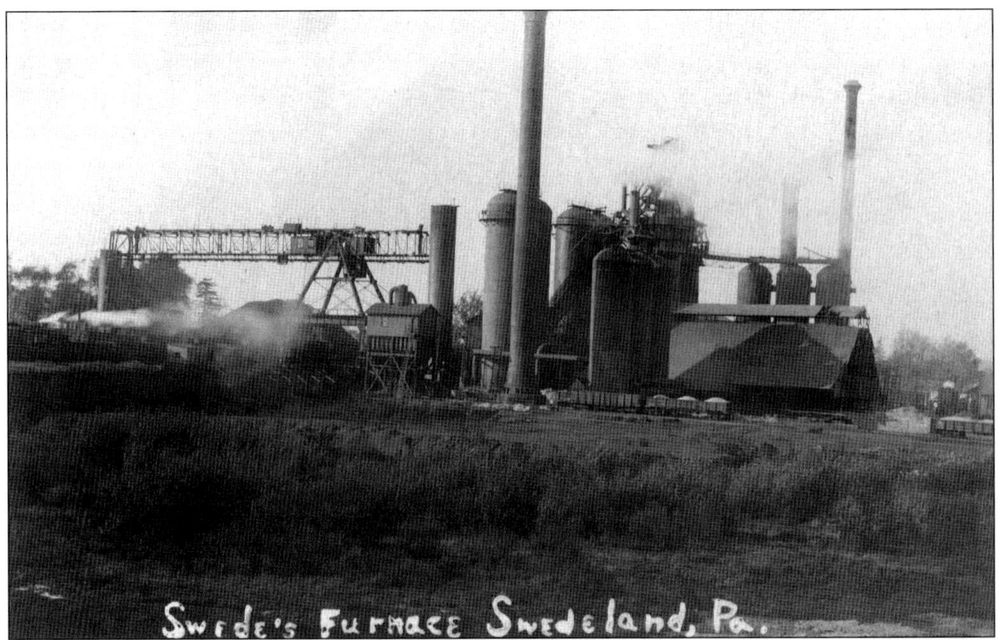

Here is a great view of the Alan Wood Steel Company. At the time of this 1909 photograph, it was called Swede's Furnace–Swede's Iron Works. Located on what is today Route 23 just outside of West Conshohocken in Swedeland, the company began in 1851 and went through several ownerships until it merged with the Alan Wood Steel Company in 1911. Today this is the site of the *Philadelphia Inquire.*

On February 3, 1873, there was a devastating explosion at the John Wood Company Rolling Mills. Seventeen people lost their lives. Work at the mill was very hard and dangerous. This is a close-up of the wreckage from the blast.

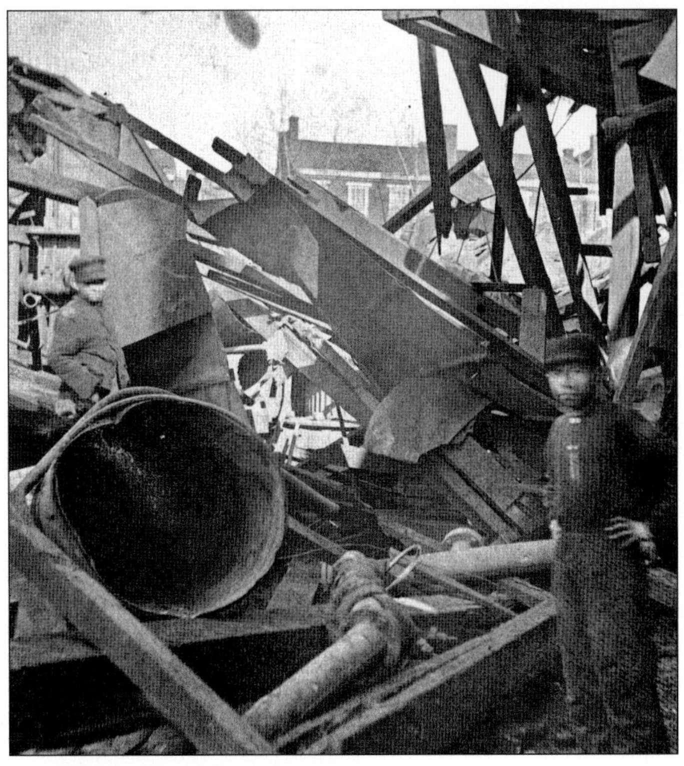

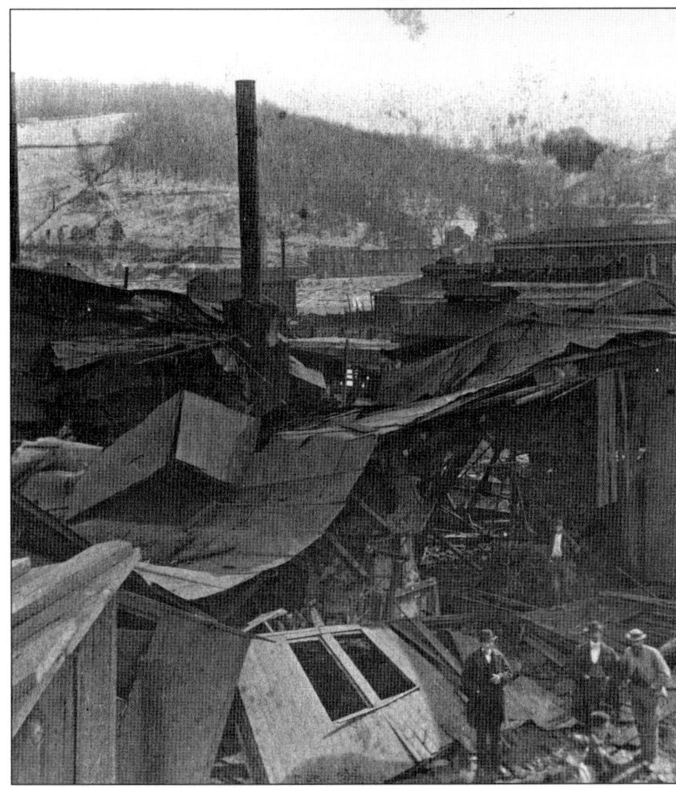

John Wood (center) and two unidentified associates survey the damage after the explosion. John "Squire" Wood not only headed the Wood iron business but also served as a justice of the peace in 1851 and a congressman in 1858.

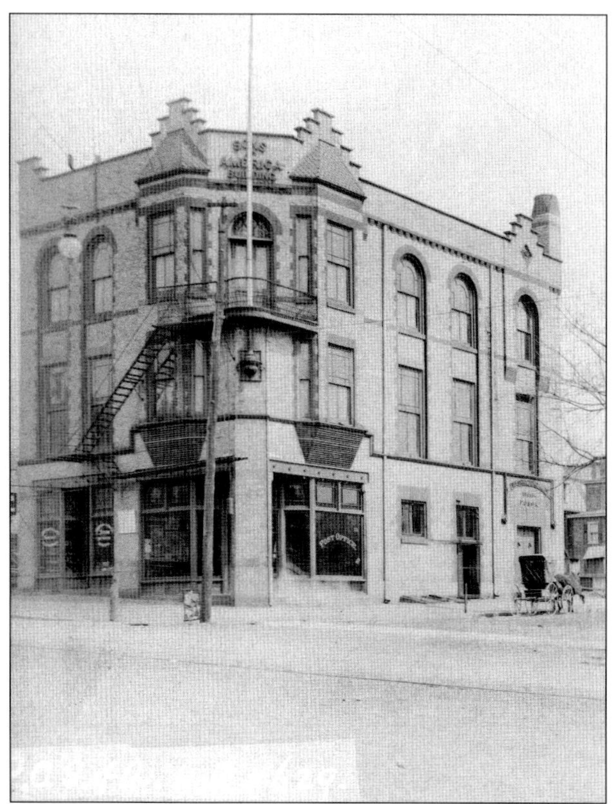

Built in 1891on the east side of Second Avenue and Fayette Street, the Sons of America building is truly a Conshohocken landmark and is still standing. As one of Conshohocken's numerous civic organizations, the Washington Camp No. 121 of the Patriotic Order Sons of America, was chartered in 1870. The land on which its headquarters were built was originally from the estate of David Harry.

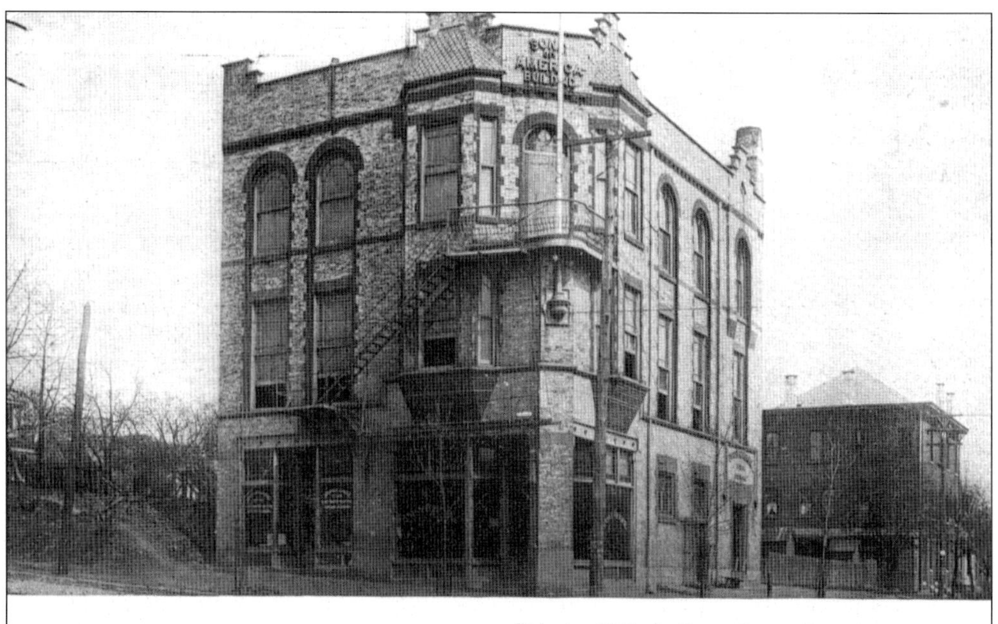

The Sons of America building was and remains home to many businesses in the community. As seen in this view from the early 1900s, it was a temporary home for the post office.

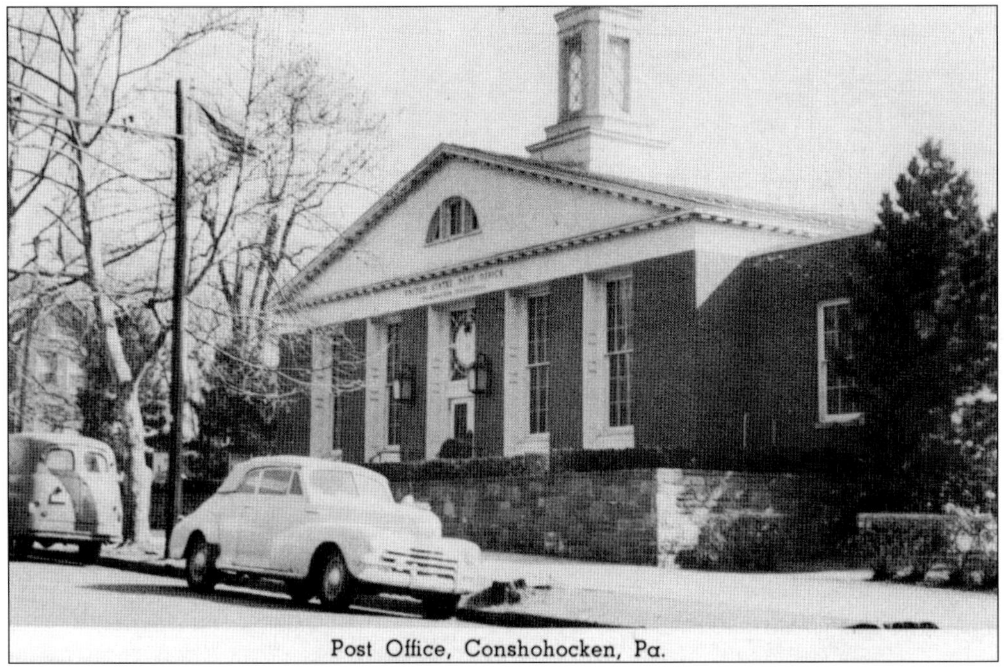

The post office began in one room on Fayette Street between Hector and Elm Streets in 1836. Over the course of 105 years, it moved to several locations in Conshohocken. In 1940, a new building was constructed on Fifth Avenue and Fayette Street as its permanent home.

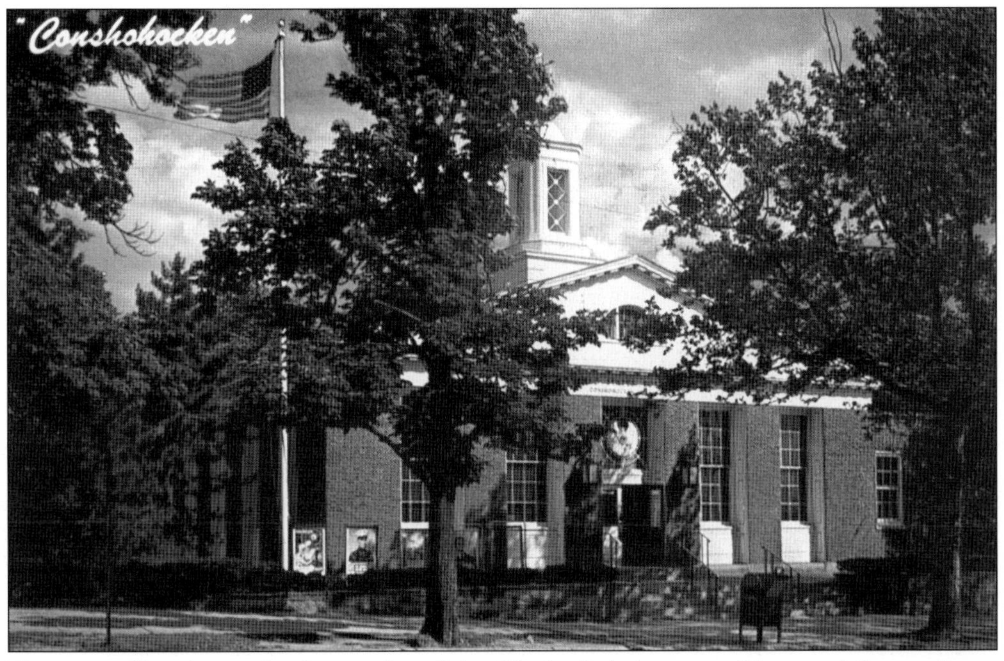

The post office sits on the former site of the Charles Lukens estate. The grand Fayette Street mansion was demolished, but the carriage house to the estate still stands today at 410 Harry Street.

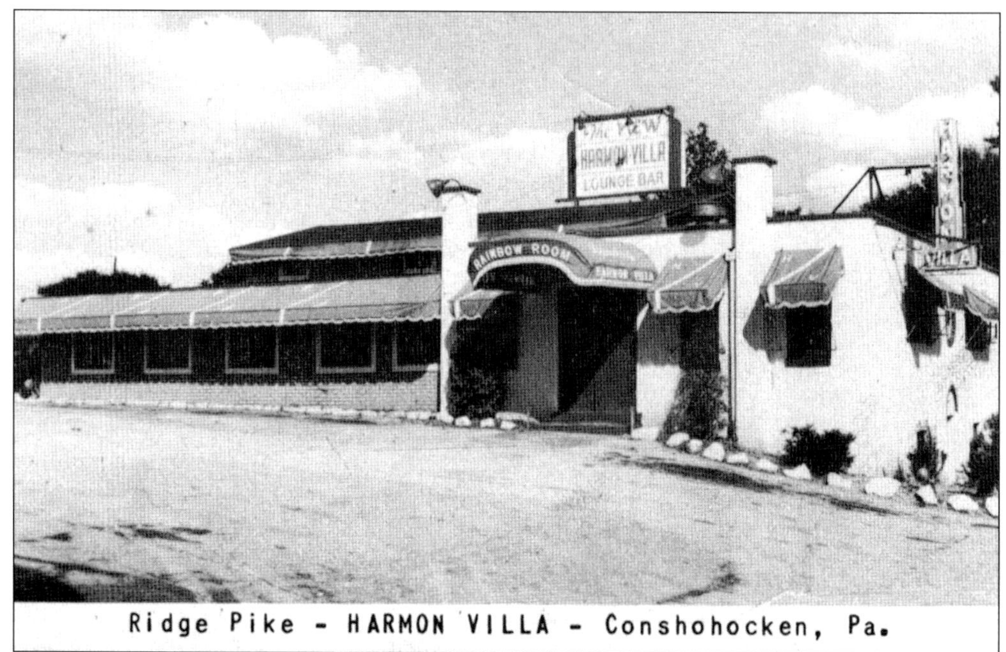

The Harmon Villa was located on Ridge Pike past Art's Skateland, just east of Belvior road. It was later called Lombardi's. The restaurant was demolished in the late 1970s or early 1980s. Today, there are automobile dealerships and a personal storage facility in this area.

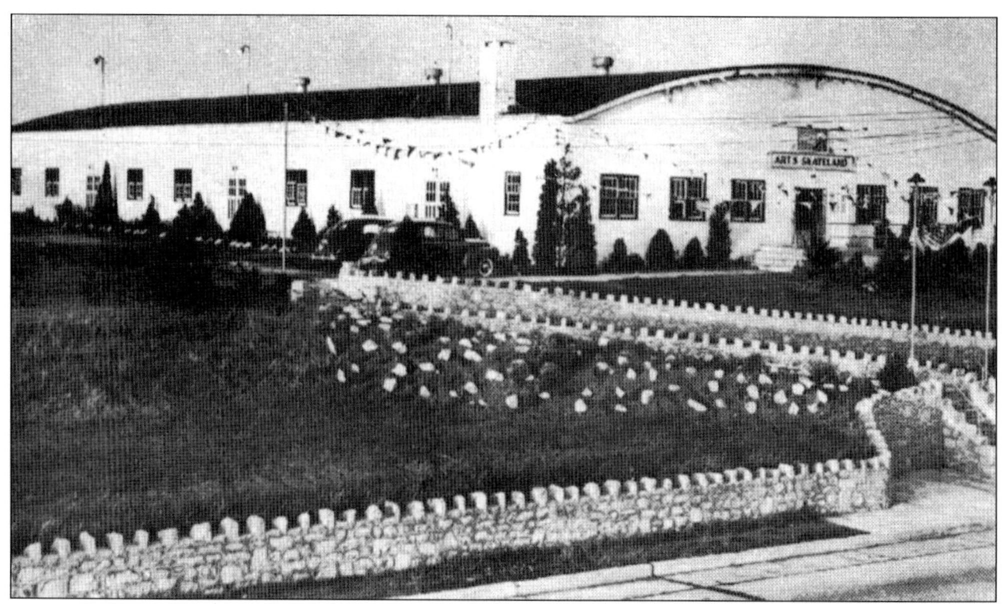

In the 1940s, Art's Skateland boasted as being one of the largest and most modern skating rinks in the eastern United States, with 13,500 square feet of skating floor. The rink was in operation until the early 1960s. The building still stands on Ridge Pike and has been home to several businesses.

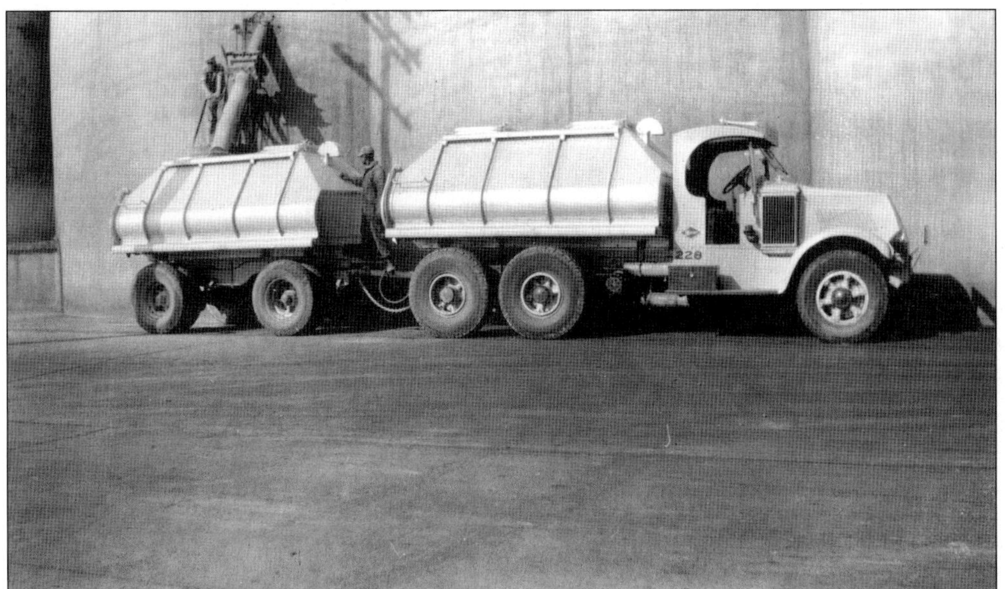

This 1937 view shows a truck loading at the Valley Forge Cement Company in West Conshohocken. The company was located at a quarry once owned by Frank H. Conrad, an early borough secretary. After the Conrad family retired from quarrying, Frank Kroch took over. Later, a group of cement manufacturers from Catasauqua, in Lehigh County, purchased the quarry and established the Valley Forge Cement Company, which later became the Allentown Portland Cement Company. These huge silos, seen behind the truck, were located on Route 23.

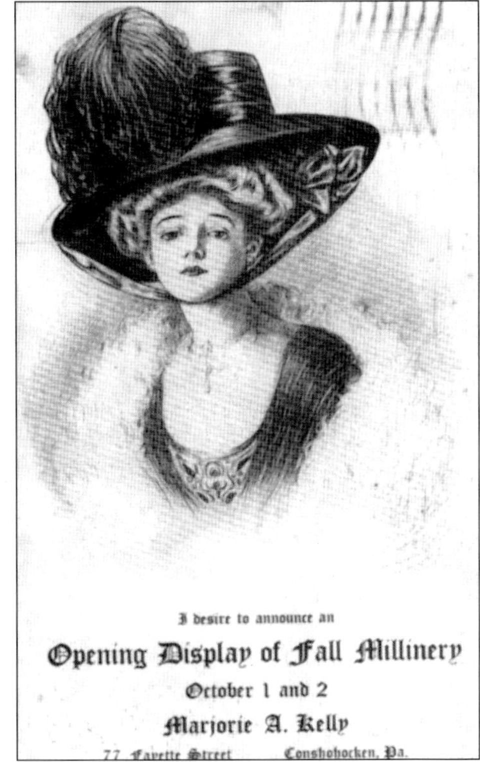

In October 1908, Marjorie A. Kelly was announcing the opening display of fall fashions at her store in Conshohocken. The store was located at 77 Fayette Street. Surprisingly, there are not a lot of store advertising postcards from Conshohocken.

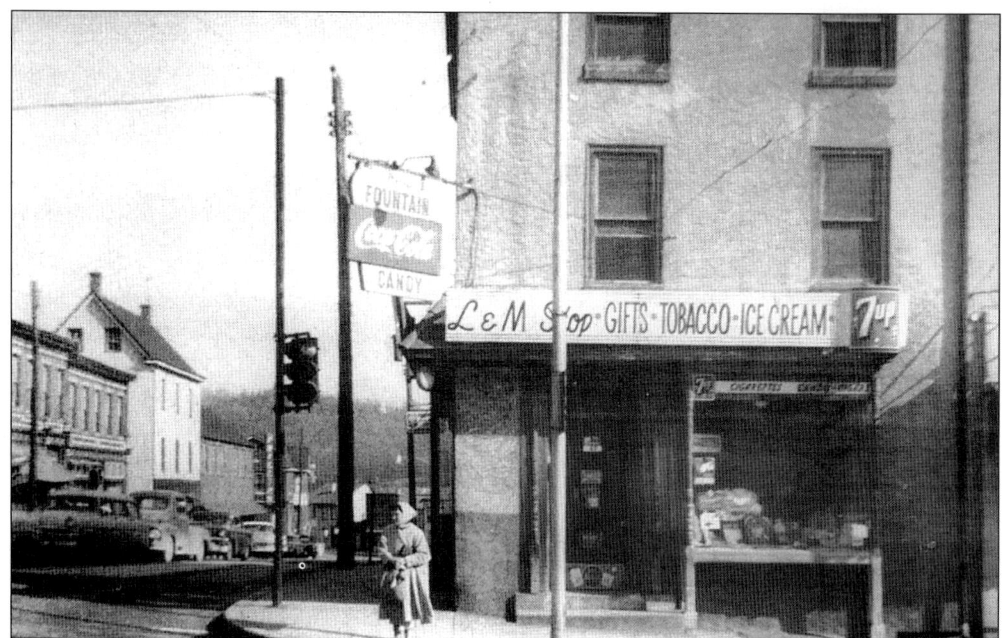

The L & M Shop was a variety store located on corner of east Elm Street. It was a popular place for school-age children to get candy or soda after school. The building was demolished under the urban development plan to make way for a turning lane off the Matsonford Bridge.

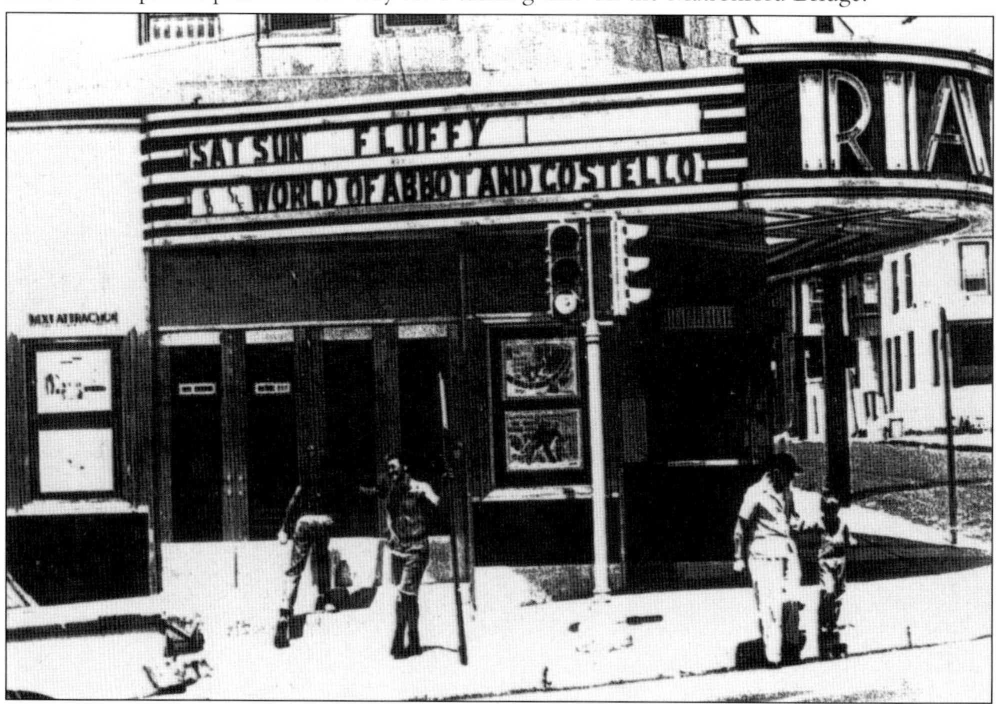

Saturday afternoon at the Riant Theater was a great way to spend a couple of hours. The Riant opened its doors on November 11, 1921. It was located at the corner of First Avenue and Fayette Street. It closed in the early 1970s, and the building was demolished. Today it is the site of Lucent Technologies. (Courtesy of Jack Coll.)

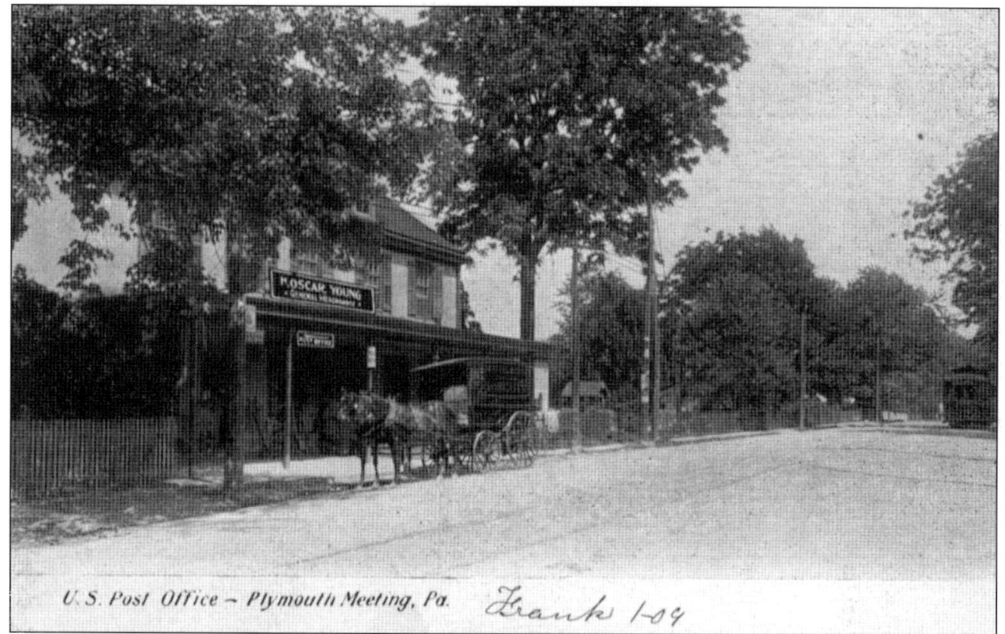

This is a great 1909 view of the Oscar Young general store on Germantown Pike across from Butler Pike. In front of the store is a biscuit wagon bringing fresh supplies to the store. The store also had a small post office inside for the local residents. The trolley on the right is heading east on Germantown Pike. Today this is an office building.

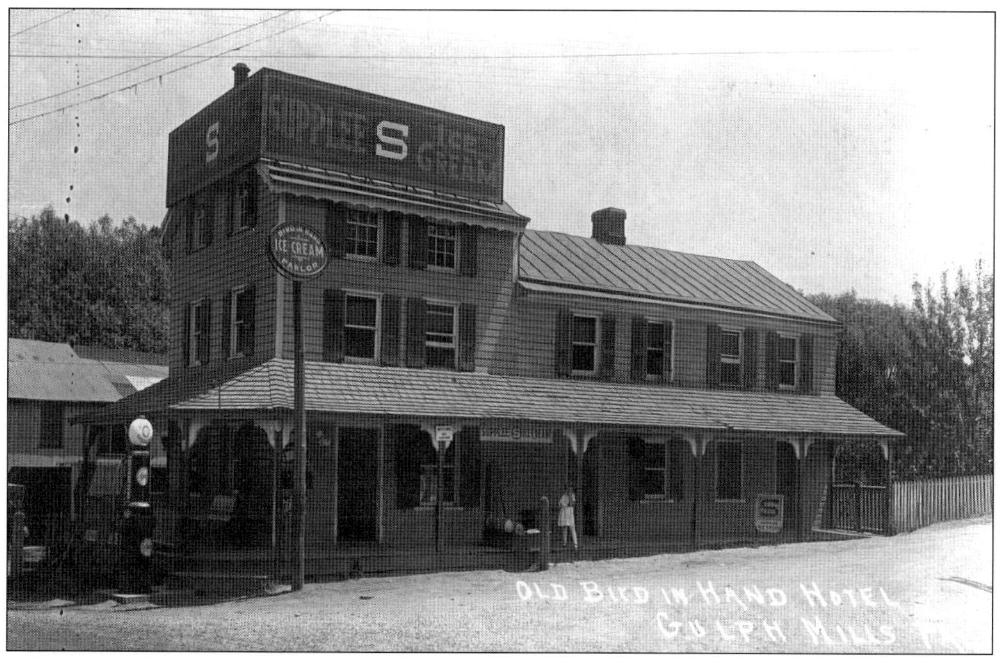

The Supplee ice-cream parlor was located on Gulph Road below the Gulph train station. At one time, it was called the Bird in Hand Hotel. This 1930s picture features an old Atlantic Gasoline pump.

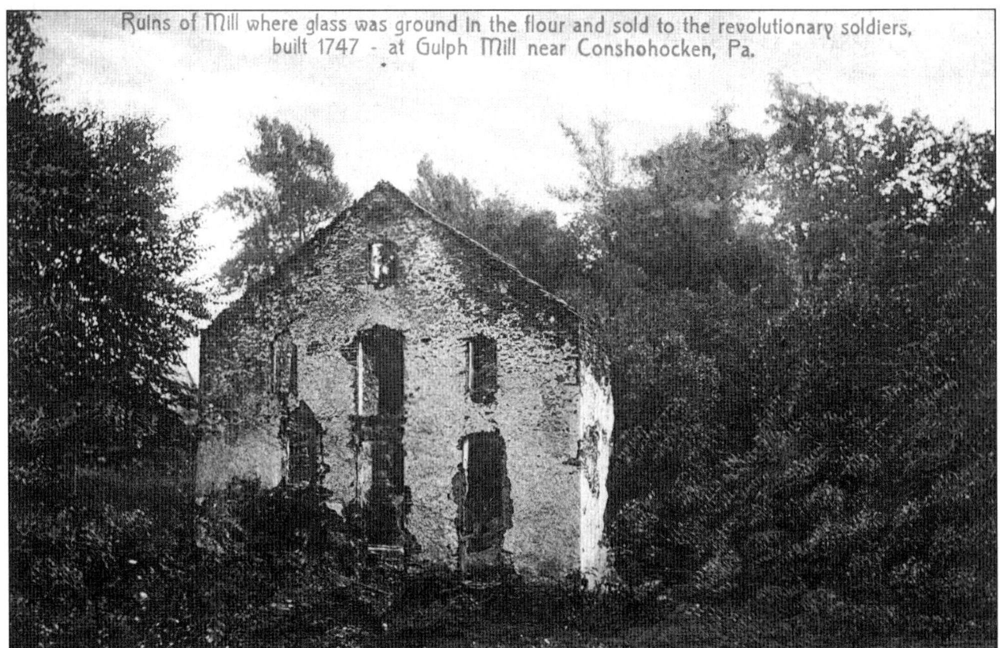

In 1895, fire destroyed the last remaining gristmill erected at Gulph Mills. This mill and later mills powered by water from Gulph Creek gave Gulph Mills its name. For a number of years, this forlorn stone skeleton of the 1747 mill remained as a local landmark. It was later torn down.

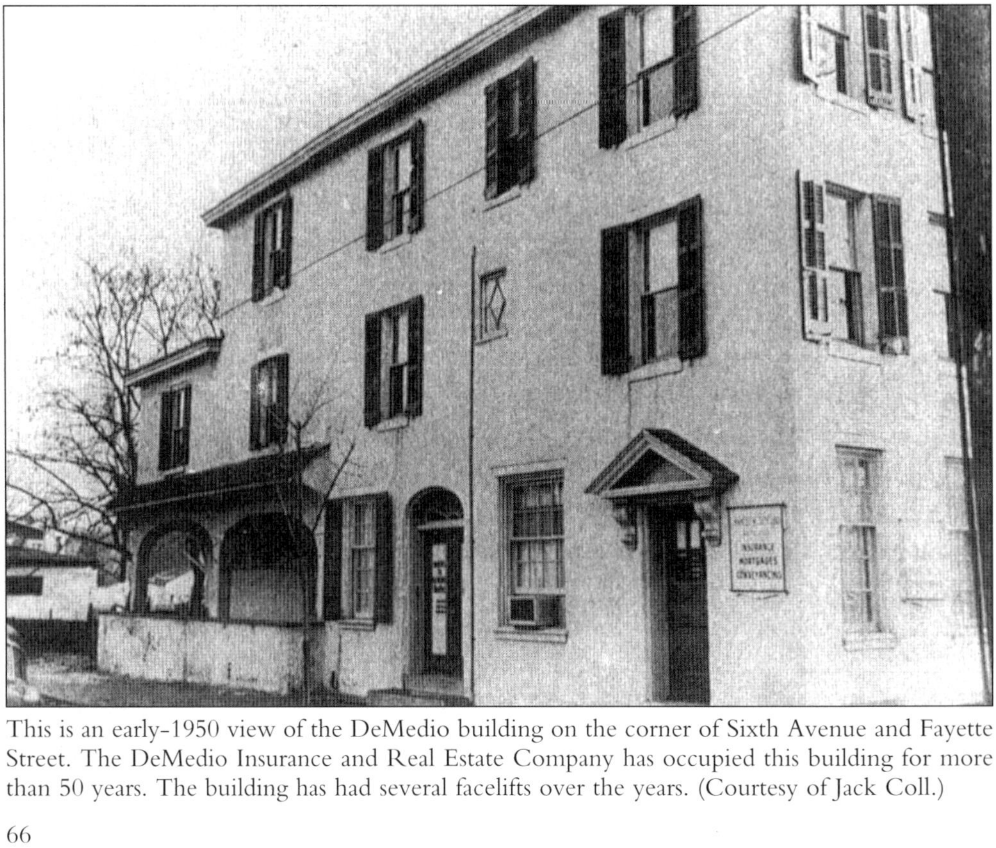

This is an early-1950 view of the DeMedio building on the corner of Sixth Avenue and Fayette Street. The DeMedio Insurance and Real Estate Company has occupied this building for more than 50 years. The building has had several facelifts over the years. (Courtesy of Jack Coll.)

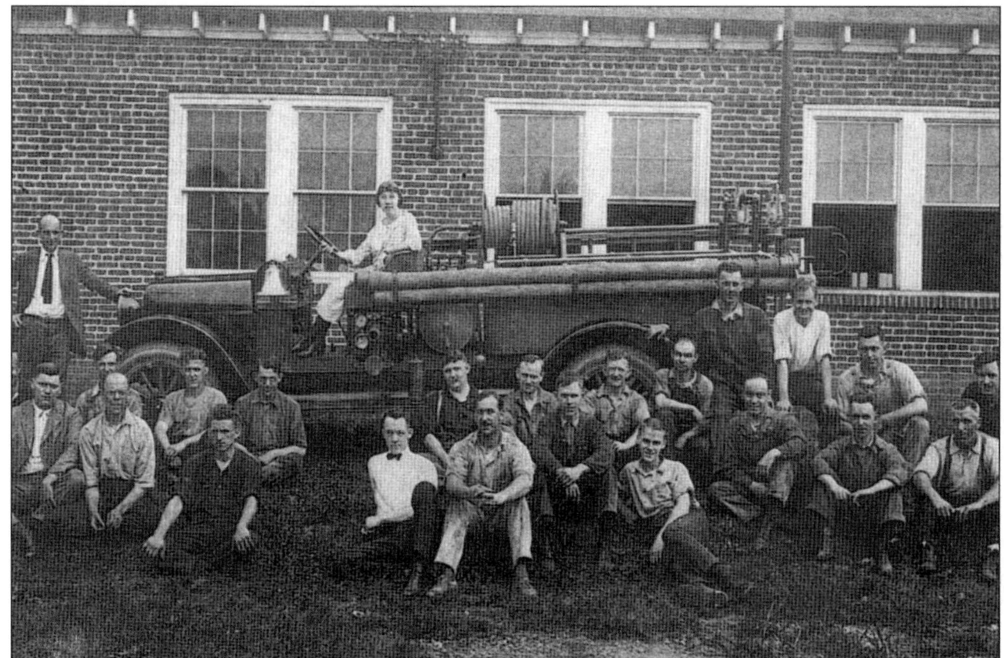

Hale Fire Pumps is one of the oldest industrial companies in Conshohocken today. C.H. Young, E.J. Wendell, and Alan C. Hale (who stayed with the company only long enough to lend it his name) started the company in 1914. It is known worldwide for manufacturing quality fire pumps. This is a company photograph of dedicated employees in 1922. (Courtesy of Jack Coll.)

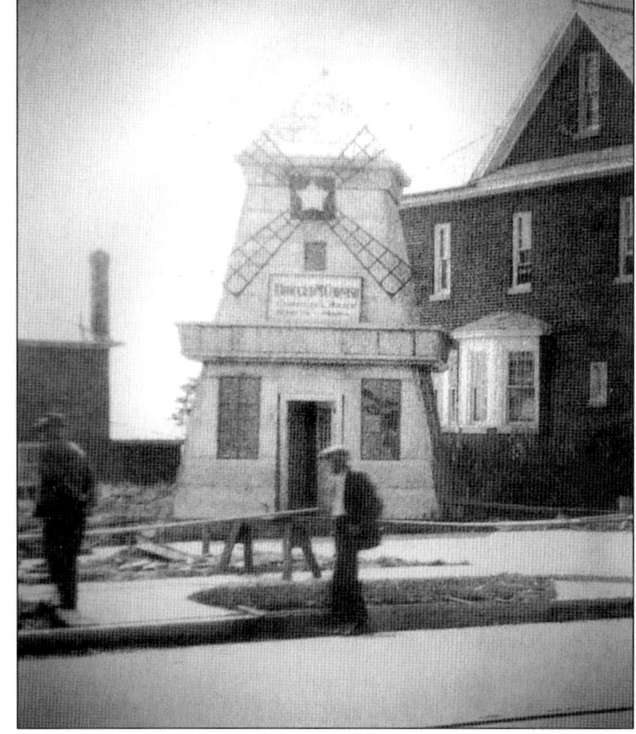

Conshohocken Windmill no longer stands at the corner of Eleventh Avenue and Fayette Street, but it was a landmark for many years. This quaint little place was home to many businesses, such as an ice-cream and candy store, a used-car lot, an insurance company, and a builder's office. The building was demolished, and an office building now occupies the site.

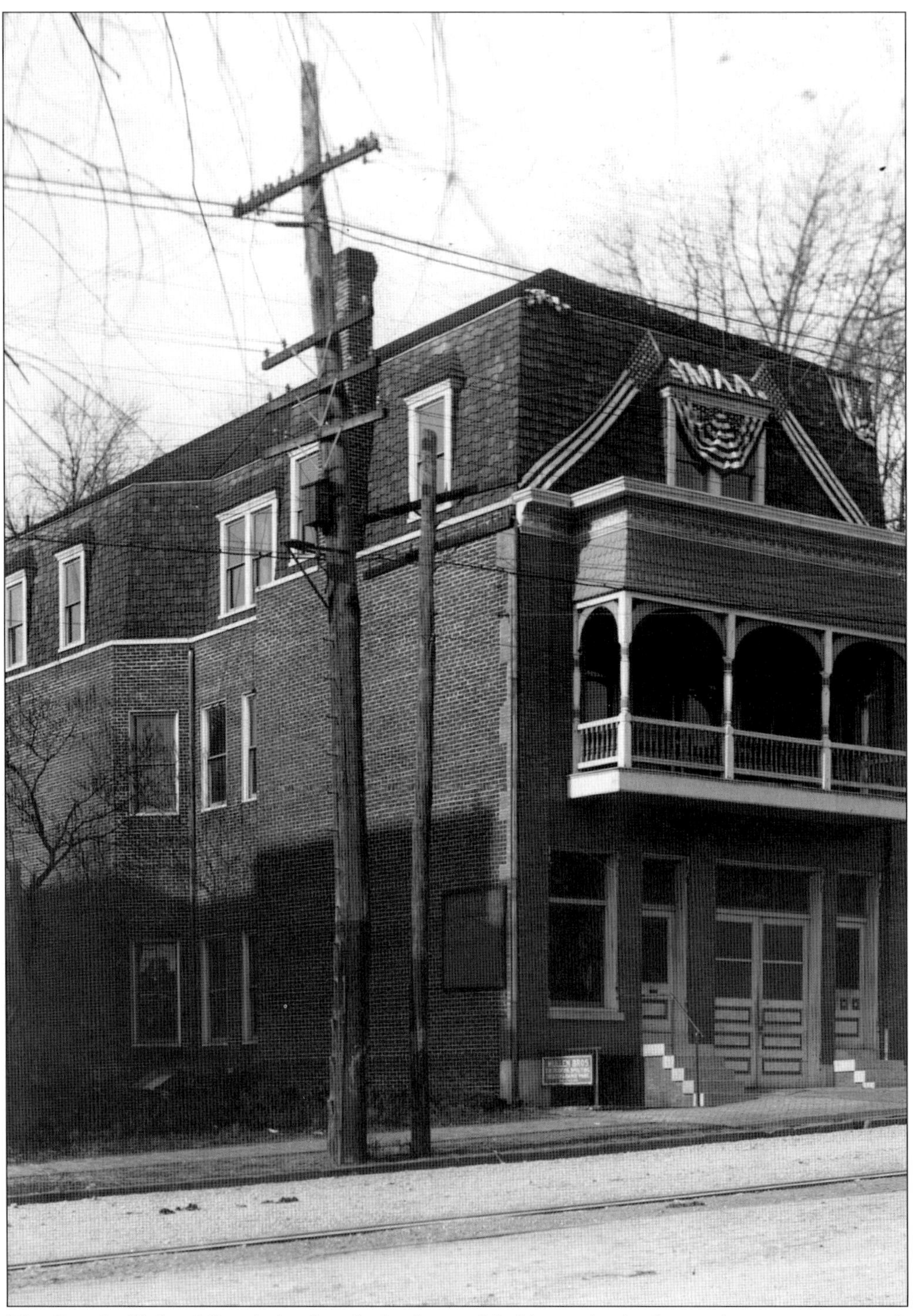

The Penn's Club of Conshohocken had a long, rich history in the borough as a young men's athletic association. The club organized many town events, and typically the town fathers belonged to the club. This *c.* 1908 photograph was taken on lower Fayette Street before the Penn Club built new quarters on West Second Avenue, where the organization met until the 1950s.

Six

Bravely Serving the Community

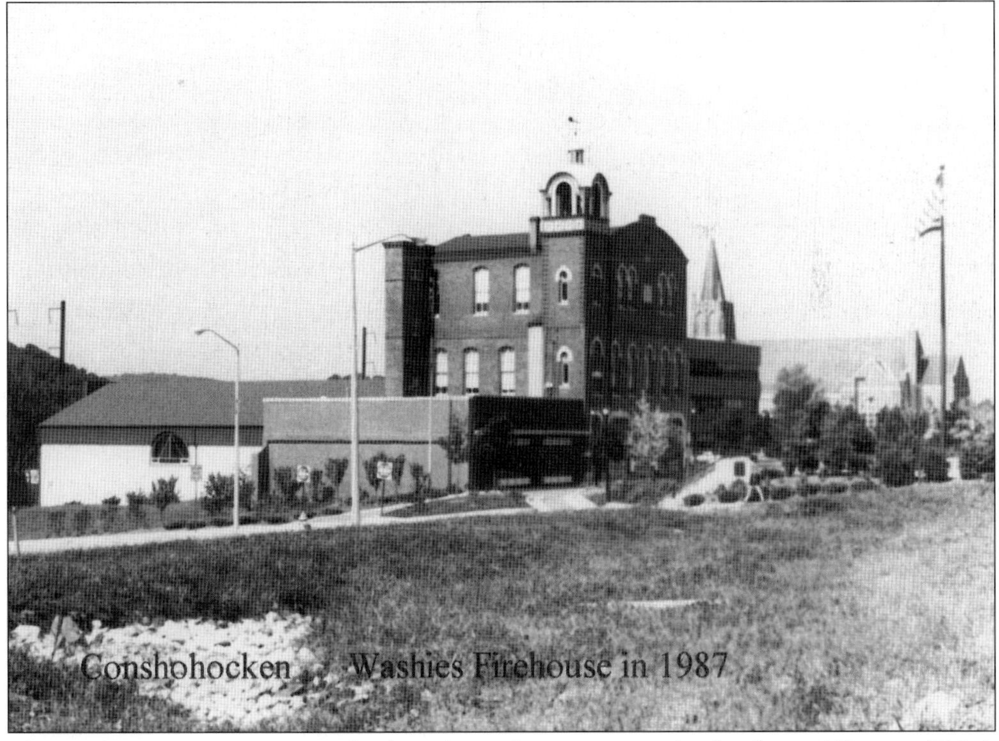

The Washington Fire Company has been in service to community for almost 130 years. This is an unobstructed view of the old firehouse on West Hector Street and the new firehouse building that faces West Elm Street. The vacant lot in the foreground was once a thriving retail area for the town. Today, professional buildings are located in this area. (Courtesy of Doreen DeSantis.)

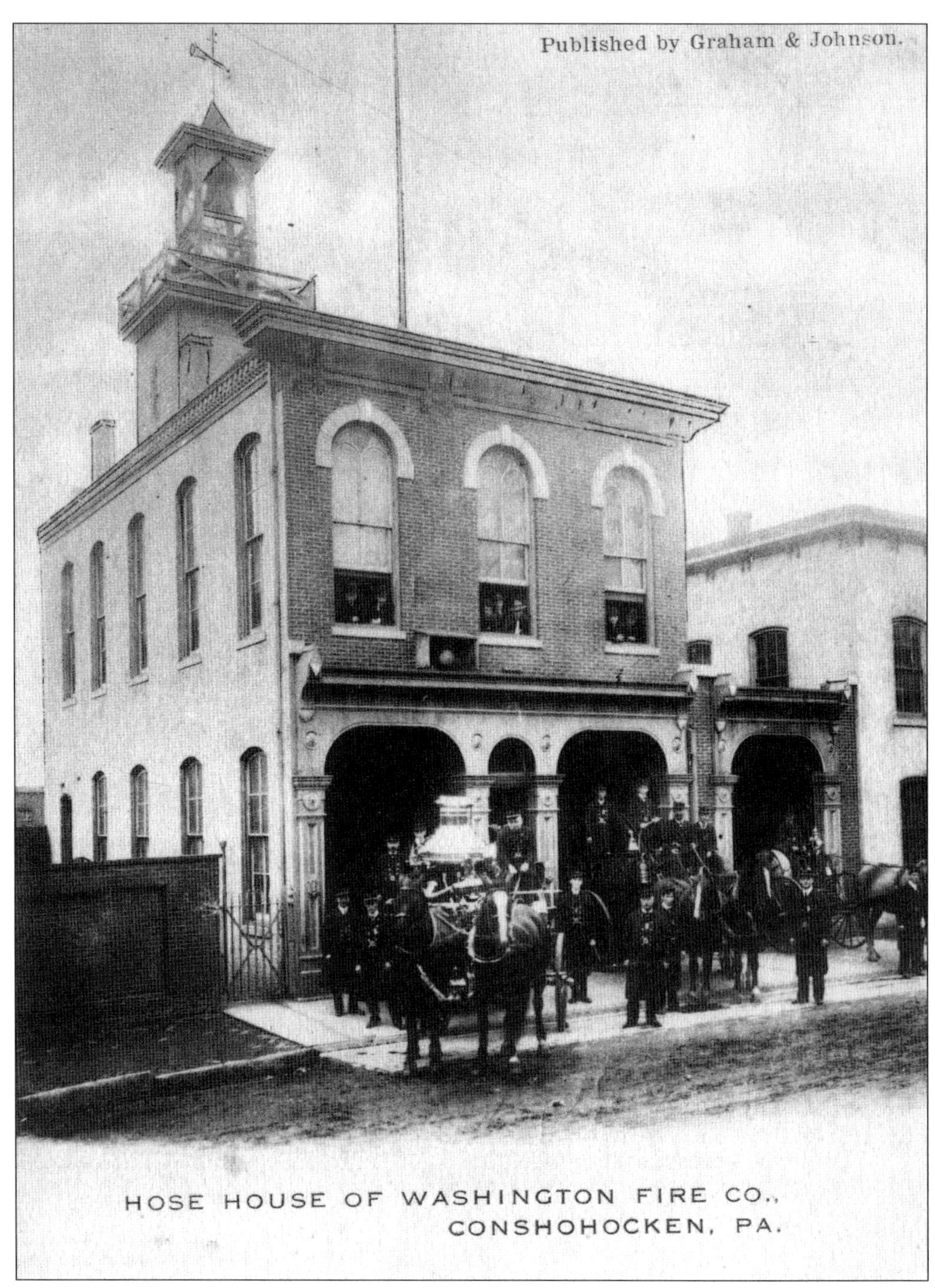

Washington Fire Company No. 1 was formed as a result of a raging fire at the Colwell Furnace. Thirty-eight concerned citizens gathered at Stemple Hall on December 13, 1873, to form the fire company. Their first steam engine was housed in a stable that was owned by George Washington Jacoby, owner of the marble works. On September 7, 1878, the company moved into its newly built two-story home on West Hector Street. A one-story addition was built on the lot between the borough hall (far right) and the firehouse in 1886.

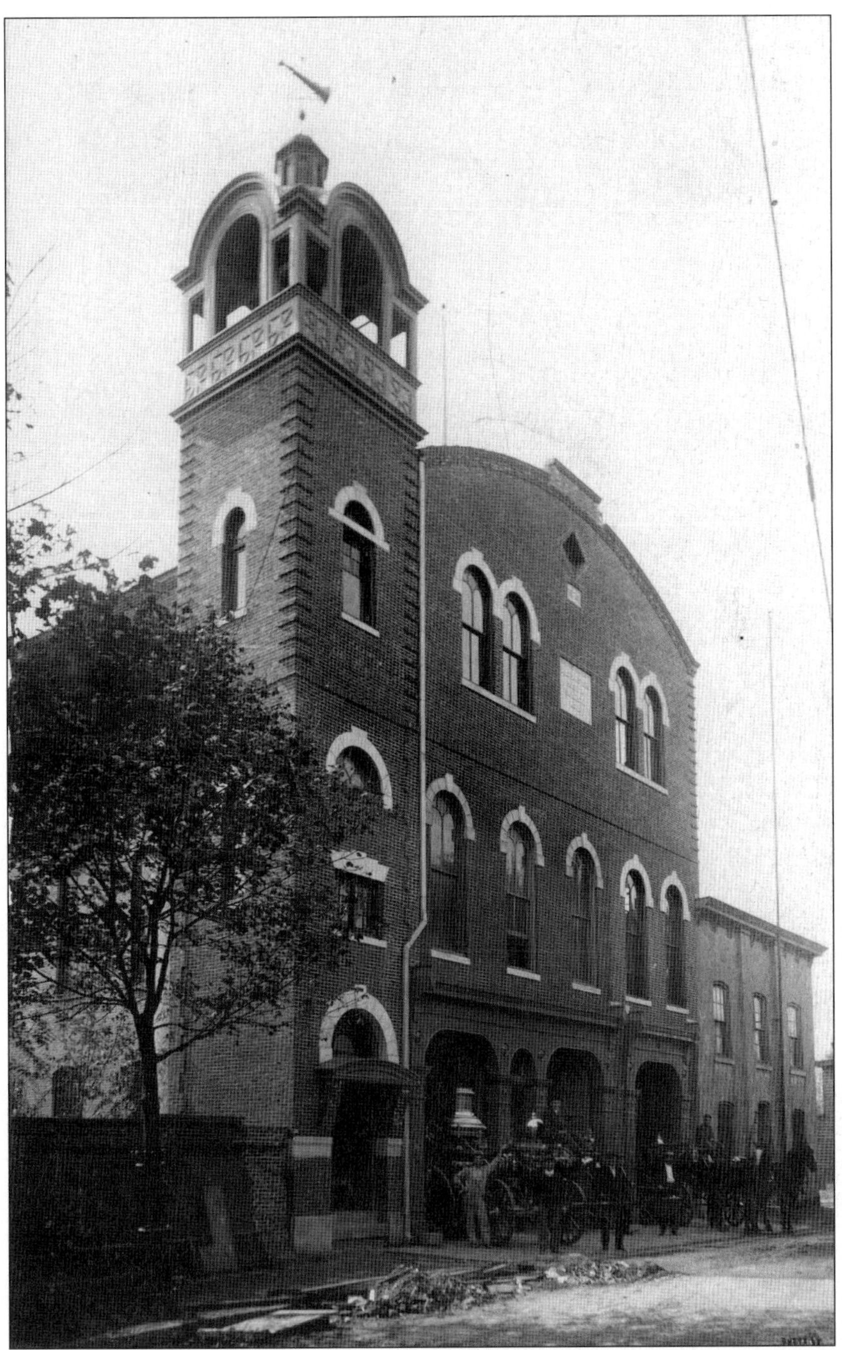

In 1908, a bell tower and a third story were added to the Washington Firehouse for a public hall. The fire equipment was horse-drawn at that time, and the firehouses could not afford to keep their own horses, so the fire company rented horses from a local farmer. In 1914, "Washies," as the company was known, bought its first gasoline-driven engine. In 1975, the firehouse on West Hector Street was placed on the National Register of Historic Places, saving it from destruction during the town's urban development. The current home of Washington Fire Company No. 1 is located on West Elm Street.

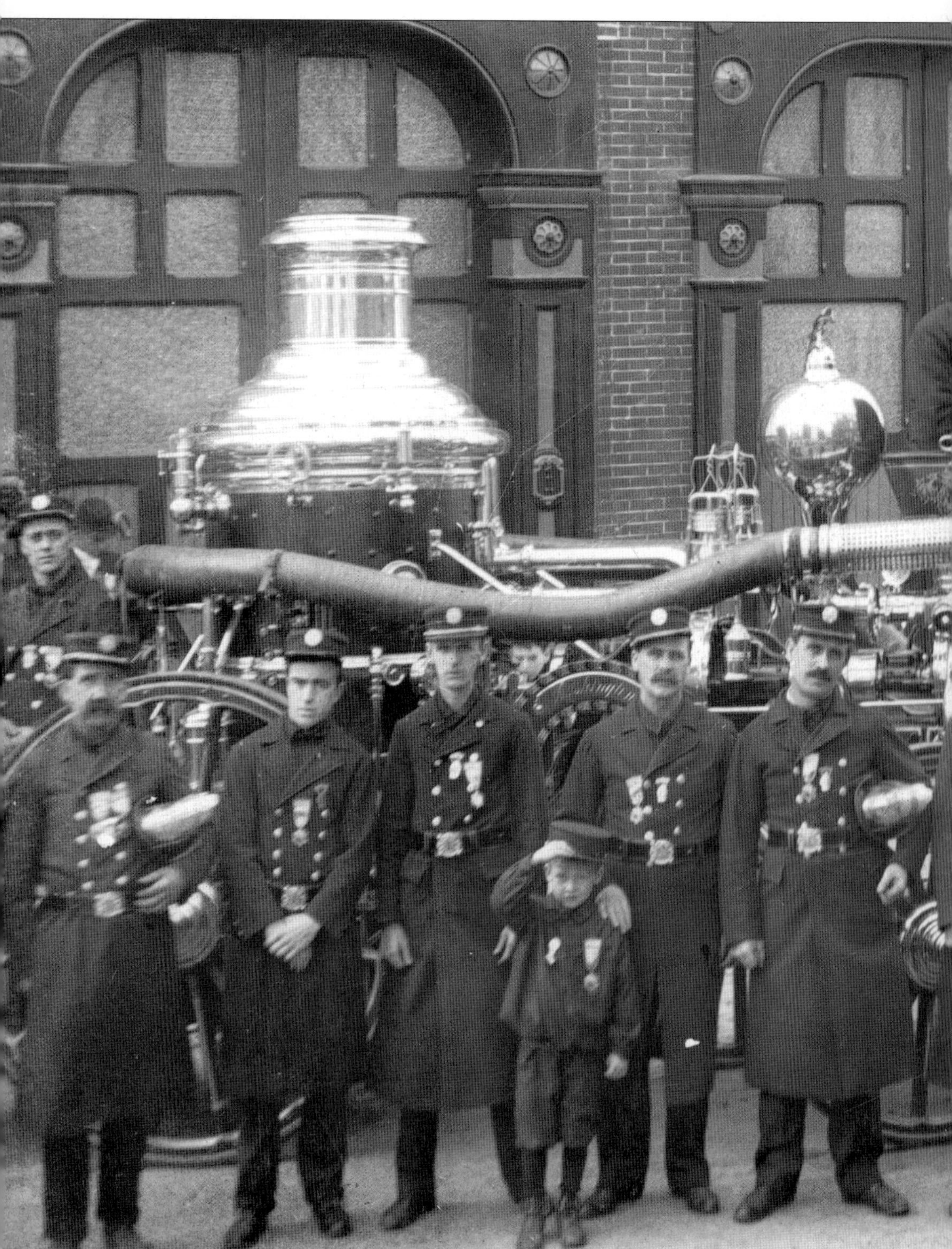

Pictured in 1908 are the members of Washington Fire Company No. 1. Dressed in their parade finest, these courageous volunteers were always ready to serve when needed. This photograph

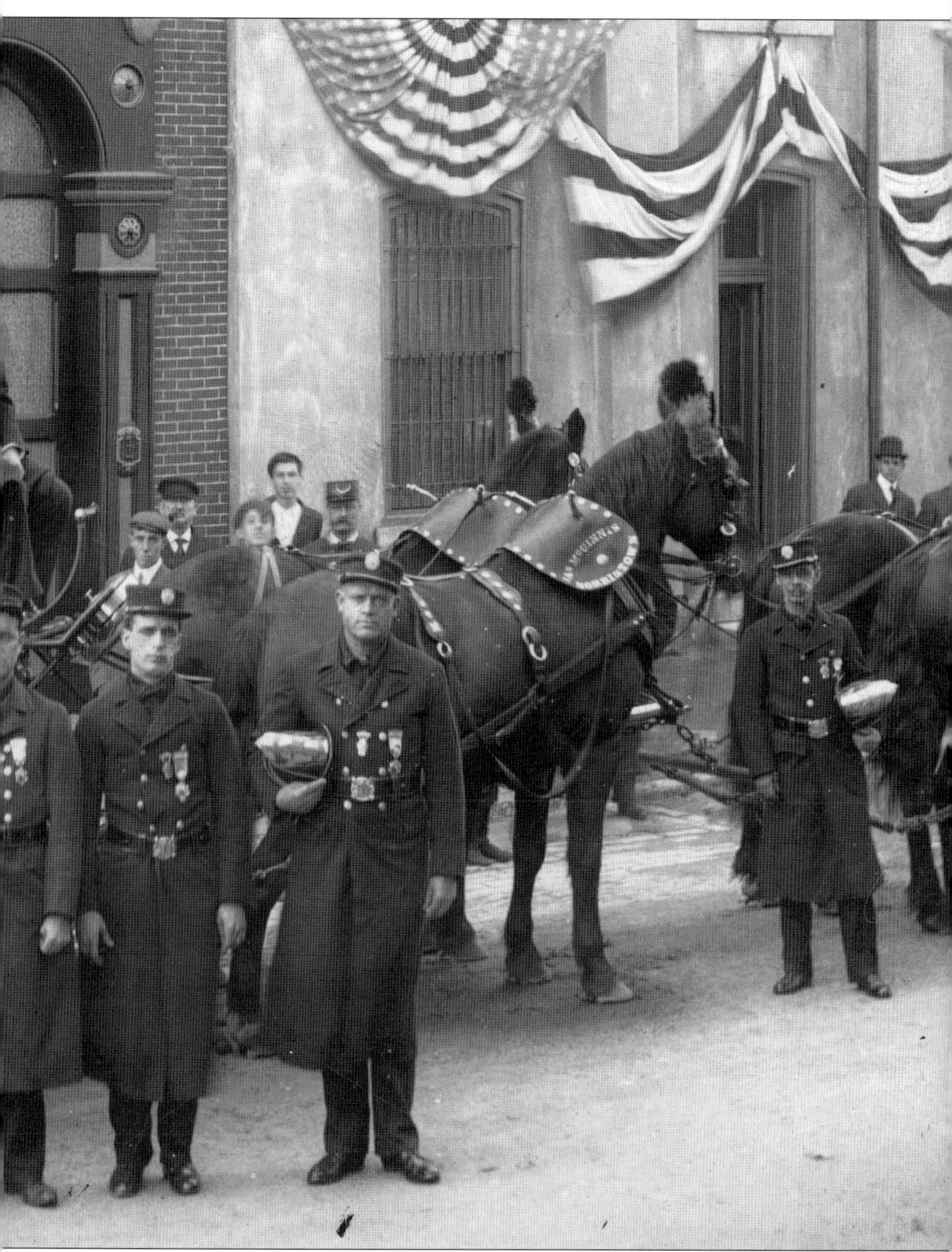

was taken during an Independence Day celebration while they were getting ready to march in the parade. To the right is a good view of the borough hall, decorated for the event.

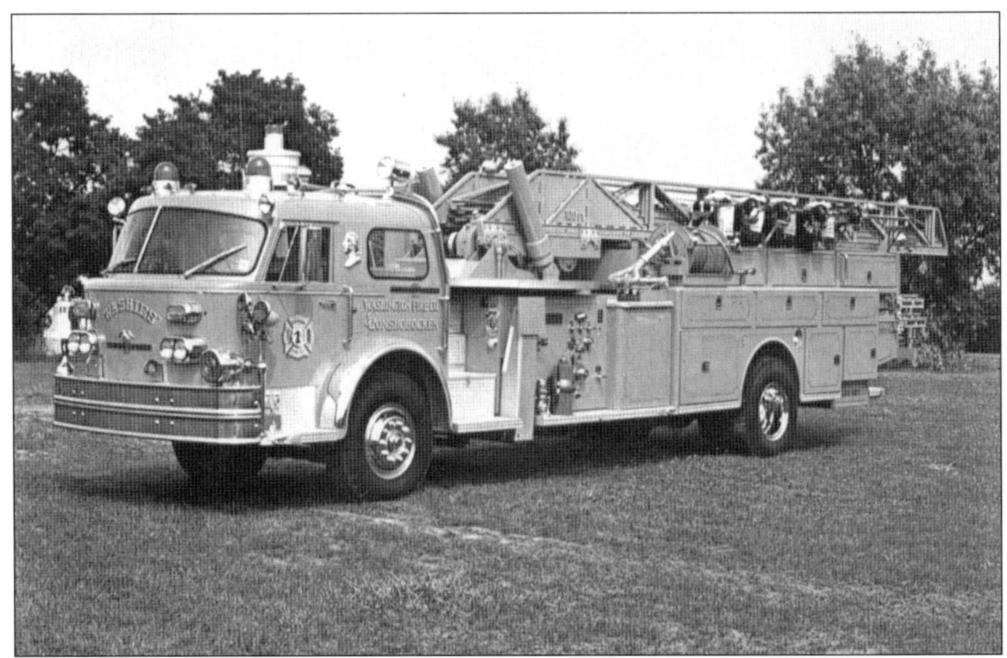

This is a shot of the Washies' 1974 American La France 100-foot aerial truck. Washies marked its centennial in 1974 by hosting the 95th-annual Pennsylvania State Fireman's Convention. Fire companies from all over the state paraded down Fayette Street in celebration.

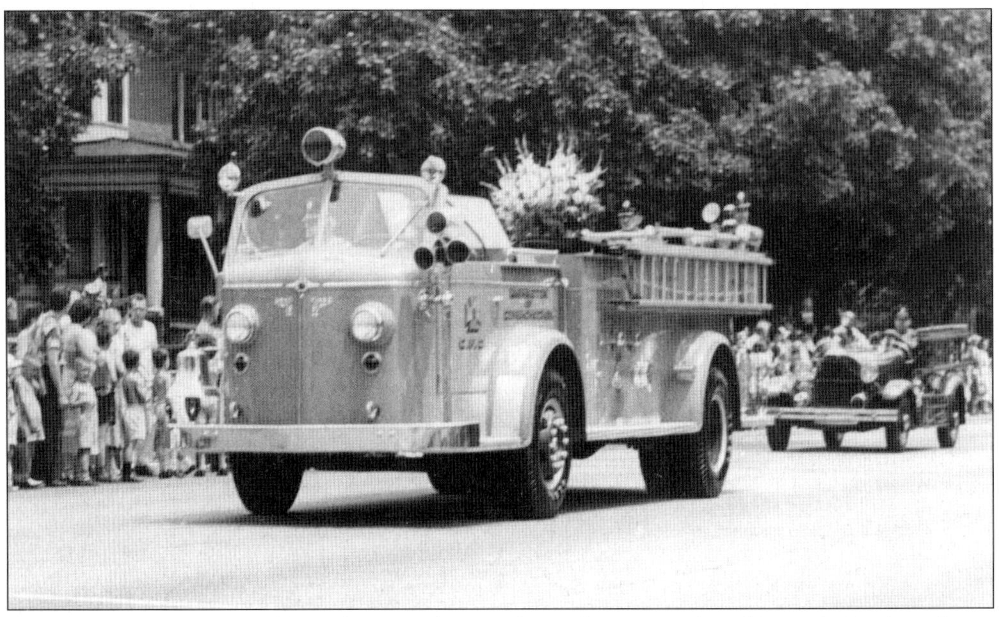

A hometown parade would not be complete without the fire truck. This *c.* 1950s view shows the Washington Fire Company's 1,000-gallon American La France truck traveling down the tree-lined upper avenues of Fayette Street in the summer.

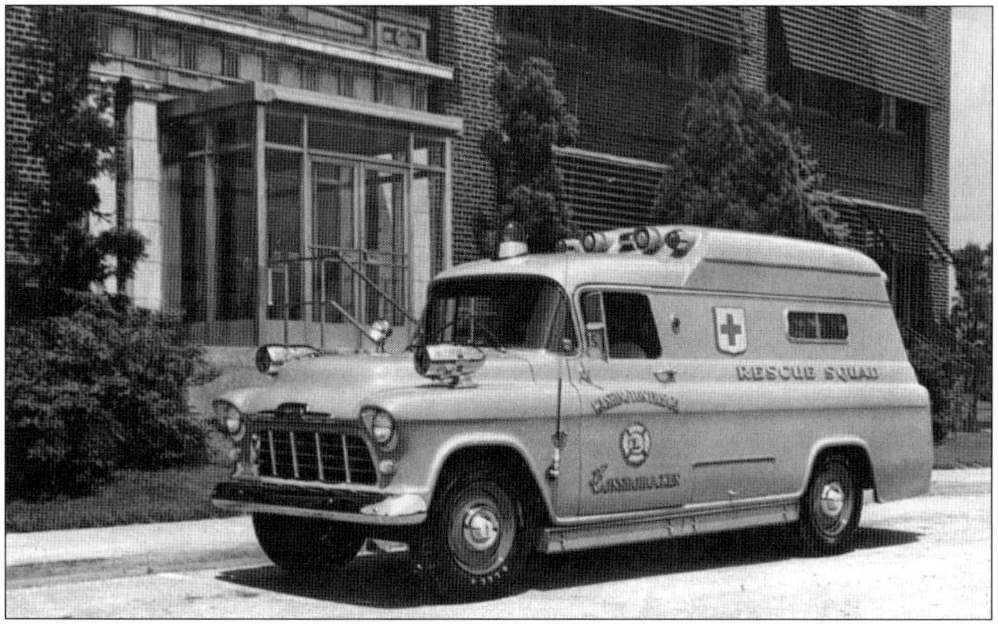

The Washington Fire Company is a volunteer organization serving the borough and vicinity. These two postcards were sold in the mid-1970s to raise funds for the rescue squad. Above is the all-purpose rescue unit. The three-in-one unit could be used as an ambulance, rescue truck, or squad truck. Below, the company displays its firefighting power. The building in the background was the main office of the Alan Wood Steel Company. It is now the 1000 Conshohocken Road office complex.

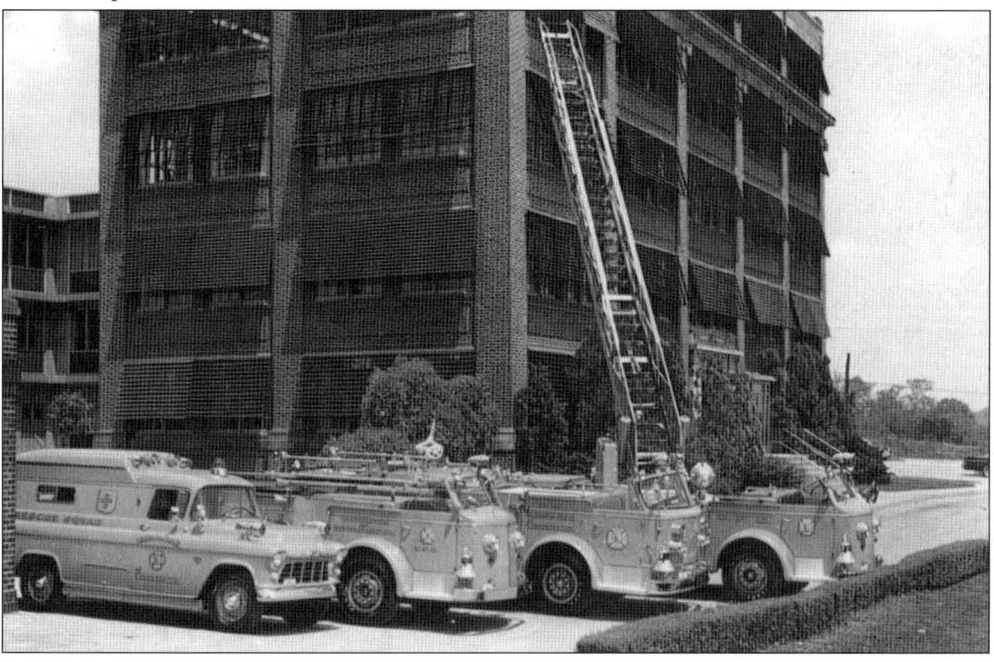

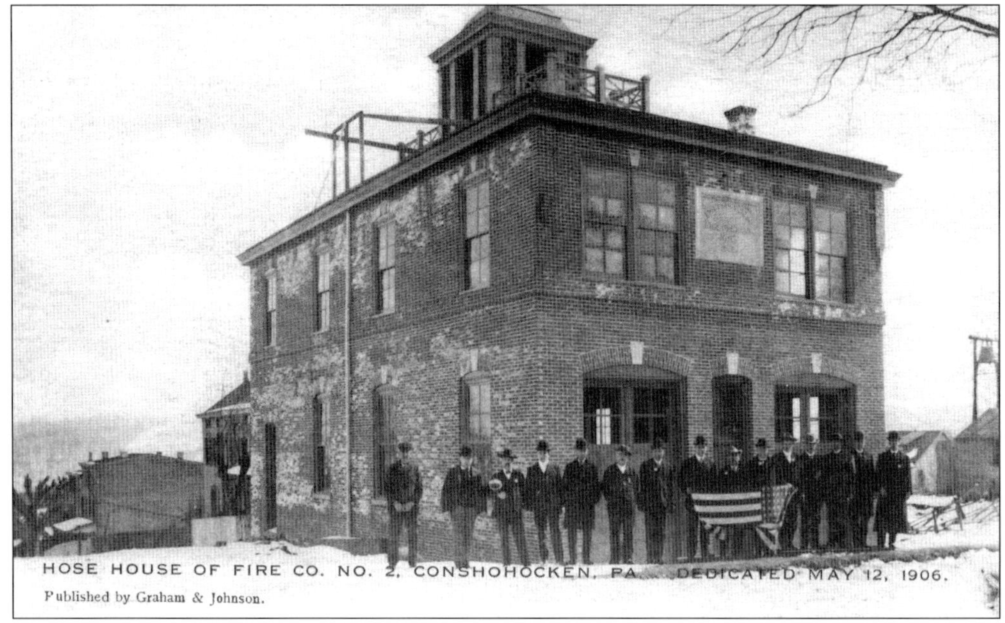

The Conshohocken Fire Company No. 2 was founded in 1903 by a group of concerned citizens who felt the need for a firehouse in the upper end of the borough. The new firehouse, located at East Ninth Avenue and Harry Street, was dedicated on May 12, 1906. The company at first had hand-drawn carriages and later horse-drawn ones, but it could not afford to keep its own horses. The company was given unlimited use of the horses from the Lee Surgical Supply Company, then located one block from the firehouse at East Eighth Avenue and Harry Street.

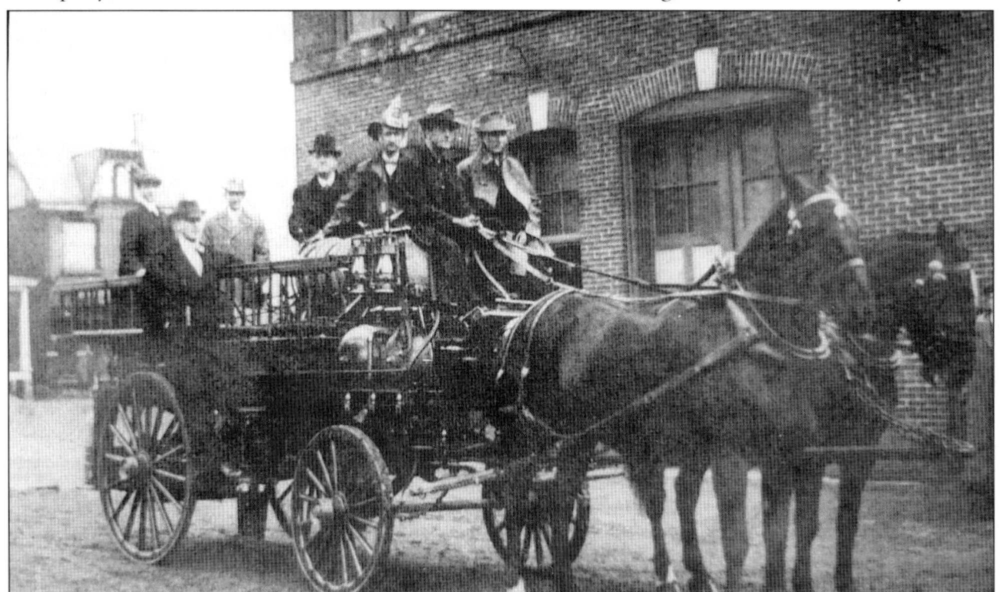

Members of the Conshohocken Fire Company No. 2 are the first to test-ride the company's new fire apparatus in 1906. George "Highley" Slavin sits in the driver's seat. The fire carriage was drawn by horses donated by the Lee Surgical Supply Company. Slavin was experienced with driving equipment because he was also one of the borough's early trolley drivers. (Courtesy of Jack Coll.)

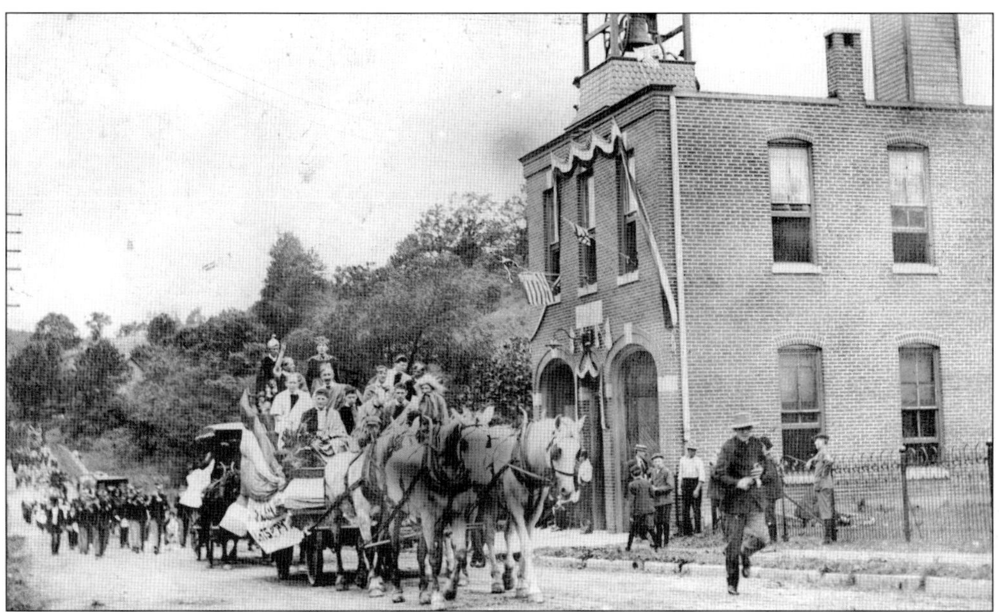

An Independence Day parade passes the George Clay firehouse on Ford Street in 1908. This was a big town event with horse-drawn floats and carriages. It looks like the whole town turned out for the celebration. The firehouse was erected in 1900 and later expanded due to the growth of the community.

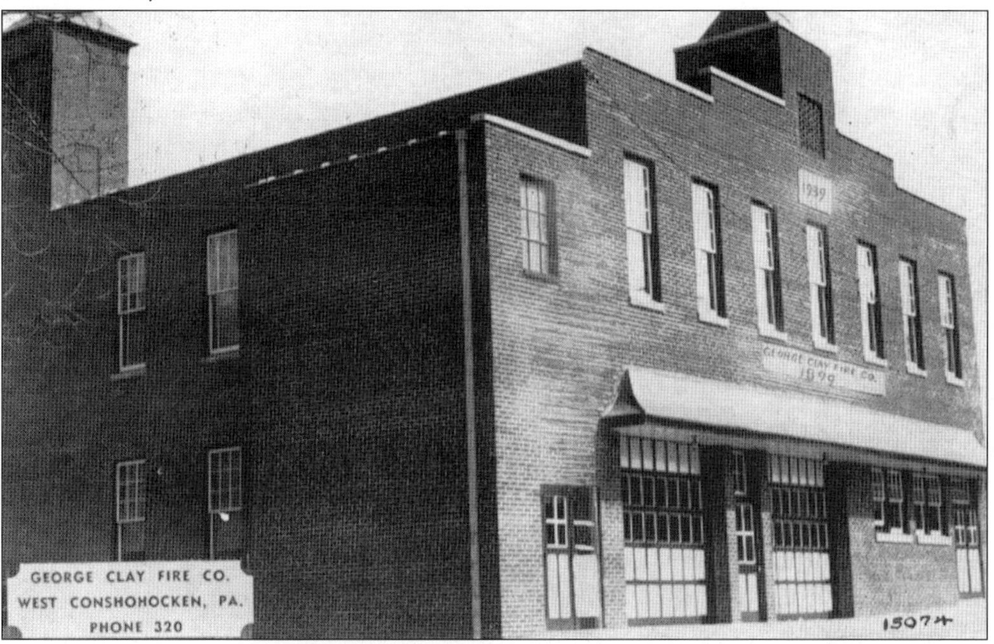

In 1898, 47 West Conshohocken citizens met in Odd Fellows Hall to take the preliminary steps to organize a fire company. An apparatus committee was formed to discuss a proposal from John Clay of Philadelphia. Clay presented the fire company with a hose carriage built for $800, provided that the company erect a suitable building to cost no less than $1,500 and that the company be named for Clay's brother George. The offer was accepted, and the firehouse was erected in 1900.

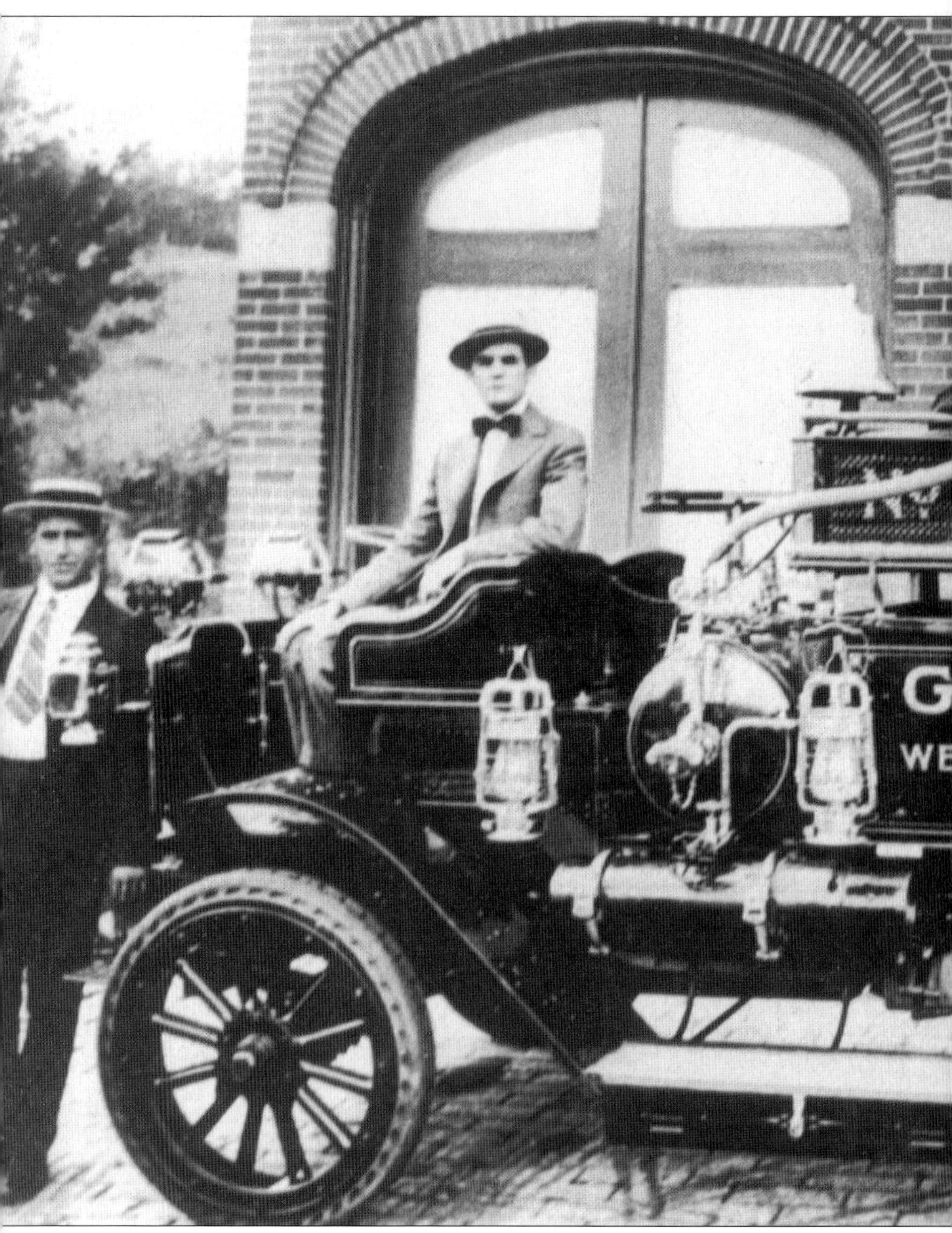

This photograph was taken outside the George Clay Firehouse on Ford Street in West Conshohocken. It shows a 1912 two-cylinder autocar chemical truck. Standing in front of the truck is Herman "Dicker" Adams, and in the driver's seat is George Mclaughlin. In the back of

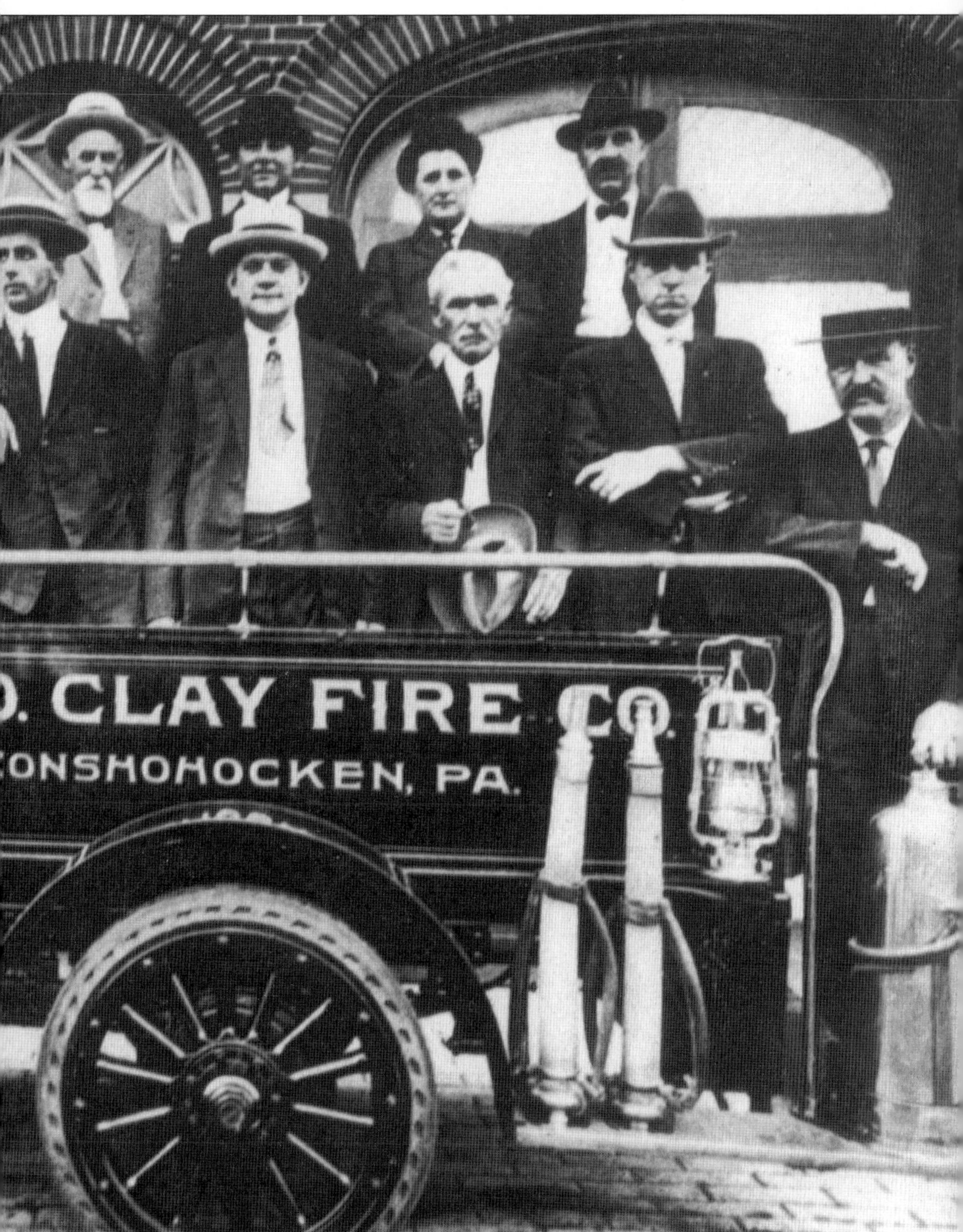

the truck are, from left to right, the following: (front row) Jerry Adams, Abe DeHaven, Howard Whithead, Perry Ramey, and Harry Hammond; (back row) John Murphy, Ben Riles, Ed Cassey, and Ed Woodward.

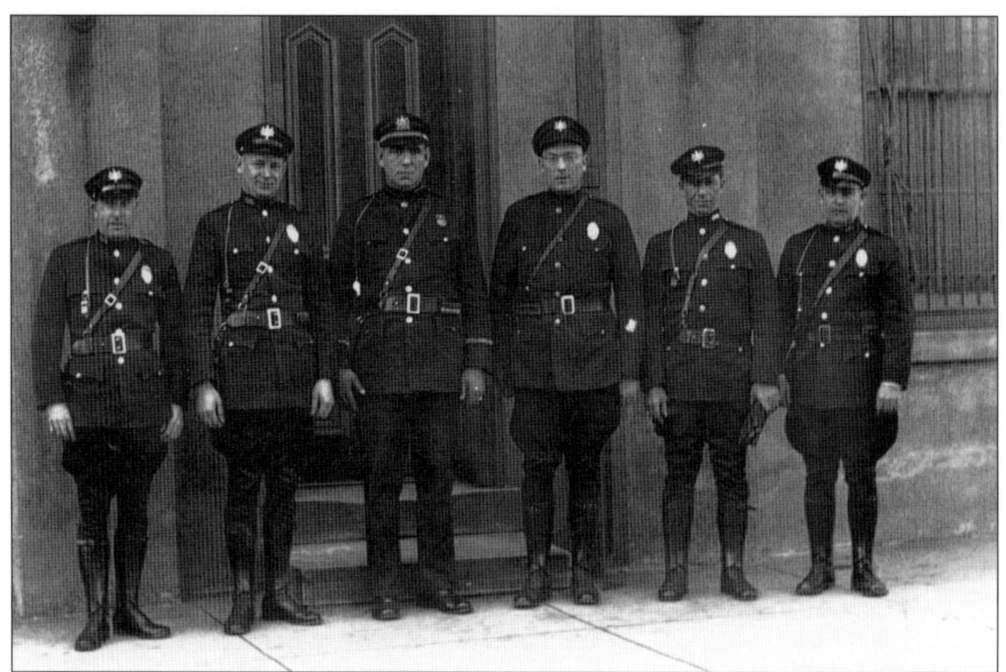

The entire police department poses outside the borough hall, then located at West Hector Street next to the Washington Fire Company. The officers are, from left to right, Harry Snear, Walter Phipps, Francis "Bunny" Blake, Pat Donovan, ? Stallone, and Zeake Kirkpatrick. (Courtesy of Jack Coll.)

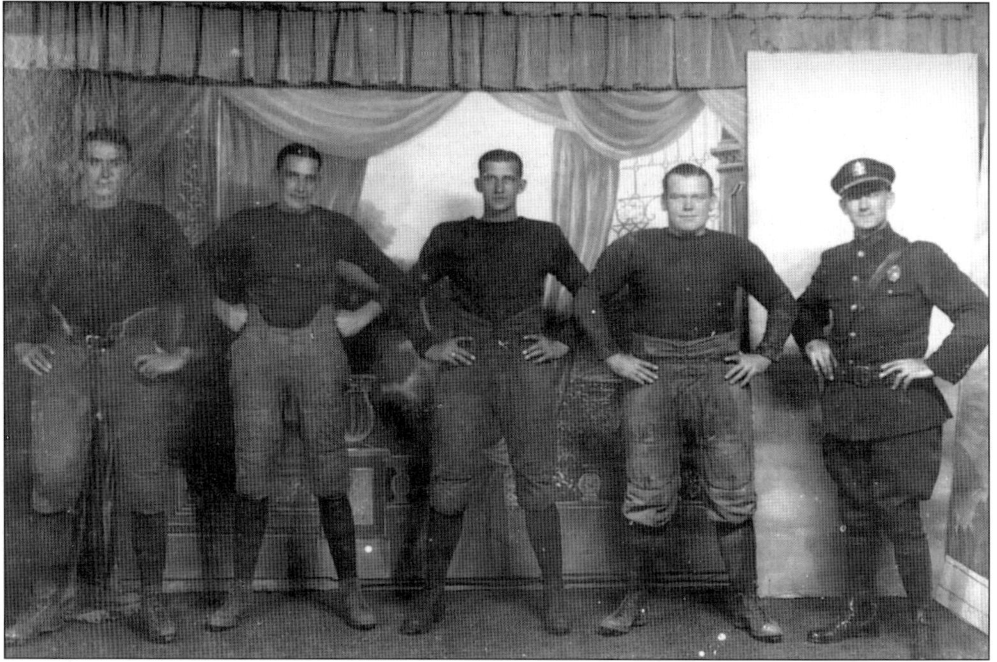

These football players are the four horsemen of the Conshohocken Professionals, a 1928 football team. They are seen here with Chief Donovan of the Conshohocken Police Department. (Courtesy of Jack Coll.)

Seven
ON THE FIELD

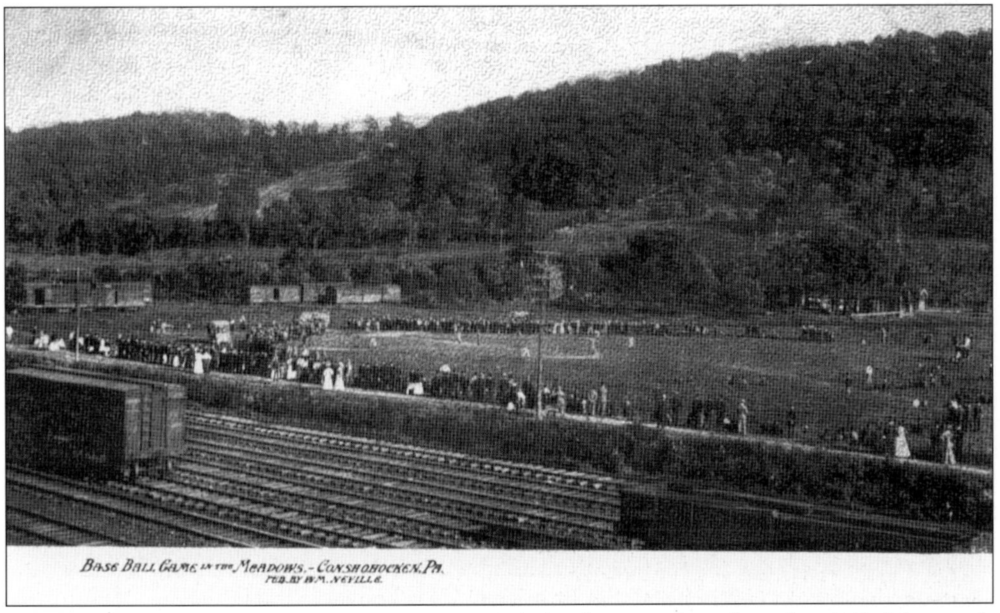

As in many communities across America, Conshohocken residents love baseball. Thousands would gather to enjoy a Saturday or Sunday afternoon at the Meadows to watch local teams play. The Meadows was located along the river on Washington and Cherry Streets. It is the current site of Hale Pumps Foundry.

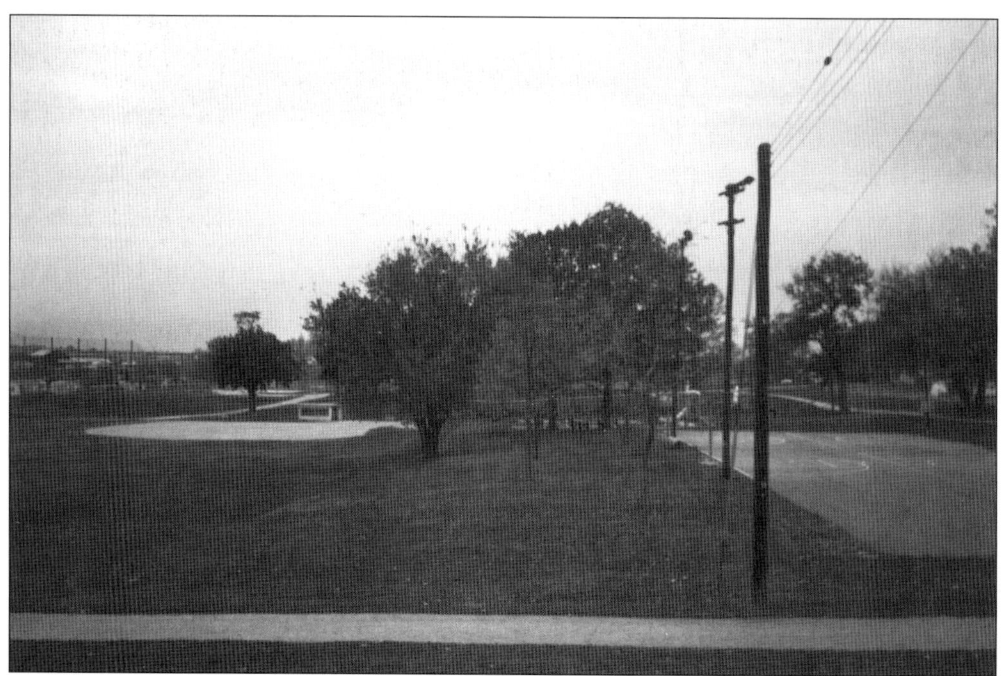

In 1930, Frank Sutcliffe, then president of the John Wood Company, donated 17 acres between Seventh and Tenth Avenues west of Freedley Street to Colwell Lane for a park in memory of his wife, Mary Jane "Polly" Sutcliffe. The park serves the community with five baseball fields, a basketball court, a walking trail, swings, and a slide.

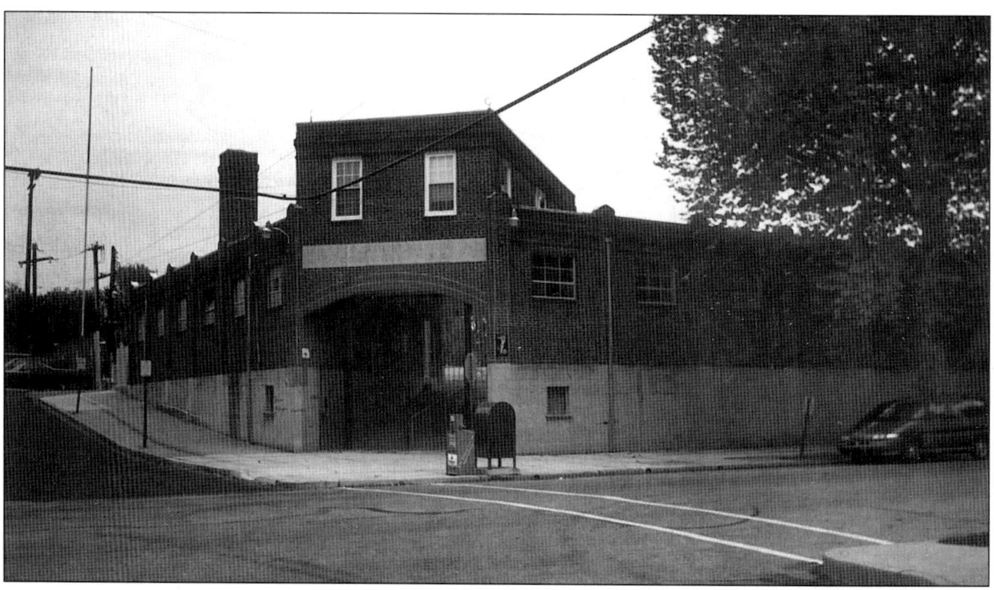

Conshohocken's A.A. Garthwaite Field, more commonly known as the "A" Field, is located on Eleventh Avenue and Harry Street. The field has been used for sporting events from as early as 1914, when the Conshohocken Professionals played football games there. Many rivalry Thanksgiving Day football games have been played at the field. It has also hosted rallies, concerts, square dances, and softball and baseball games.

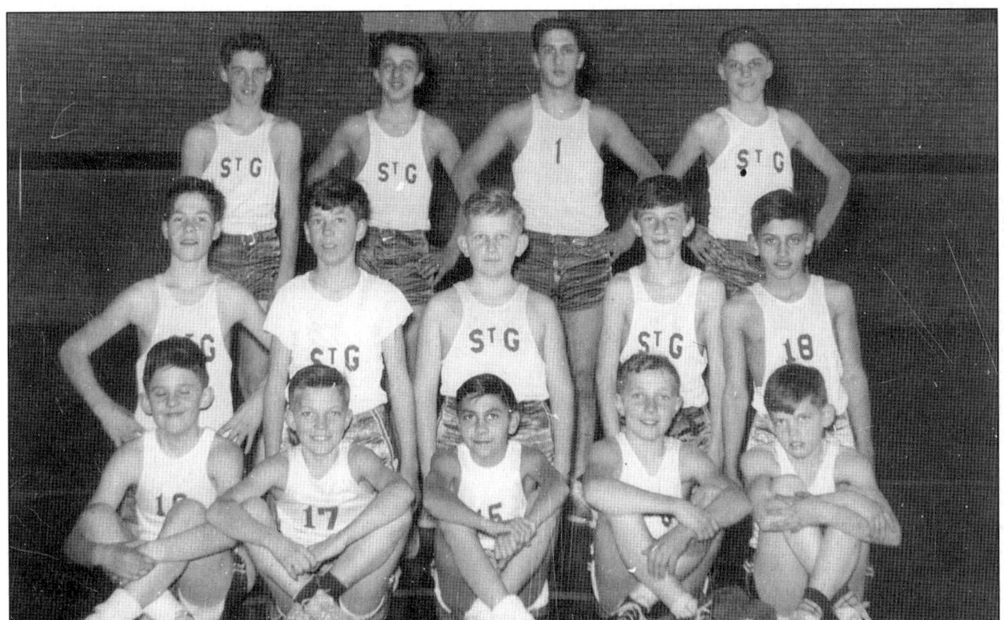

Sports are very important to the area schools. Each school had Catholic Youth Organization teams that would play local schools. Many of these games were played at the Fellowship House. This is St. Gertrude's Catholic Youth Organization basketball team of 1954–1955. That year, the team had a winning season of 20-1. (Courtesy of Jack Welsh.)

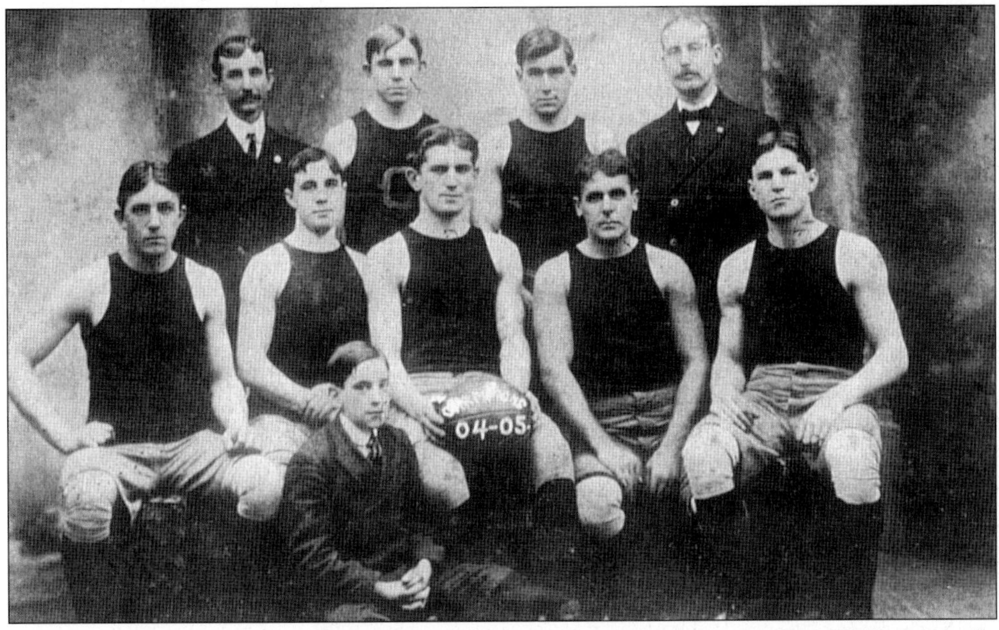

This is a photograph of the 1904–1905 Champion Pioneer Club team. In 1904, William Neville and his team barnstormed through Pennsylvania and the Midwest, defeating all opponents. Neville issued the challenge to play any team anywhere. A Chicago team took up the challenge but then canceled. Neville proclaimed the first World Championship of Basketball for Conshohocken in the 1904–1905 season, and the claim has never been disputed. The Pioneer Club team is honored in the Basketball Hall of Fame in Springfield, Massachusetts.

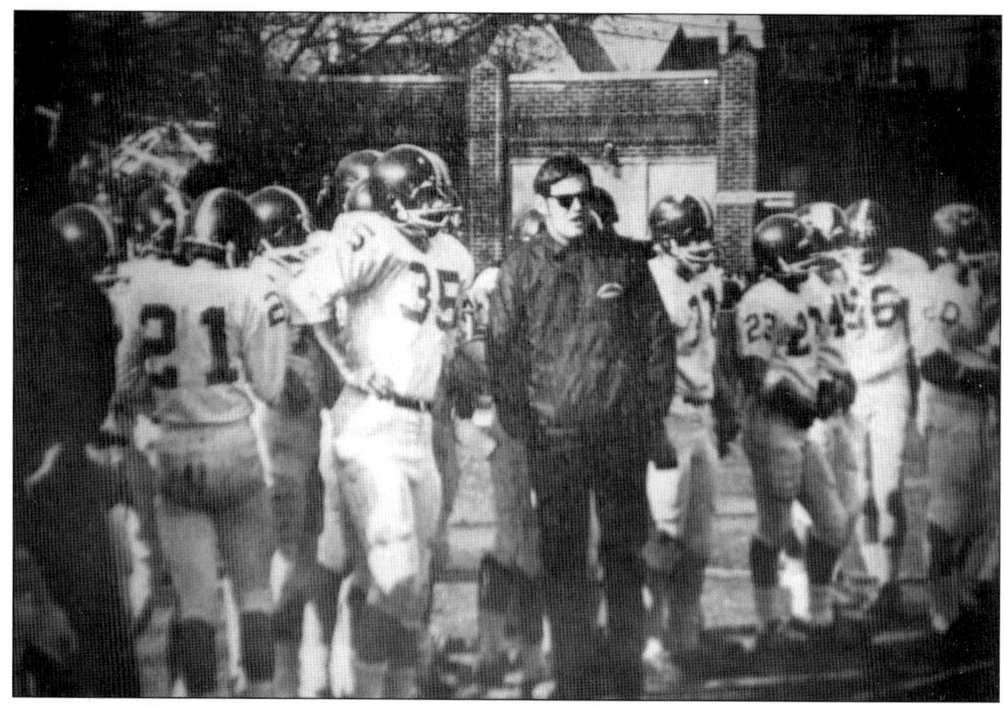

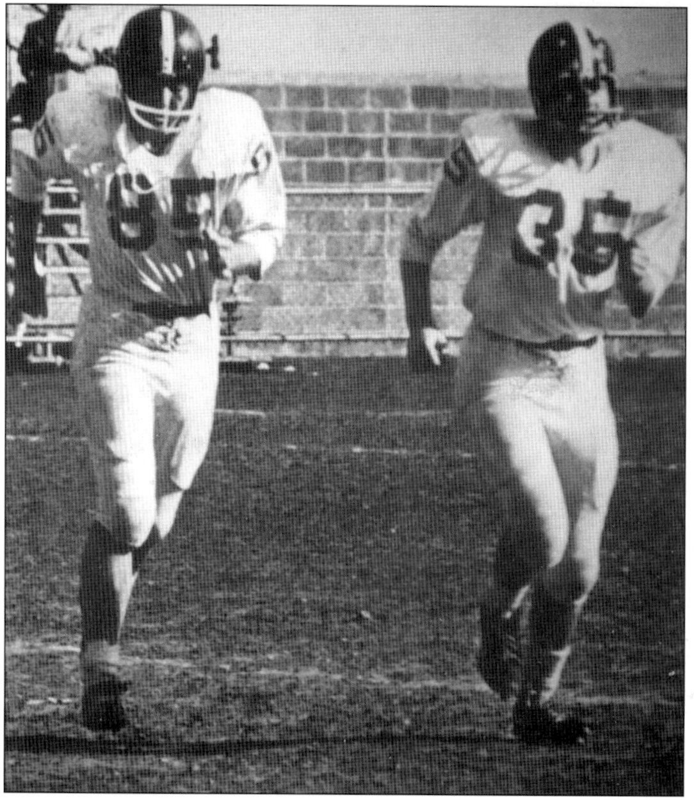

On Fridays and Saturdays from August through November, Archbishop Kennedy School's football team would play at its home field. Above, the Saints get last-minute play instructions from the coach staff. To the left, cocaptains Dennis Gordon and Phillip Welsh are coming onto the field for the last game of the season in 1970. That year, the team was 6-4, with one tie.

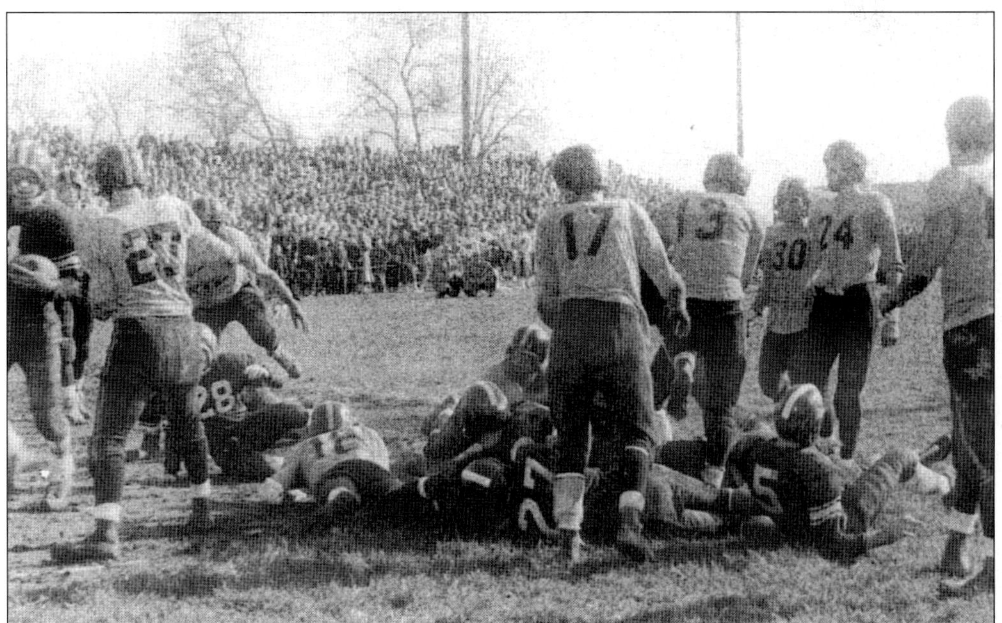
Thousands of fans watch two football rivals on the "A" Field in 1954—St. Matthews and Conshohocken High School. When these two teams would play, the whole town would turn out for the game. (Courtesy of Jack Coll.)

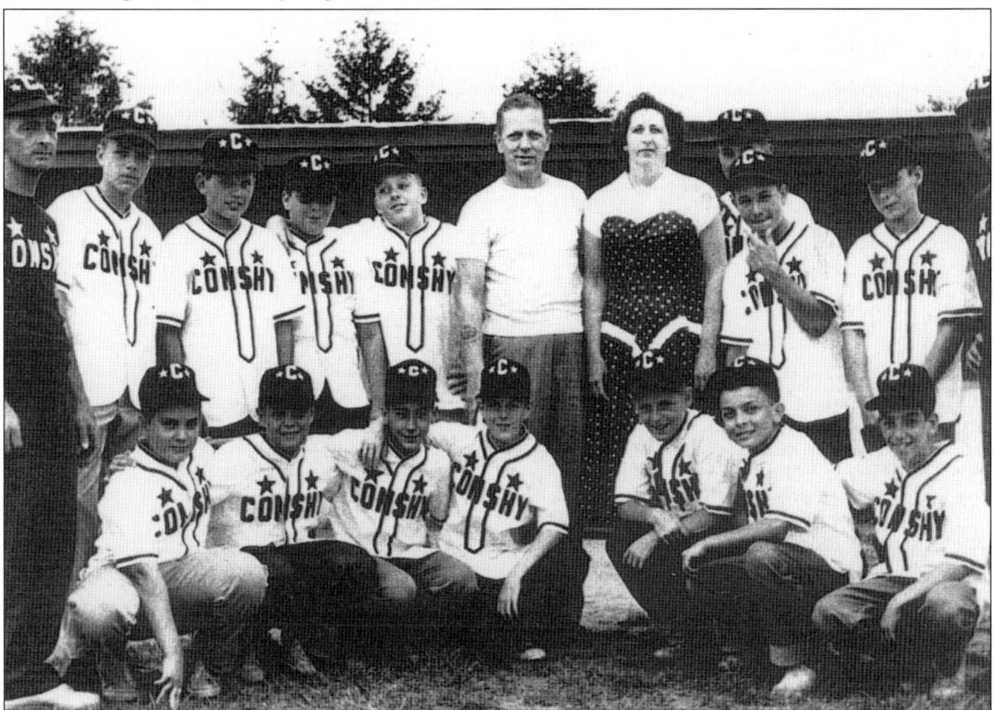
Conshohocken's All-Star Little League players are shown in front of the dugout at Sutcliffe Park. Little League baseball started in Conshohocken in 1955 and is so popular today that the park has four Little League fields and one Babe Ruth field. This photograph is of the 1961 All-Star team and includes many familiar Conshohocken faces. (Courtesy of Jack Coll.)

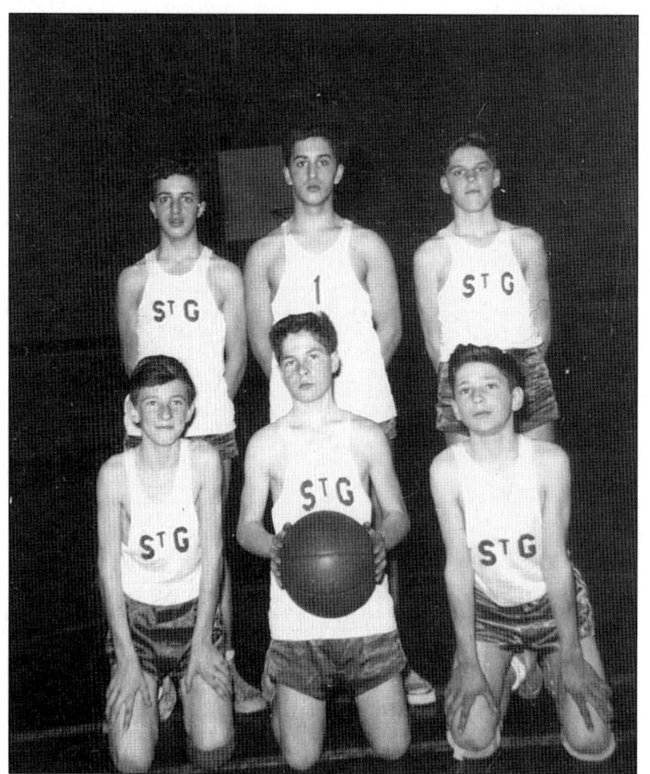

Pictured are the six starting players for St. Gertrude's 1954–1955 basketball team. These athletes excelled in the game, with a winning season of 20-1. From left to right are the following: (front row) J. Welsh, J. Barnyock, and C. Cooper; (back row) J. Venezia, T. Venezia, and D. Shaffer. Don Stemple was head coach. (Courtesy of Jack Welsh.)

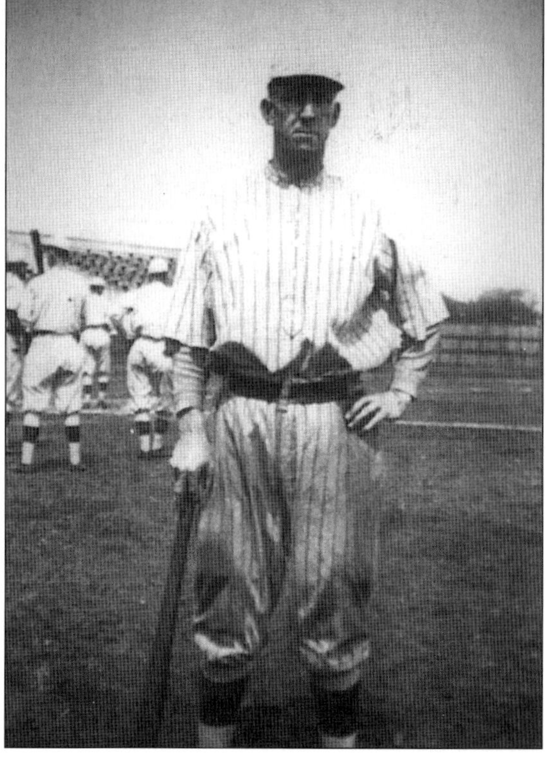

Baseball's Roy "Whitey" Ellam is said to be the greatest baseball player ever to roam the diamonds of Conshohocken. Born in West Conshohocken on February 8, 1886, Ellam lived most of his life in Conshohocken. He played for the Cincinnati National League team in 1919 and later with the Pittsburgh team. Ellam made his mark as a manager with a number of professional teams in the South. He led the Nashville team to the Southern Baseball Association championship. (Courtesy of Jack Coll.)

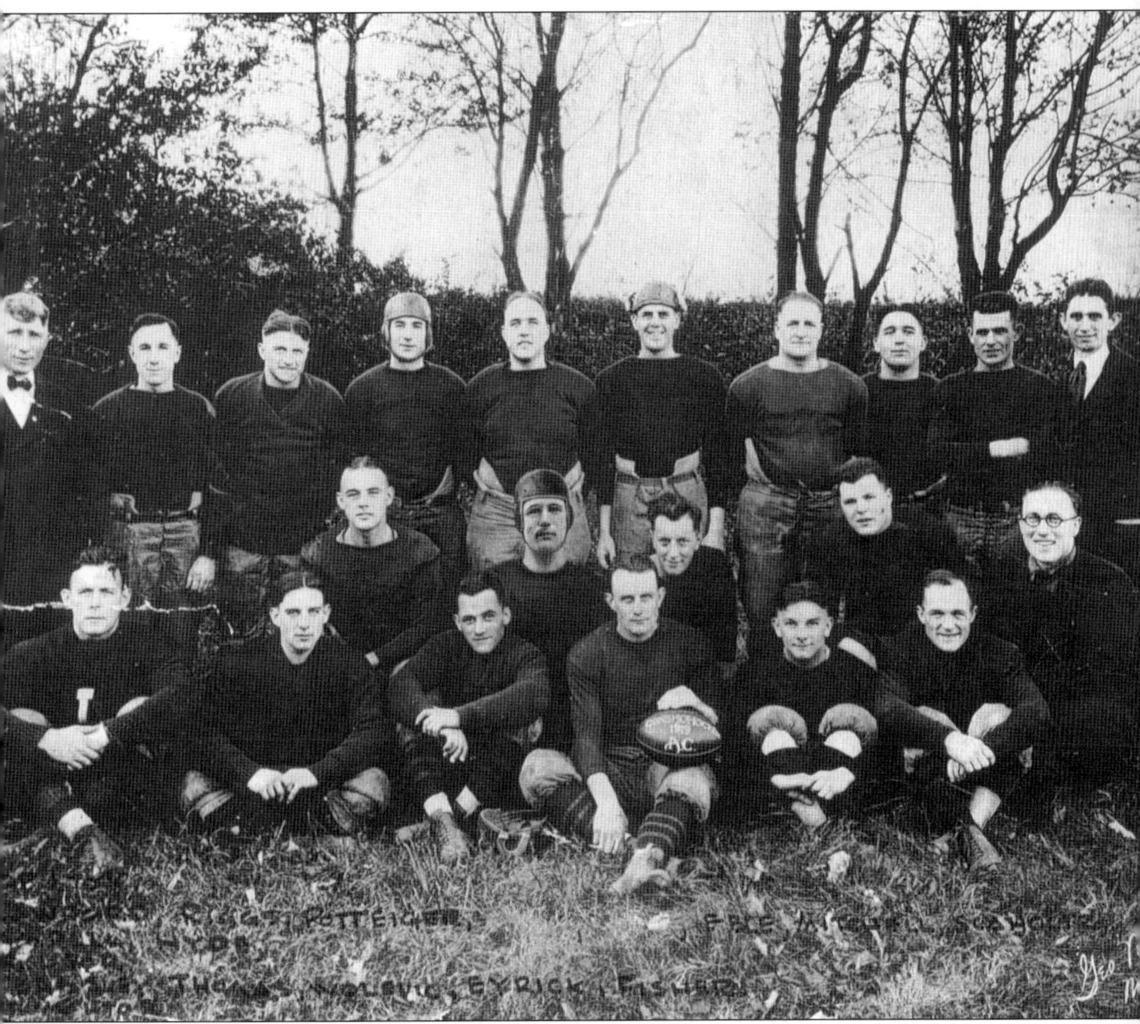

Conshohocken has fielded professional football teams since 1893. This is the Conshohocken's Athletic Club team of 1919, led by manager Bob Crawford, posted a 9-0 record, outscoring opponents 232-14 with stars like Earl Pottieger, Seth Mitchel, Pick Campbell, and Pat Ryan. When they were not on the field for a game, the team could be found practicing behind Crawford's cigar store on Second and Fayette Streets. The National Football Hall of Fame honored the team as Eastern Champions. (Courtesy of Jack Coll.)

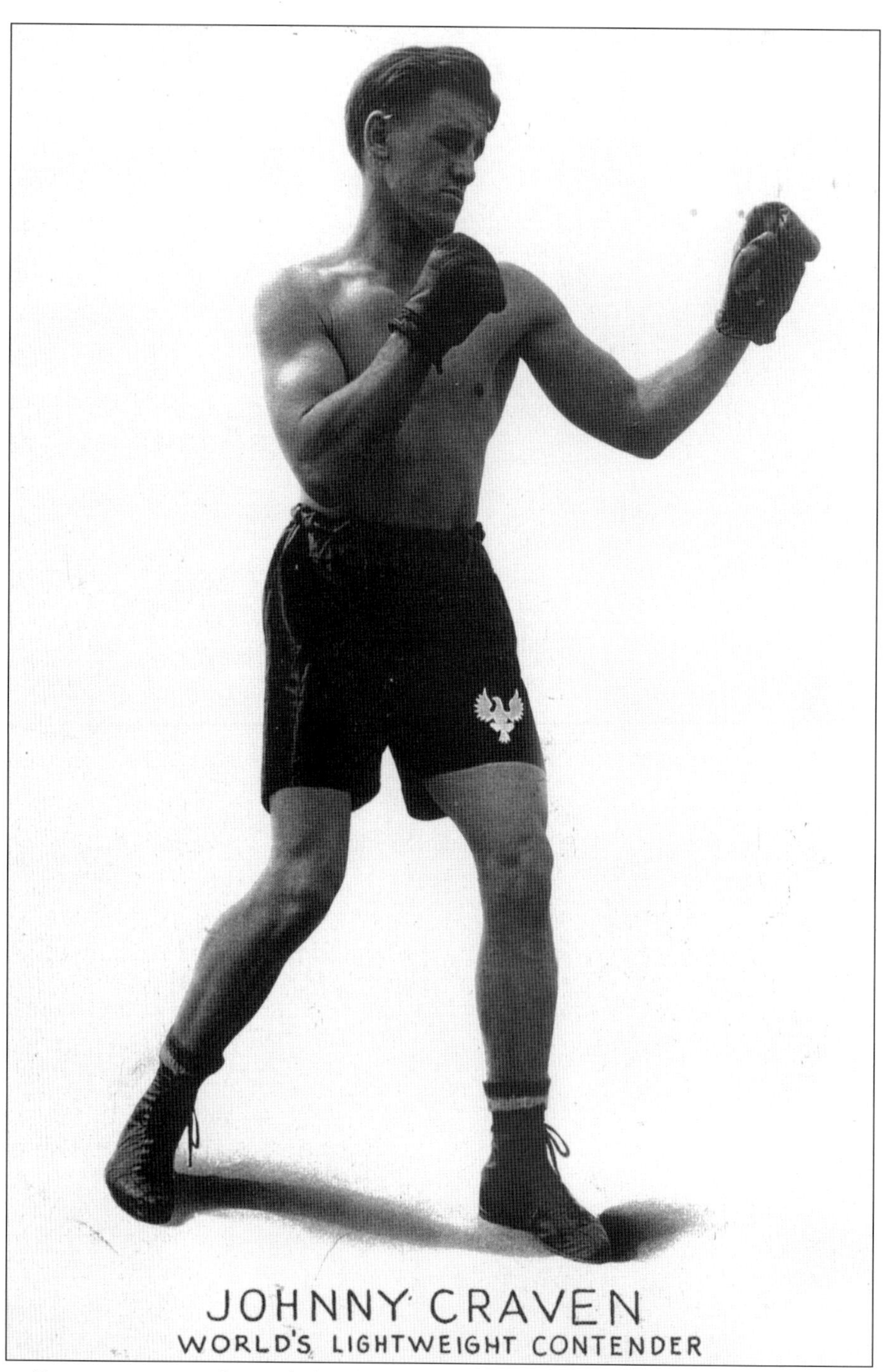

Johnny Craven was one of Conshohocken's gifts to boxing. As an amateur, he had 62 wins, including the Schuylkill Valley Championship and the Golden Glove Tournament. Craven turned professional in 1930 and, over the course of his career, had 84 wins, 44 by knockout. He quit the game several times and, during one of those brief retirements, opened the Square Circle Tavern in Conshohocken. Other great fighters of the borough included Joey Blake, Midge Fox, John Cassinelli, and Bunny Blake. (Courtesy of Jack Coll.)

Eight

Bubbling Springs

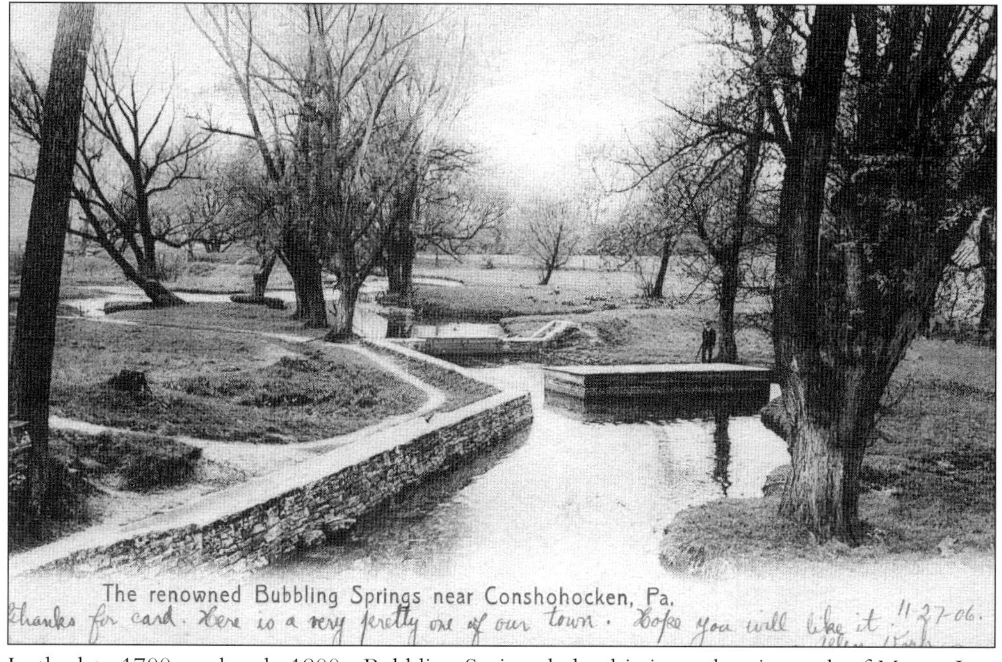

In the late 1700s and early 1800s, Bubbling Springs helped irrigate the vineyards of Mount Joy, Peter Legaux's estate. Legaux was experimenting with producing the first American wine. The beauty of the Legaux estate and the Bubbling Springs attracted notables to the area, such as George Washington and Thomas Jefferson.

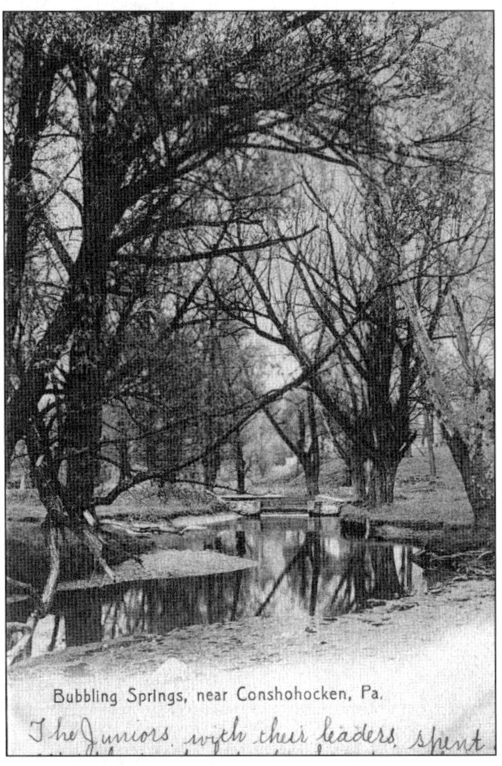

Bubbling Springs Park was located in Spring Mill just off Barren Hill Road. In fact, Spring Mill derived its name from these springs. At the beginning of the 20th century, the springs were described as pools of water forming shallow lagoons that connected with each other by deep winding channels. The pools were set among a grove of oak and willow trees and scattered over a half acre of meadow. Although the springs still exist, the site is overgrown and no longer visible from the road.

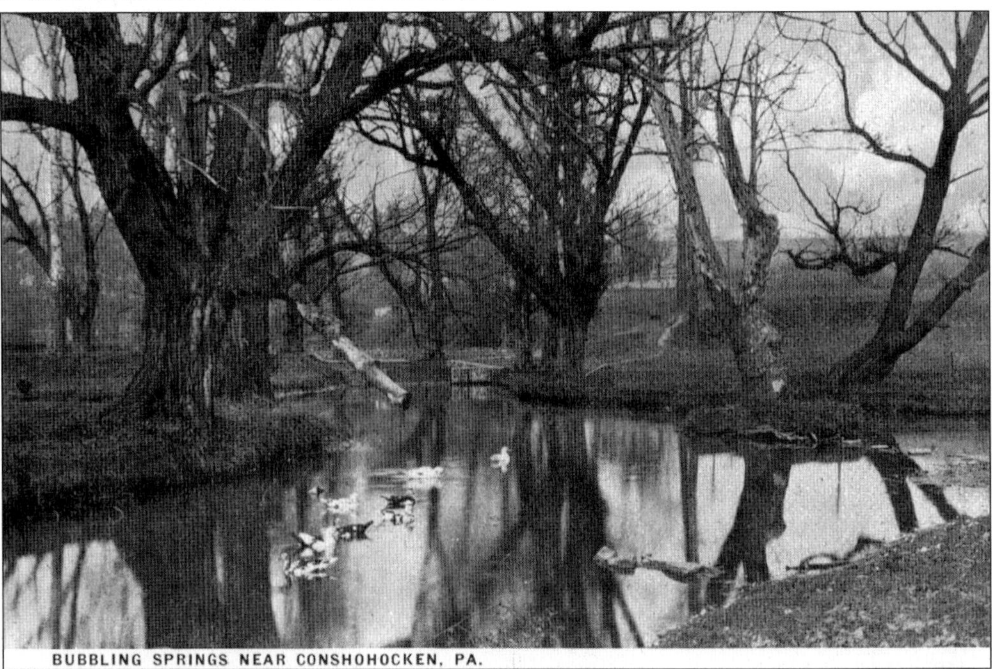

In the 1700s, a flour mill was built near the springs—hence, the name Spring Mill. The springs provided waterpower for the gristmill, which operated for more than 250 years. A public ferry was also maintained in this area for easy access to the mill, for river transportation, and as a shipping point for the marble quarried in Whitemarsh Valley.

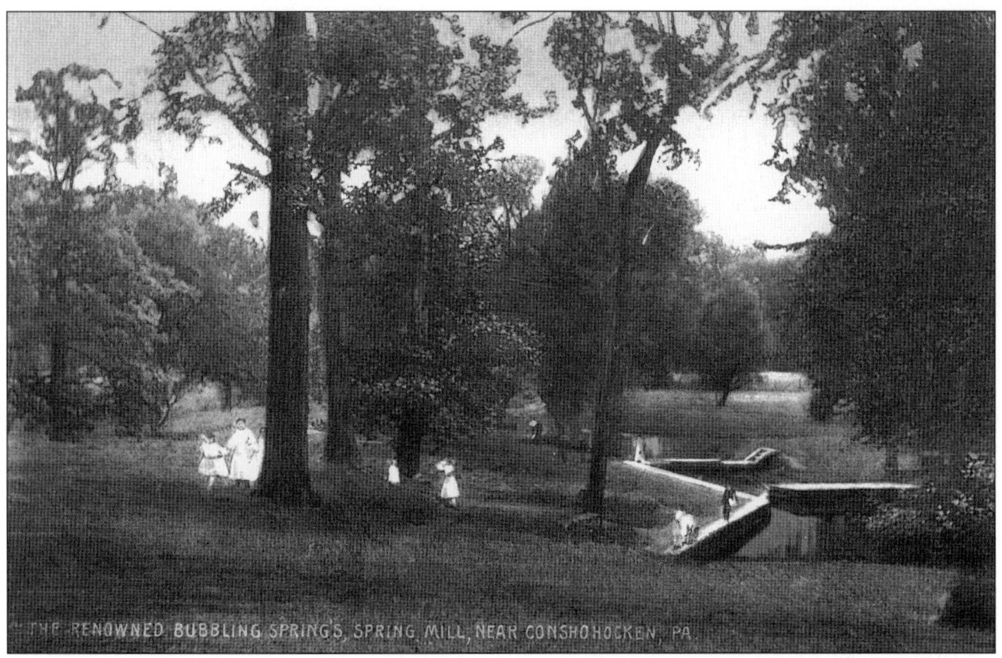

By the late 1800s, Bubbling Springs had become a popular tourist area for family picnics and church socials. The newly formed Spring Mill Band performed Sunday concerts in the park.

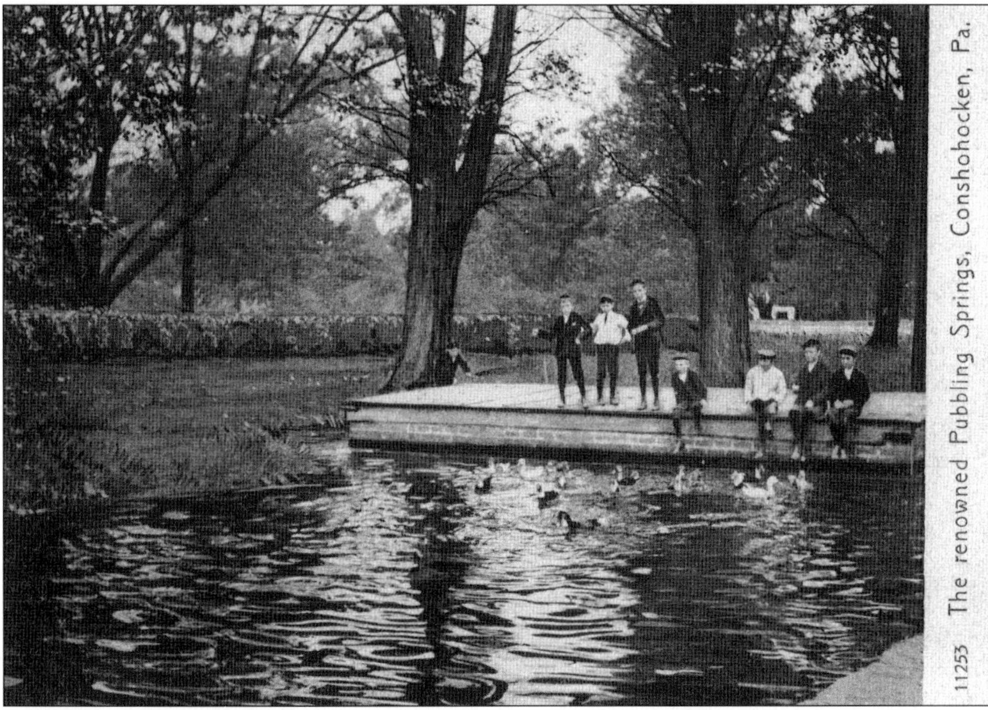

Boys in their Sunday best feed ducks in the water at Bubbling Springs. Young and old alike enjoyed the park and springs. In the early 1900s, children swam in the spring, and young couples had picnics on the banks.

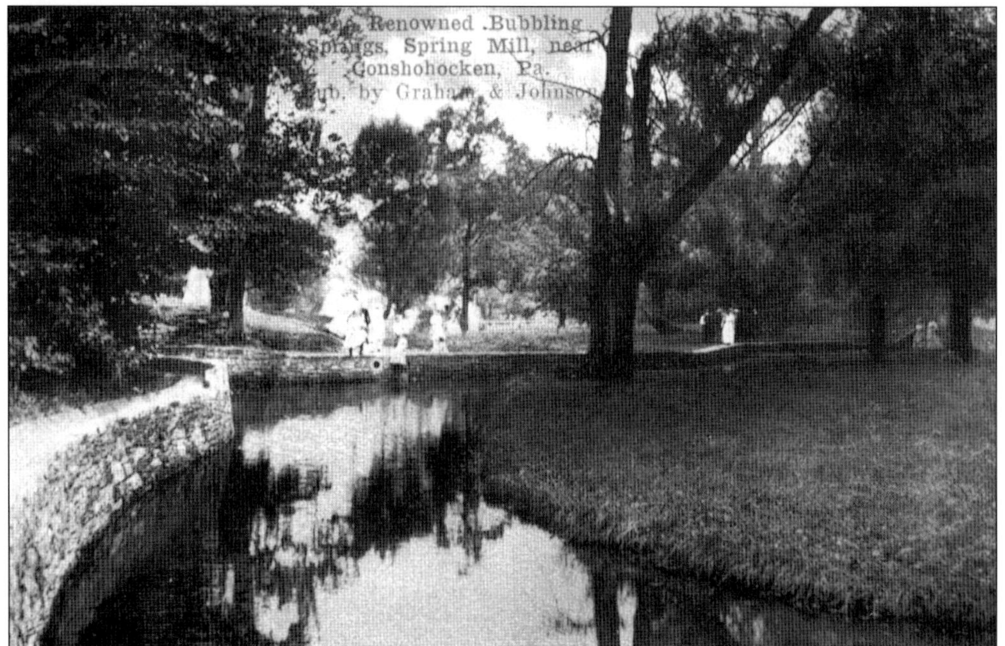

It is unfortunate that this once beautiful park at Bubbling Springs can no longer be enjoyed. With the growth of industry in the Spring Mill area came the loss of this peaceful natural park.

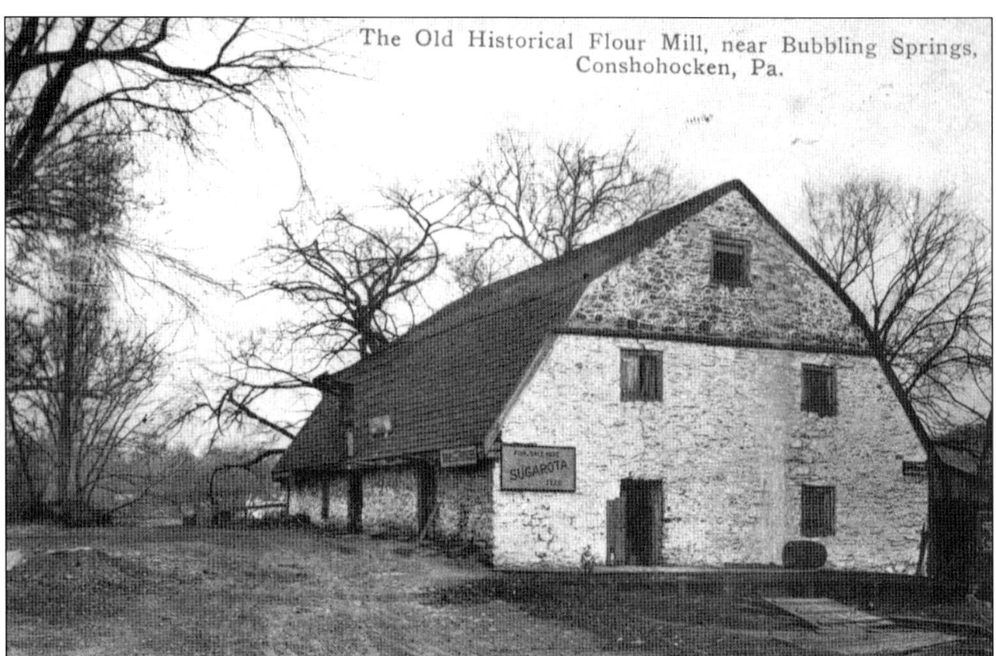

Farms were a common sight in the area in the 1700s. The Old Spring Mill was a place for farmers to sell their wheat so that they could pay the quitrent due to the proprietor, William Penn. At that time, when a proprietor of large parcels of land sold segments of the property, they still retained political control over the property. The quitrent was a loyalty payment that the smaller landowner would pay to the proprietor.

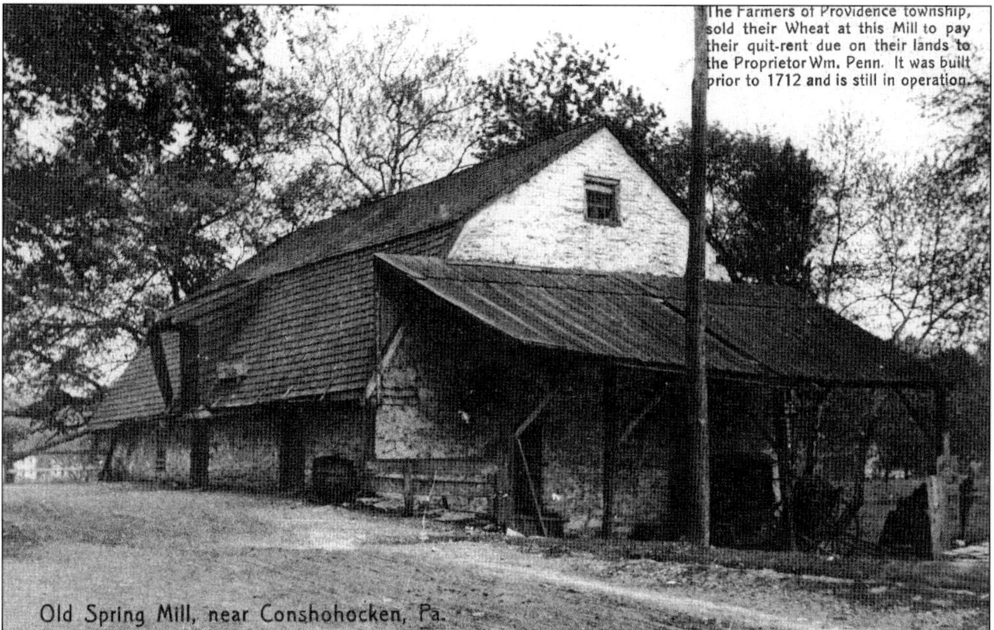

The Old Spring Mill was in operation for more than 200 years. Located in an area now known as East Hector Street and North Lane, the mill provided flour for Washington's troops on their way to Valley Forge in 1777. The mill was ideally located at Bubbling Spring near the Schuylkill River. A ferry dock on the river made the mill easily accessible to farms across the river.

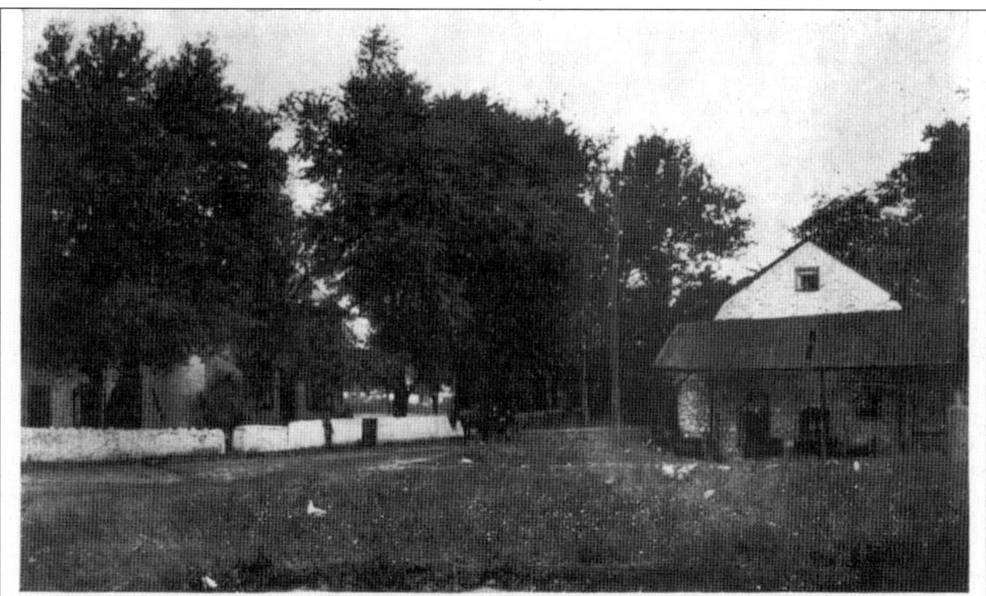

The gristmill and house were built prior to 1712 and were once part of the Peter Legaux estate. The mill was powered by water from Bubbling Springs. It was said that regardless of river or weather conditions, the spring always provided an even flow of water year-round, making it the best gristmill in the area.

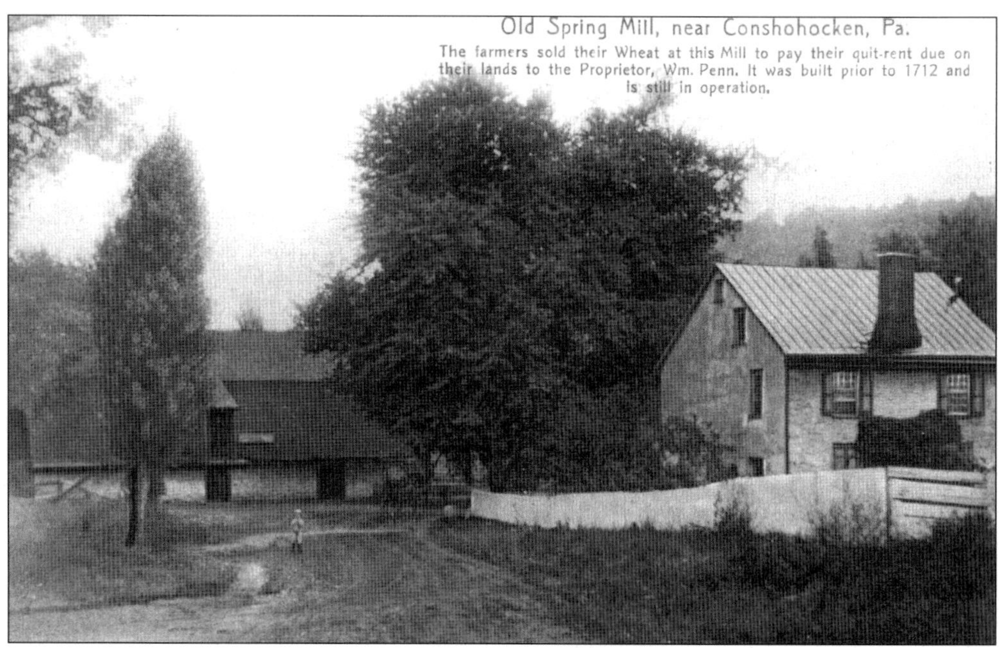

The Old Spring Mill operated through World War II. Shortly afterward, it became a feed store until a fire demolished the building in 1968. The house is still standing today at Hector Street and North Lane.

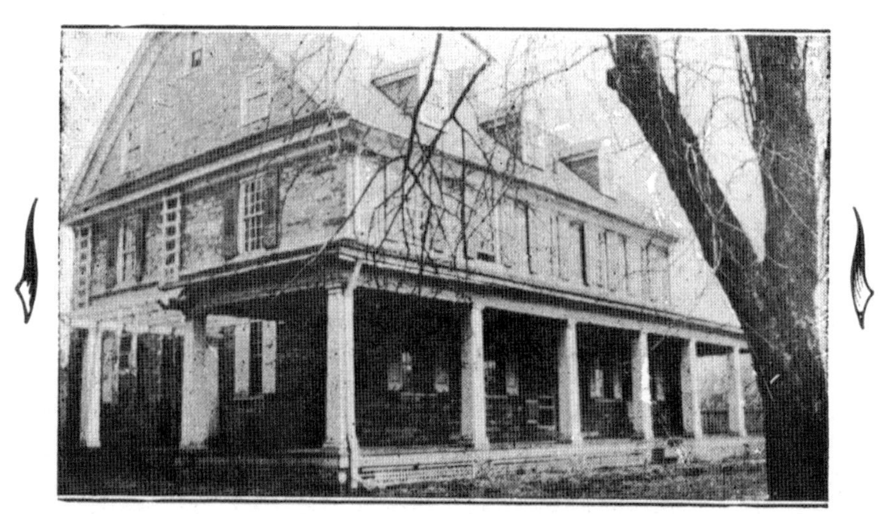

"MOUNT JOY," home of Peter Legaux, famed French refugee and scientist of Revolutionary times, still standing and occupied at North Lane and Hector street, Spring Mill near Conshohocken. In this house, Peter Legaux entertained General Washington, General Lafayette, Benjamin Franklin and many other Colonial notables.

In 1786, Peter Legaux purchased the estate known as Mount Joy. Legaux was a wealthy French refugee, entrepreneur, and scientist. He cultivated grape vineyards and bee gardens on the sunny slopes of his estate in Spring Mill. The beauty and grandeur of the estate attracted many notable colonials of the time, such as Washington, Jefferson, and Franklin.

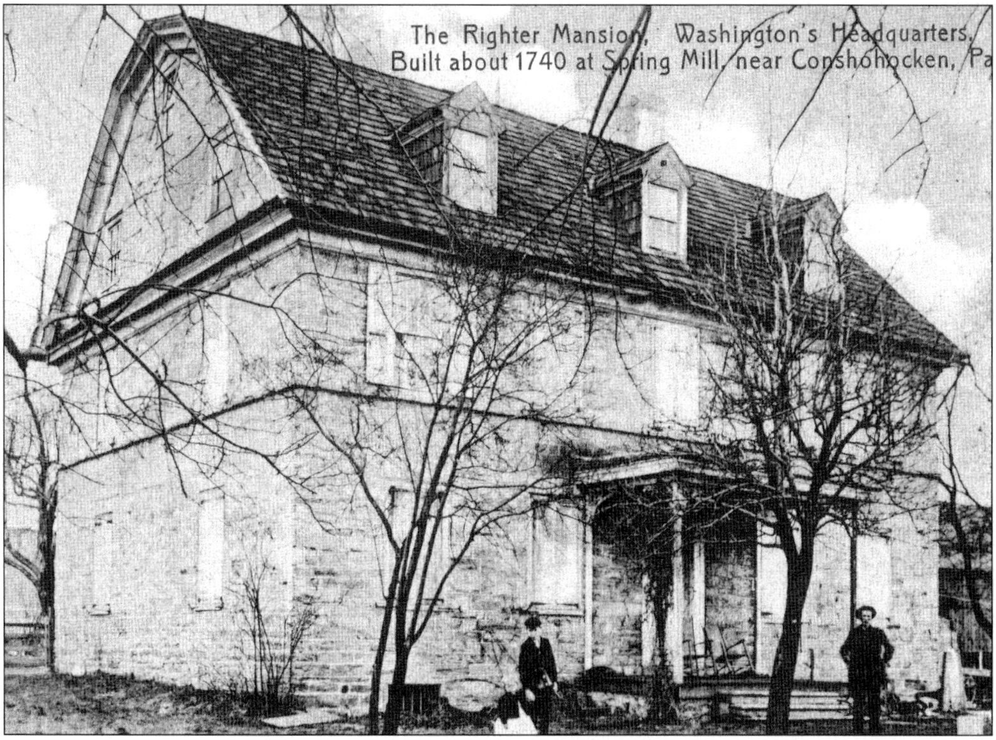

The Righter Mansion, Washington's Headquarters,
Built about 1740 at Spring Mill, near Conshohocken, Pa

This mansion has been known by many names over the last 260 years. The home is believed to have been built in the 1740s. In the course of its history, the Spring Mill plantation, located in an area now know as North Lane and Hector Street, was owned by Col. Samuel Miles from 1773 to 1783. He named the estate Mount Joy. Colonel Miles was a valiant Revolutionary War officer. It is believed that during his ownership of the home, it was used for a headquarters for George Washington.

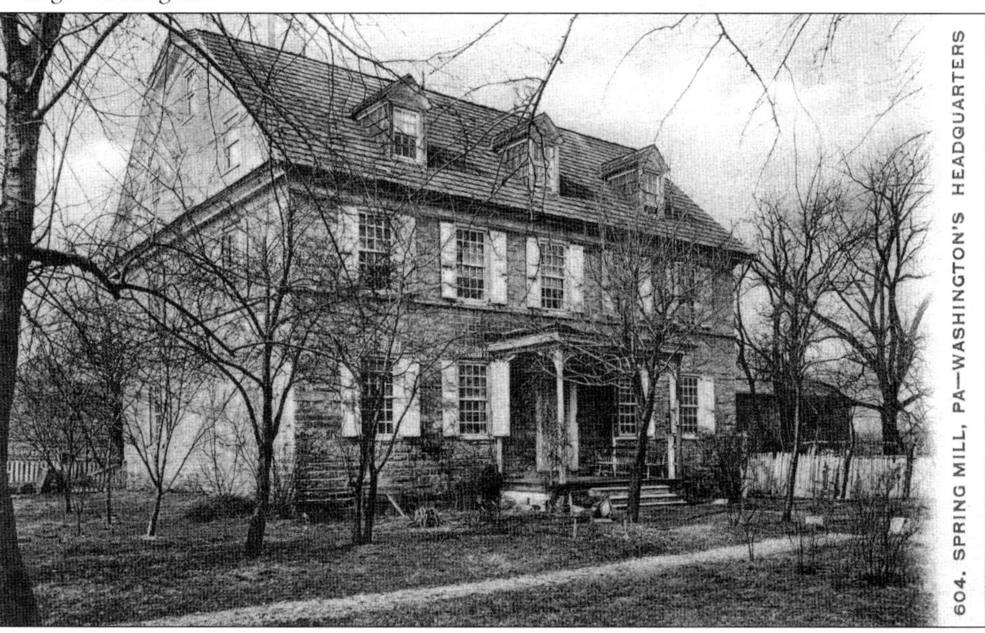

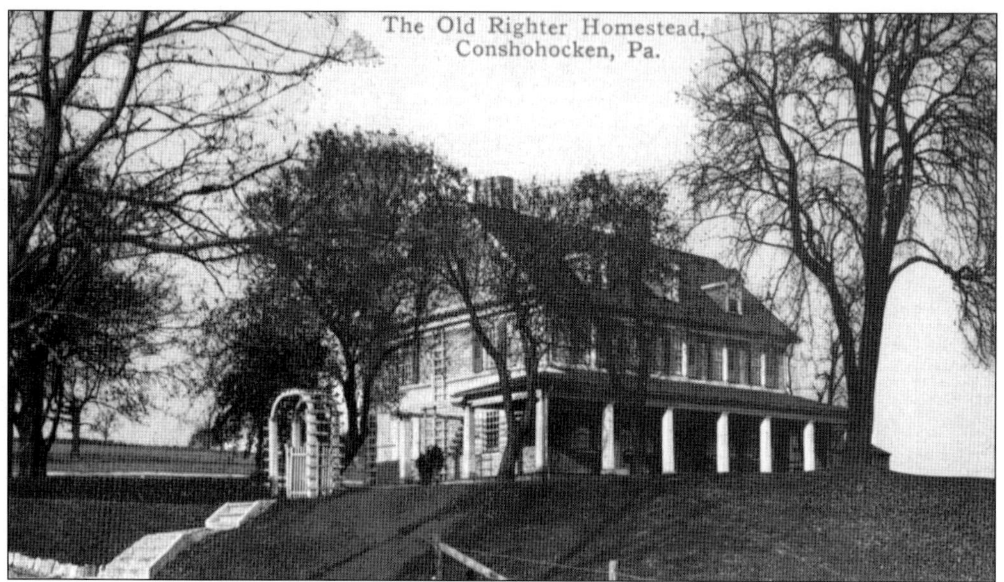

The first attempt at making wine in America took place in Spring Mill. In 1793, the *Daily Advertiser* stated, "The first vintage ever held in America would begin at the vineyard, near Spring Mill. Peter Legaux will begin to make American wine. We shall no longer be indebted to foreign wines." Unfortunately, the cost of producing the wine did not make it competitive with the foreign market, and the little company collapsed. John Righter, son-in-law of Legaux, rescued the property from bankruptcy.

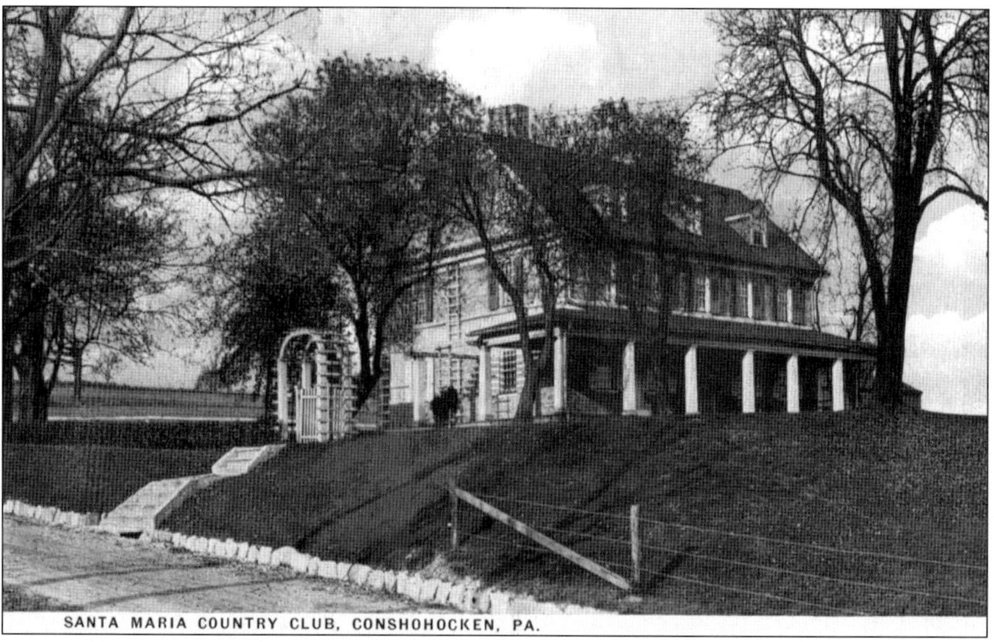

After Legaux's death in 1827, Mount Joy was referred to as the Righter Homestead. The Righter family sold their house in 1921 for use as the Knights of Columbus Country Club. The property then became known as the Santa Maria Country Club. The Spring Mill Fire Company bought the house in 1928 and used it as its headquarters. Today, the house is occupied by professional offices.

Nine
FAITH AND WISDOM

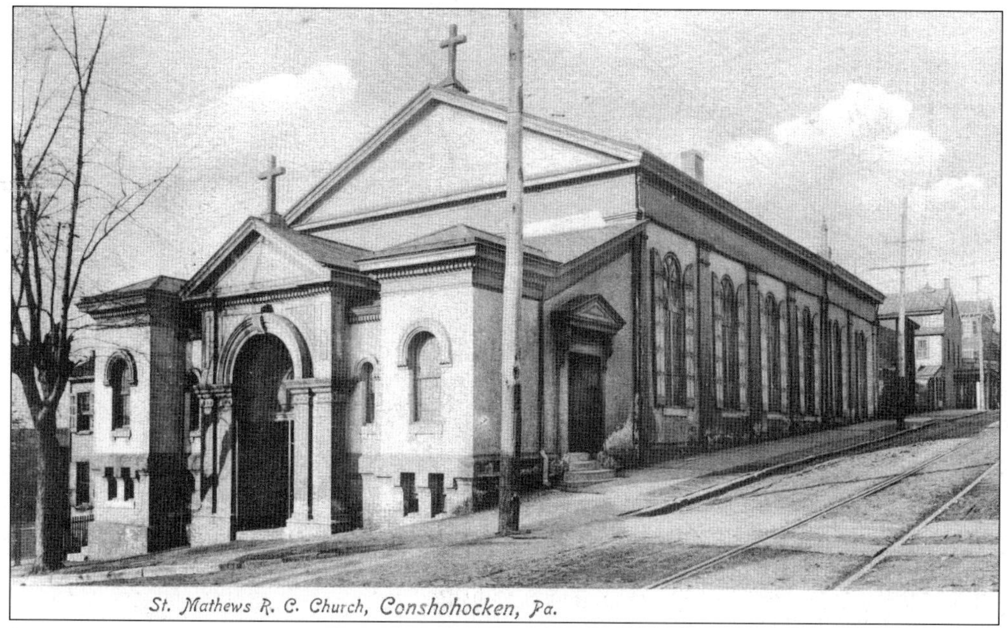
St. Mathews R. C. Church, Conshohocken, Pa.

St. Matthews Roman Catholic Church was established in 1851, one year after the town incorporation. It was the first of several Catholic churches in Conshohocken. The first church building was located at the corner of Harry and Hector Streets.

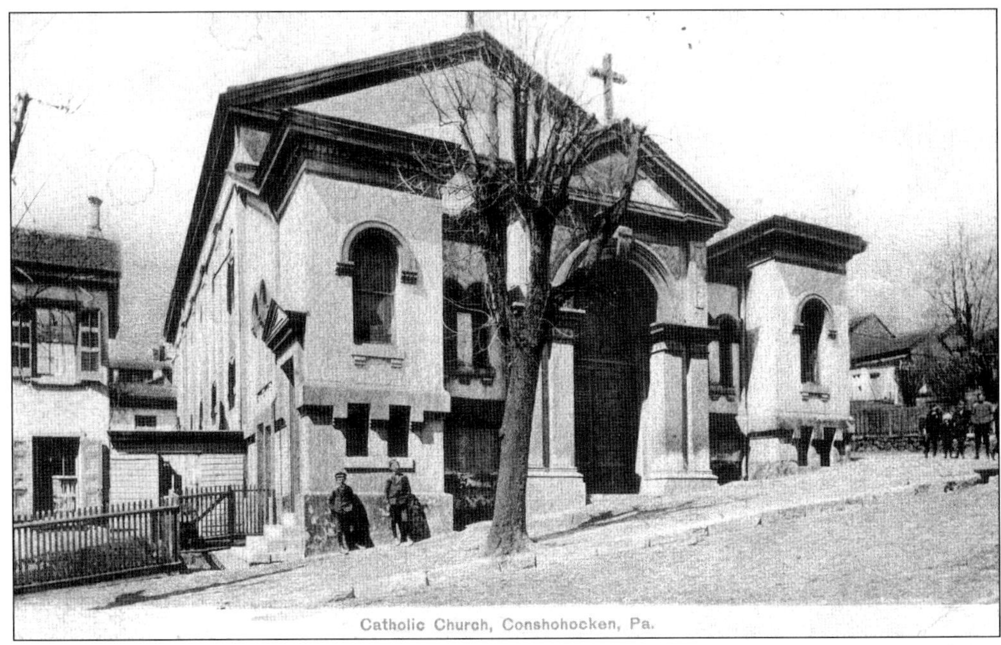
Catholic Church, Conshohocken, Pa.

This Catholic church was the original building for St. Matthews. The church was established to address the religious needs of the Irish Catholics who had immigrated to Conshohocken to work in the mills and quarries.

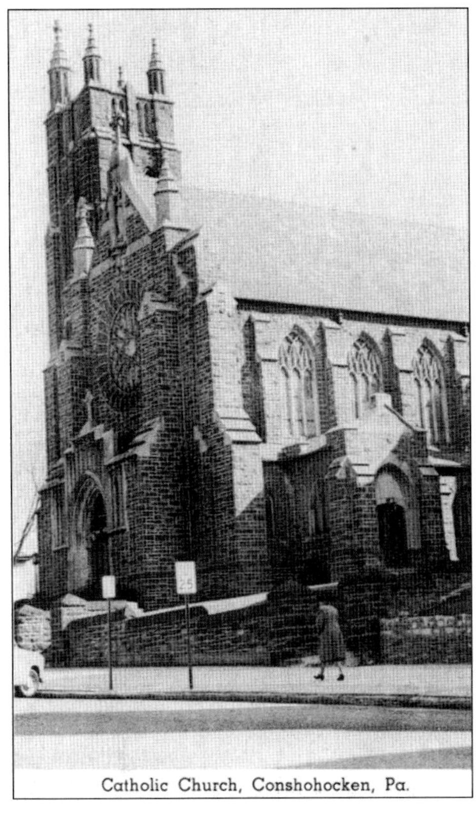

Catholic Church, Conshohocken, Pa.

Due to the continued growth of the Irish Catholic community, St. Matthews pastor Rev. James Parker purchased ground on the corner of Third Avenue and Fayette Street to build a new church. In 1915, St. Matthews laid the cornerstone, and the building was completed in 1919.

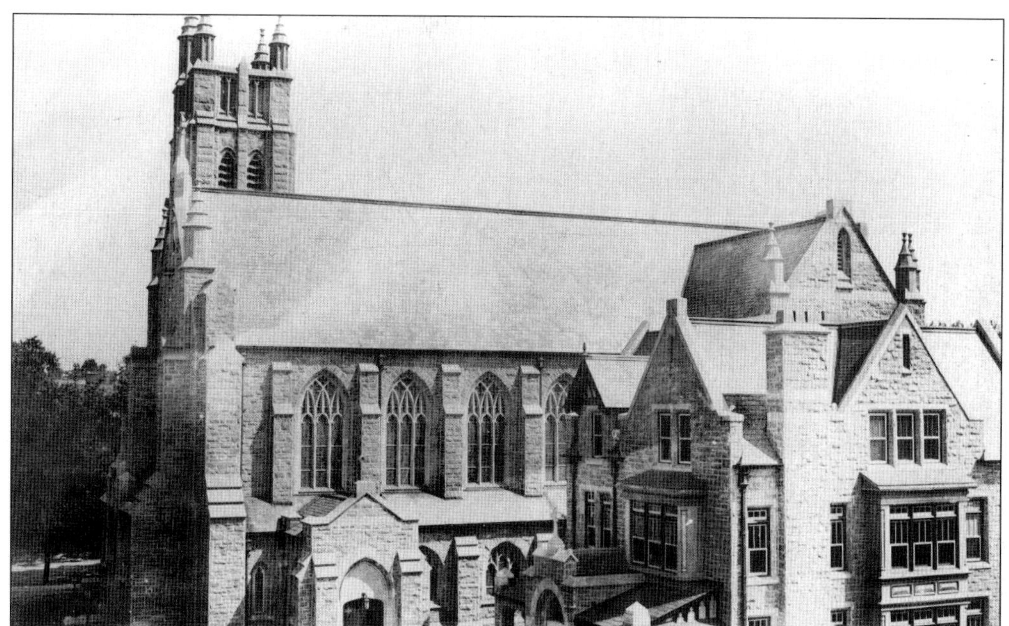

The new St. Matthews building was dedicated on September 21, 1919. The church represents the prosperity, maturity, and growth of the Catholic population of Conshohocken in the early 20th century. The building is 13th-century Gothic in design. The rectory (foreground) was also constructed in 1919.

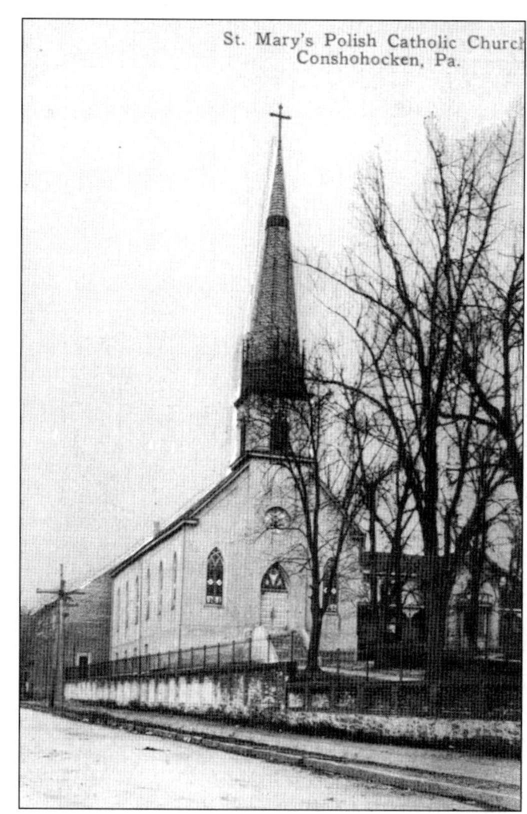

St. Mary's Polish Catholic Church was organized in 1905 with 60 Polish families. The building in this postcard was located at West Elm and Maple Streets and was the former site of the Conshohocken Presbyterian Church. In 1949, ground was broken for a new church at the corner of West Elm and Oak Streets, and the new Gothic building was dedicated on December 7, 1951.

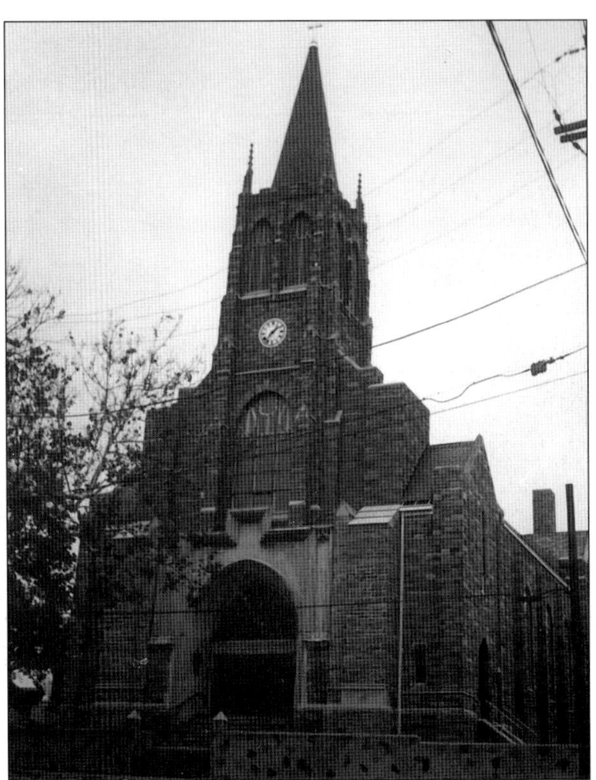

St. Mary's Polish Catholic Church began when Rev. Benedict Tomiak traveled to Conshohocken to get acquainted with the Polish people who had been attending his church, St. Josaphat's in Manayunk. With his own funds, Tomiak purchased a two-story stone house with a garden that had belonged to William Wood and had been built by John Wood at Oak and Elm Streets. He celebrated the first mass on May 1, 1905. This temporary chapel was quickly outgrown, and the church moved several times until ground was broken for a permanent site at West Elm and Oak Streets.

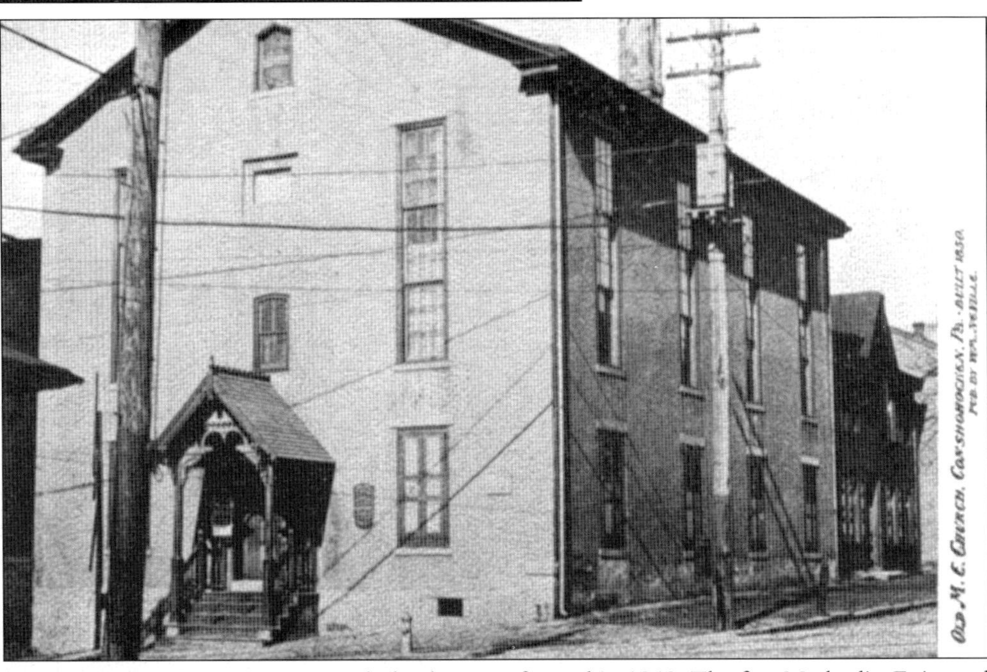

The Methodist community in Conshohocken was formed in 1848. The first Methodist Episcopal church was built at Elm and Fayette Streets. By *c.* 1900, however, it could no longer house the growing congregation. Ground was purchased at Sixth Avenue and Fayette Street for a new church site.

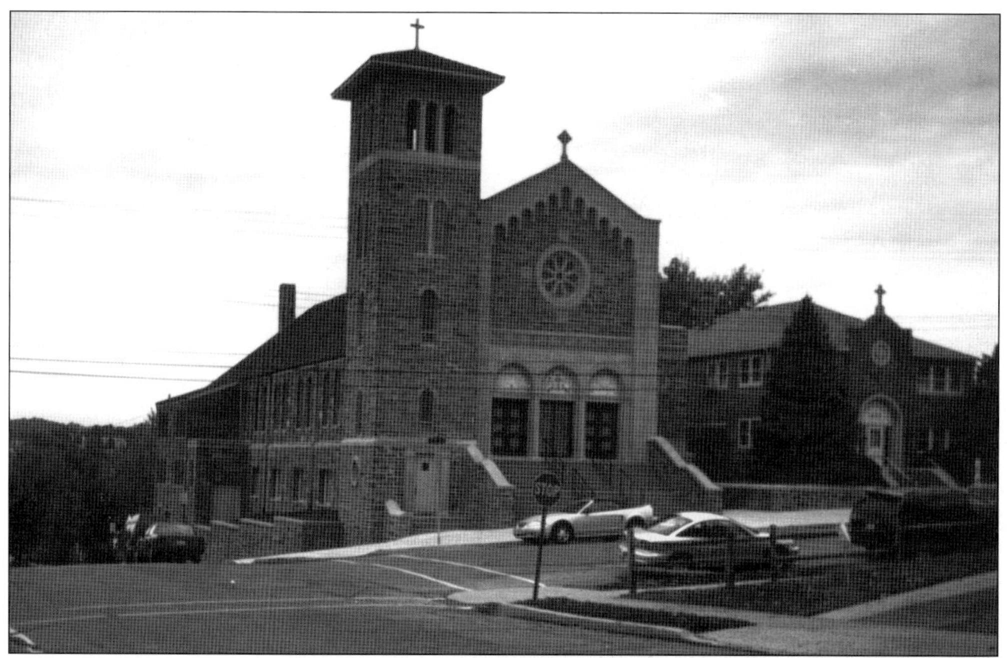

In 1912, permission was granted to a group of Italian Catholics in Conshohocken to establish a church, and the first mass of SS. Cosmas and Damian Church was held at the Little's Opera House. Ground was purchased from the estate of Hiram Corson on Fifth Avenue and Maple Street, and construction began. A small, red brick building was constructed high above street level at the rear of the lot. It was intended to be a temporary structure; plans for a larger church had to wait until after World War I. In 1926, a basement church was constructed and served as the foundation of a permanent church. In 1952, a new church was constructed in the Italian Romanesque style. Above is the current church, and below is a view of the interior.

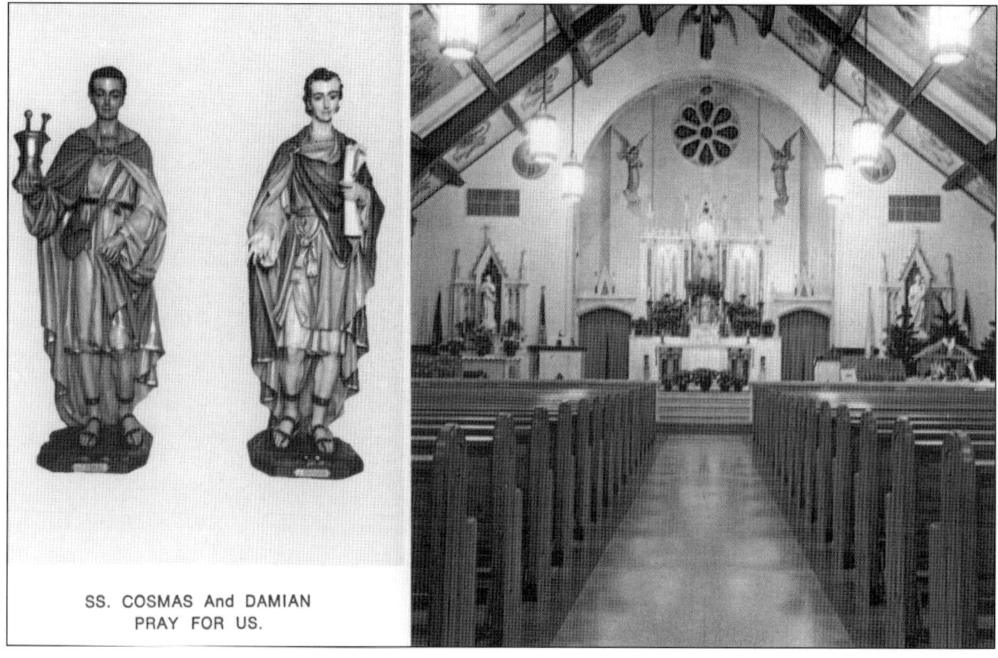

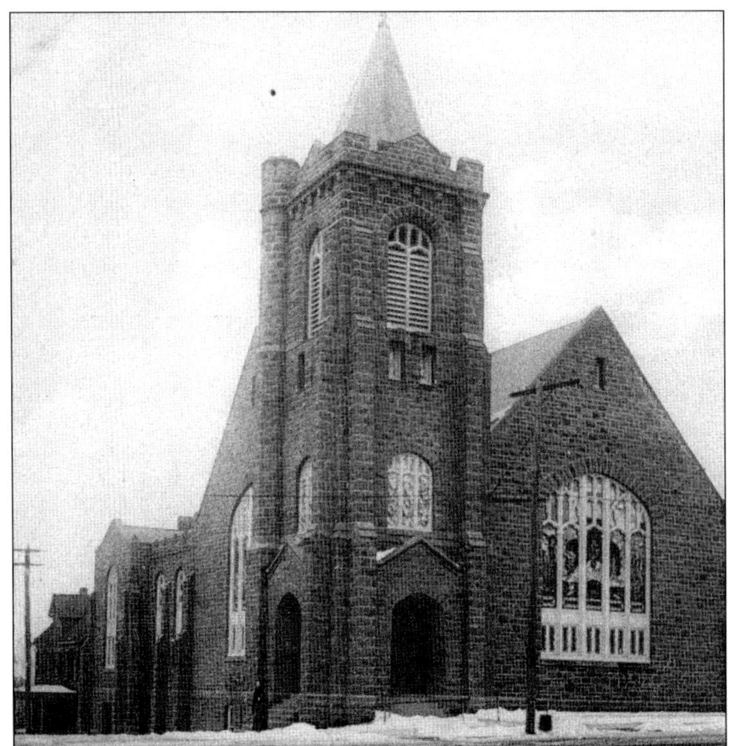

The cornerstone for the new Methodist Episcopal church on Sixth Avenue and Fayette Streets was laid on September 29, 1906. It took almost two and a half years to complete construction. The church was dedicated on January 19, 1908.

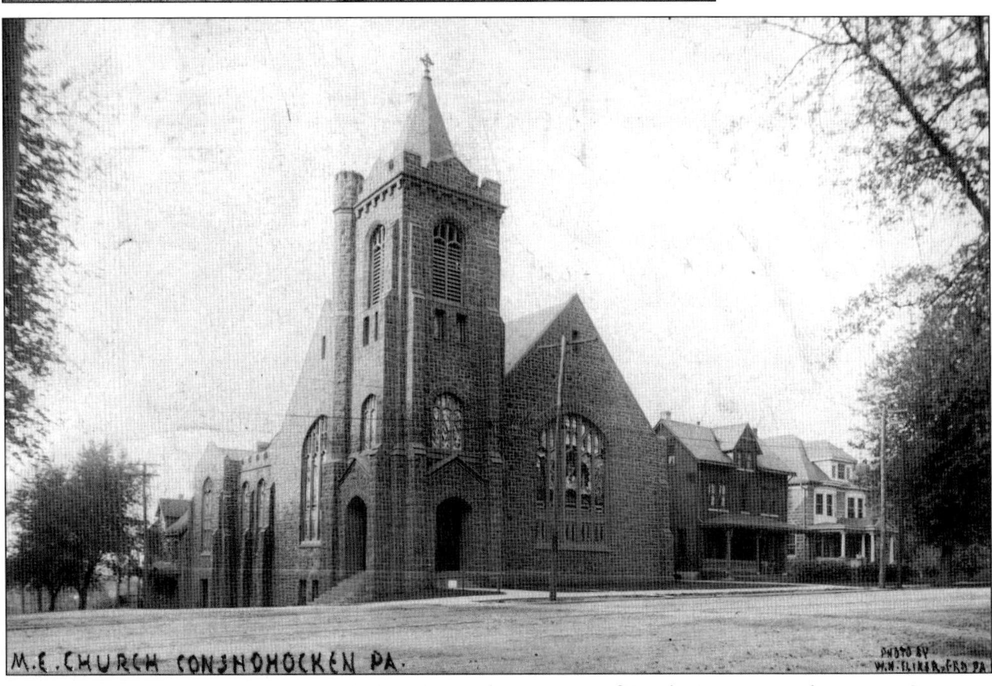

To build the Methodist Episcopal church on the corner of Sixth Avenue and Fayette Street, a home occupying that site was moved to the corner of Sixth and Forrest Streets. To the left of this photograph, facing down Sixth Avenue, is a house (near two trees) that became the parsonage for the church.

The Episcopal Church of Conshohocken, also known as Calvary Episcopal Church, began in Stemple Hall on July 25, 1858, when Walter Cresson, the owner of a mill at the foot of Matsonford Bridge, and his daughter carried an organ, hymnbooks, and a collection plate to the hall. The first church building was completed in 1860 on the corner of Fourth Avenue and Fayette Street. In 1888, this structure was replaced, and noted Philadelphia ecclesiastical architect Charles M. Burns designed the new Calvary Episcopal Church building.

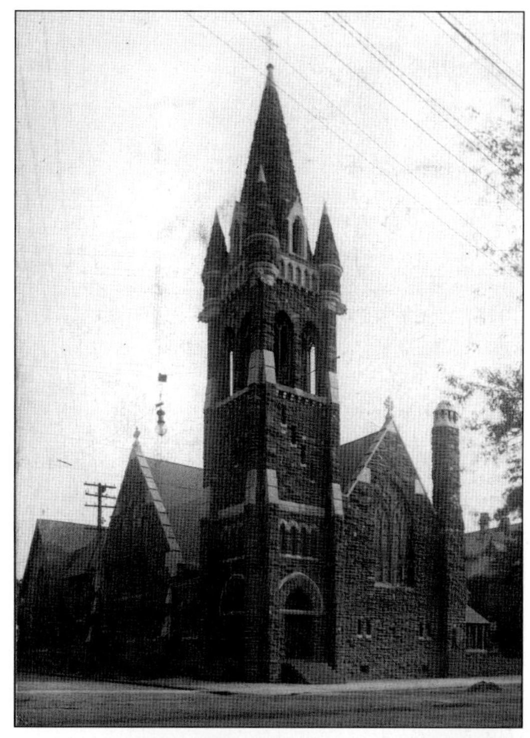

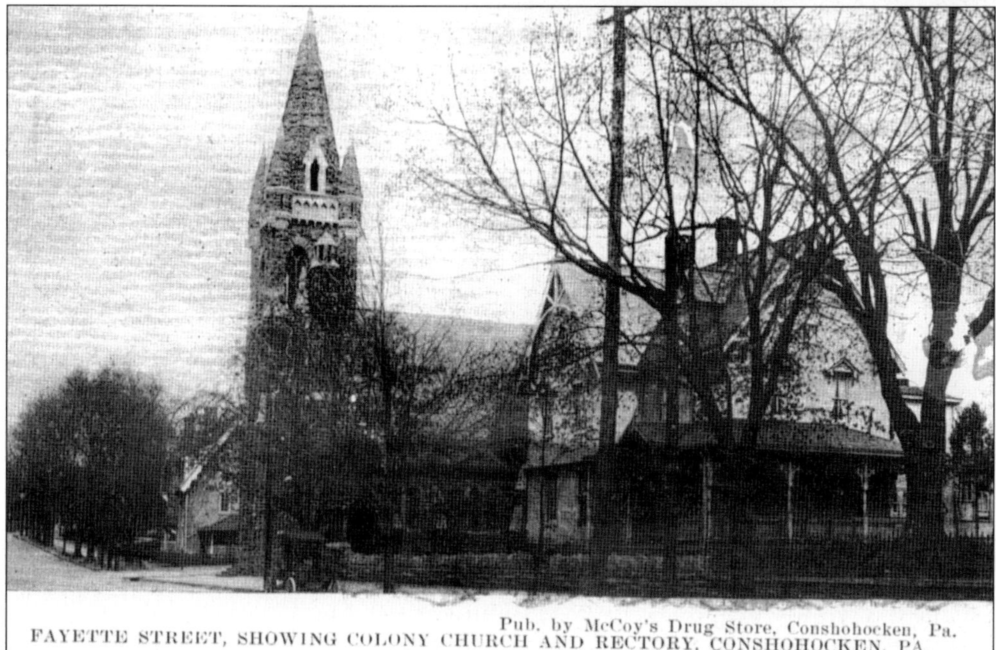

Rev. Edward L. Lycett conducted the first regular services at the Calvary Episcopal Church. This Fayette Street view of Calvary Episcopal Church shows the two-story rectory that was built in 1873 and enlarged in 1889. The construction of the new Calvary Episcopal Church in 1888 was financed in part by the Alan Wood industrial fortune. The church was paid for in full between the start and completion of its construction from 1888 and 1889.

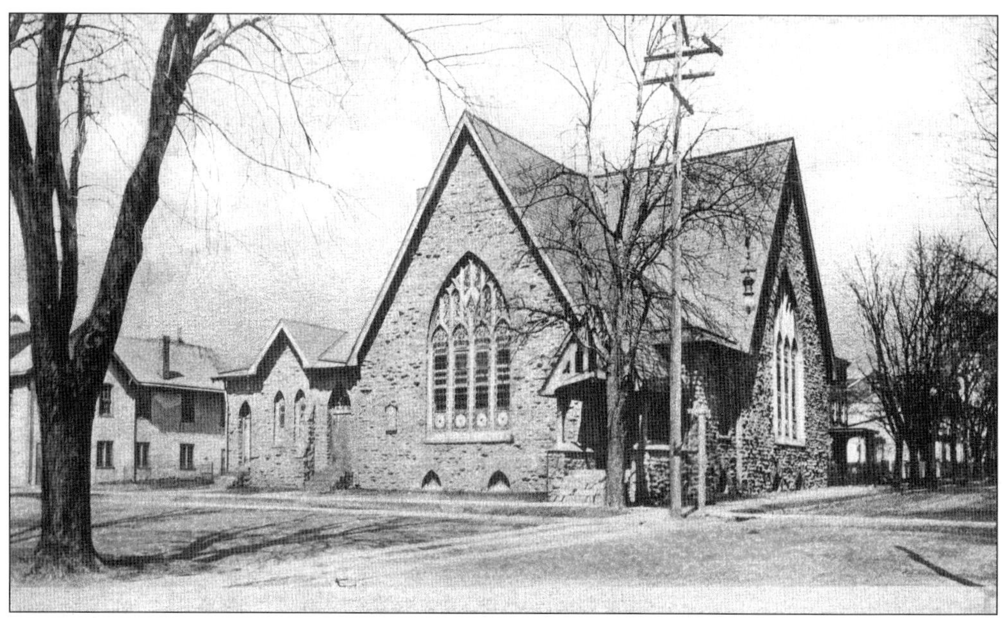

St. Mark's Evangelical Lutheran Church is currently located at the corner of Fifth Avenue and Harry Street. The church had its beginning as a Sunday school in the home of Jacob S. Moser in 1889. The church began in April 1890 with 25 people; services were held in the Women's Christian Temperance Union Hall on Third Avenue and Forrest Street.

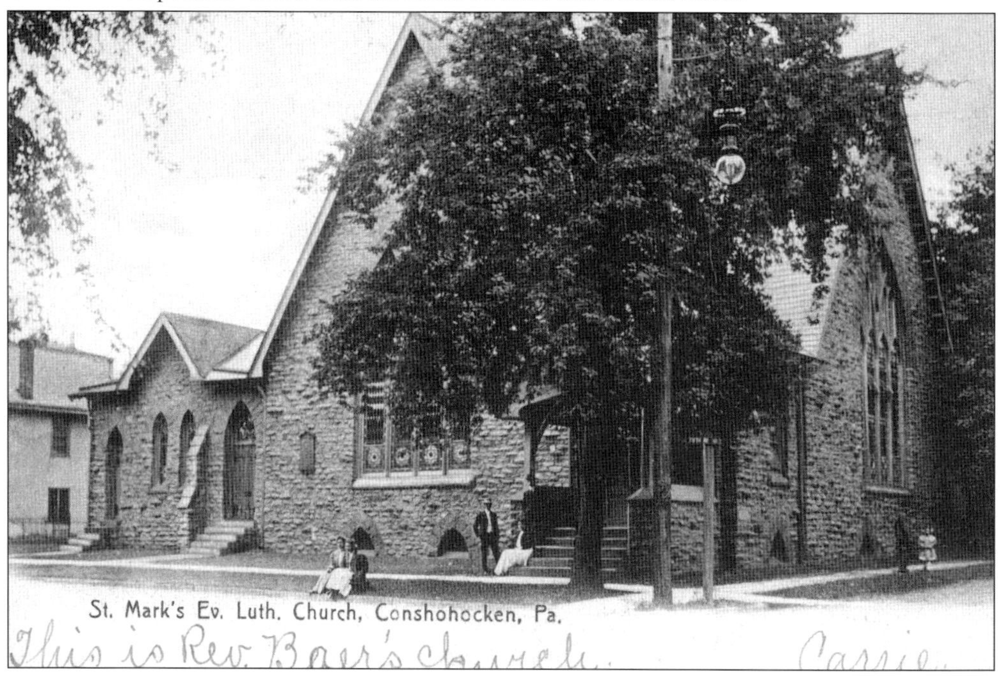

Originally, the congregation of St. Mark's Evangelical Lutheran Church purchased the Jones lot on Eighth Avenue and Hallowell Street for $1,300 as their church site. Before construction began, they decided that this site was too far from town and too sparely populated to serve the members. Several other sites were investigated and, on September 7, 1891, the congregation purchased the Brehm property at Fifth Avenue and Harry Street for $5,000.

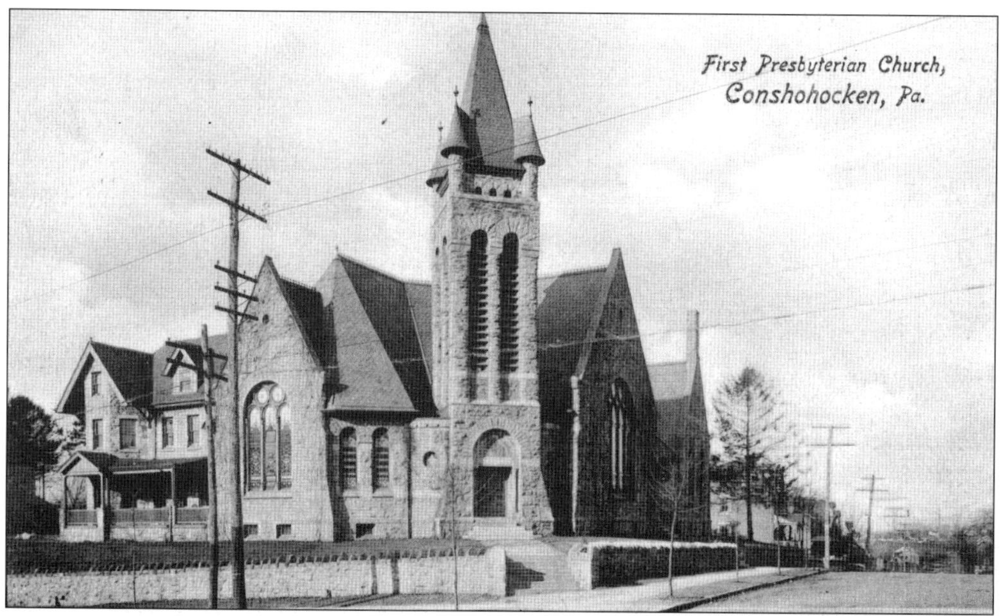

The First Presbyterian Church no longer occupies the corner of Third Avenue and Fayette Street, as depicted in this view. However, the church had a long history in the community. Before Conshohocken was incorporated, a small band of Northern Irish immigrants gathered together to worship in the Presbyterian beliefs. The First Presbyterian Church started in a one-story frame building, the Old Temperance Hall, on West Elm Street in 1847.

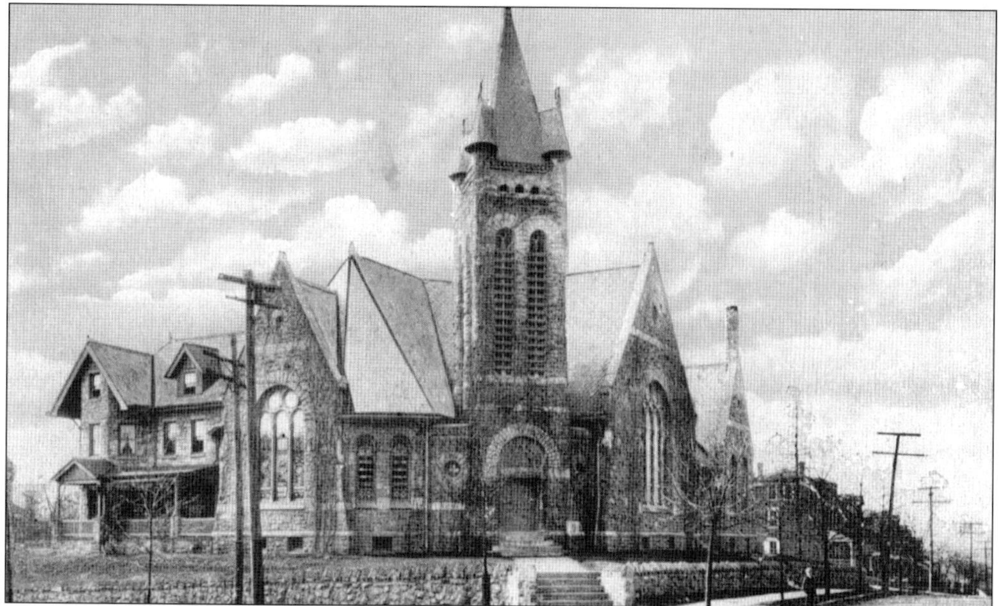

The First Presbyterian Church built its first house of worship at the corner of West Elm and Maple Streets. Soon, the church constructed a new building at the corner on Third Avenue and Fayette Street, as seen in this view. In 1966, when the congregation moved to Plymouth Meeting's Church on the Mall, this site was used by the newly formed Montgomery County Community College as a library. After the college moved to its permanent site in Blue Bell, the church was demolished and Lee Towers was constructed.

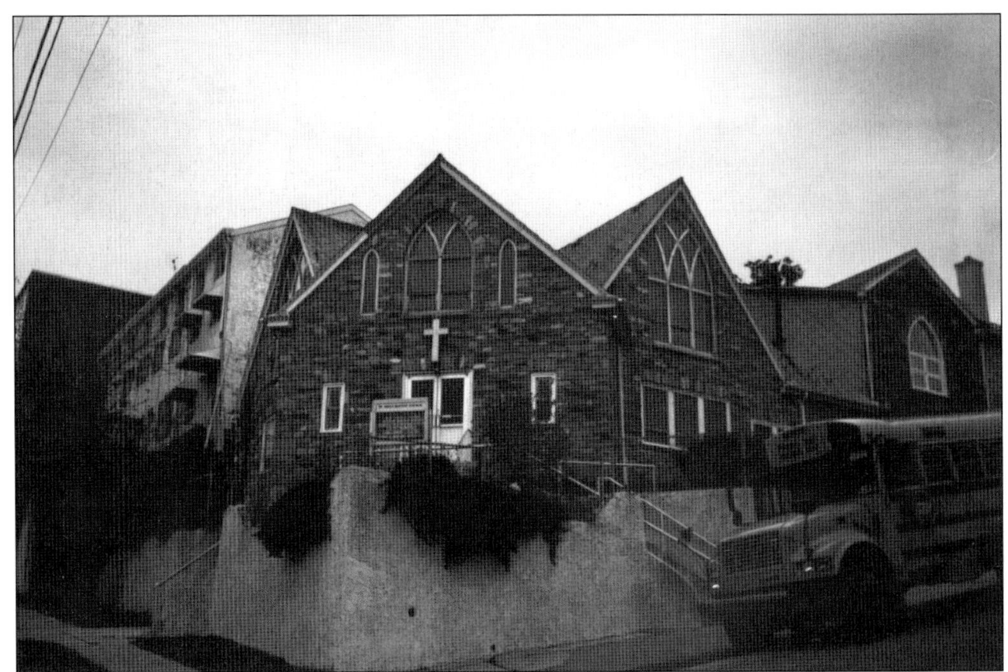

St. Paul's Baptist Church, on Third Avenue and Hallowell Street, began in April 1925, when Rev. Marshall W. Lee, minister of the Siloam Baptist Church in Norristown, began speaking to the laborers at the Alan Wood Steel Company. Meetings were held at the old James Hall Mill in West Conshohocken until a church was built on Cinder Hill (Third Avenue and Hallowell Streets). To commemorate Pastor Lee's 52 years of service to the church and community, a senior citizens' home on Third and Fayette was named Lee Towers.

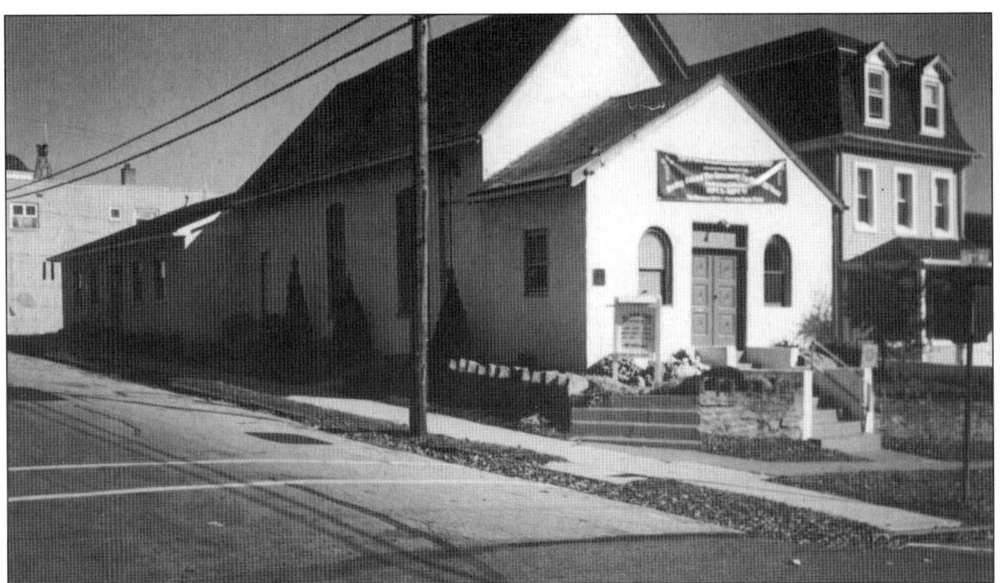

St. John African Methodist Episcopal Church, on the corner of Eighth Avenue and Harry Street, was built in 1881 under the pastorate of Rev. J.J. Campbell. Additions have been made to the front and back of the building. The church recently celebrated its 120th anniversary.

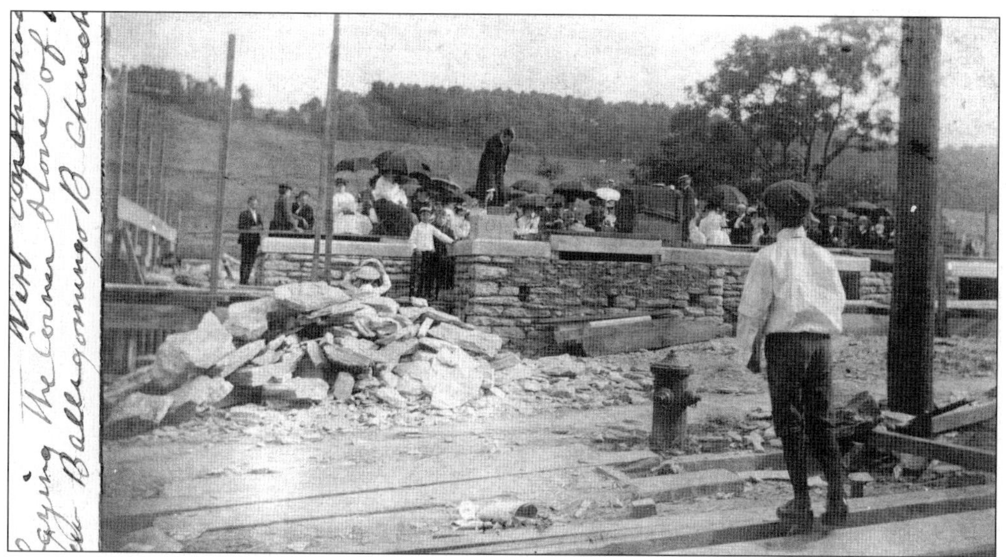

The Balligomingo Baptist Church was located on Ford Street in West Conshohocken. This is a photograph card showing the construction of the 1907 church and the laying of its cornerstone. The dedication services took place from June 21 to June 26, 1908. The church had its beginnings in 1835, when Bethel Moore, who at that time was owner of a Conshohocken woolen mill, thought the new congregation in West Conshohocken should have a place to worship of its own. He erected the first Balligomingo Church and, in 1840, the church was given its separation from the Lower Merion Baptist Church.

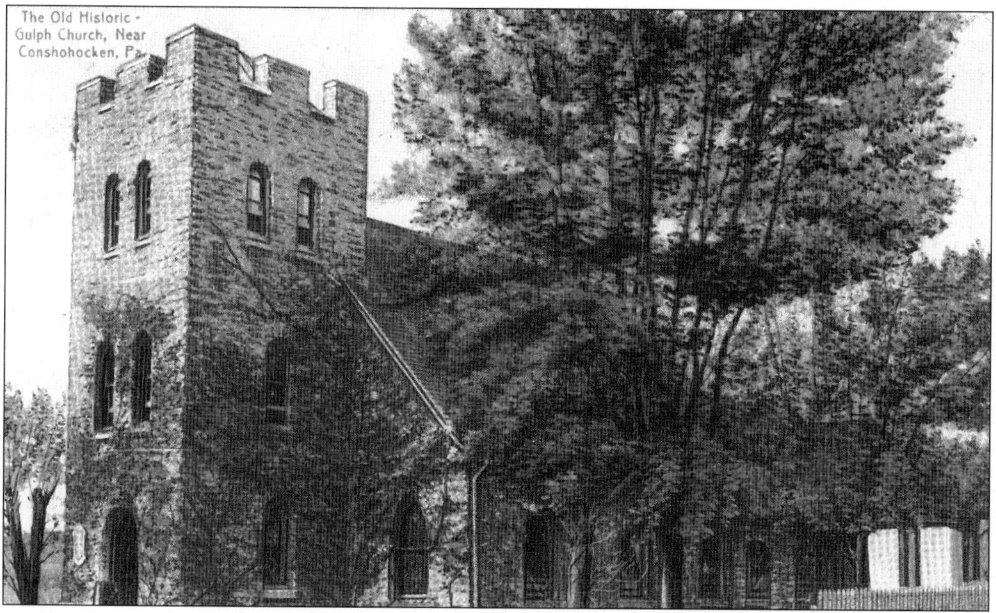

Gulph Christian Church was founded by the Christian Baptist on July 21, 1833, with 25 charter members. Revival services were held at the Gulph School, and baptisms were conducted at the Schuylkill River. In 1834, plans were made to secure a lot on Matson Ford Road and build Gulph Christian Church. The following year, the construction was complete and the church was dedicated. In 1893, a committee was organized to raise money for a new church edifice. One year later, the new church was erected debt-free.

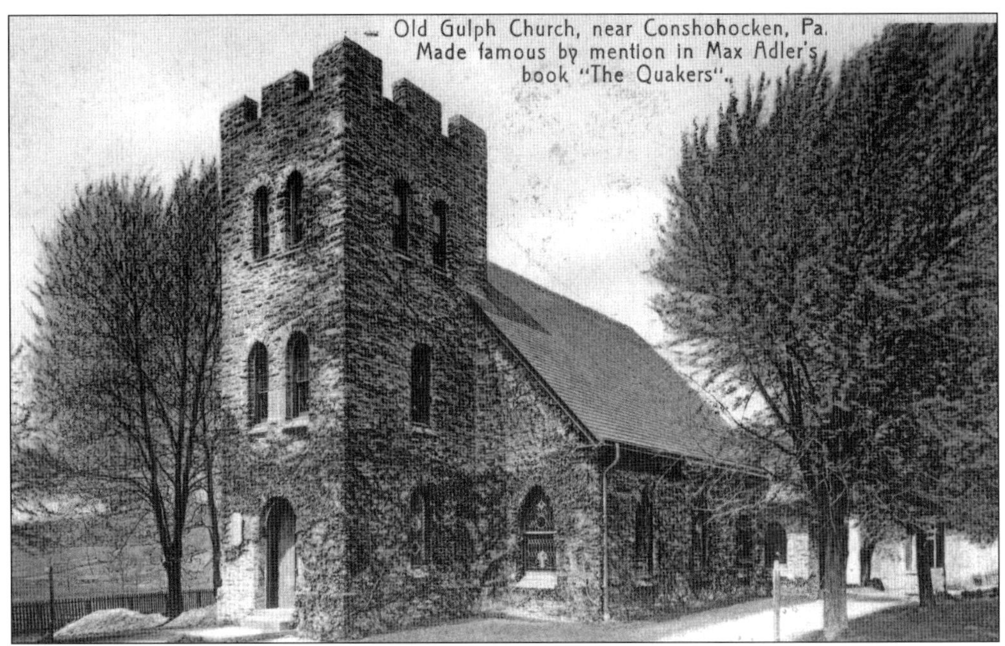

The new Gulph Christian Church was erected in 1894 in front of the old church, which still stands today as part of the present structure. The building was modeled after St. Martins Church in England. In 1905, Max Adler wrote about the church in his book the *The Quakeress*. The author describes vividly the Gulph Valley area and life at the beginning of the 20th century.

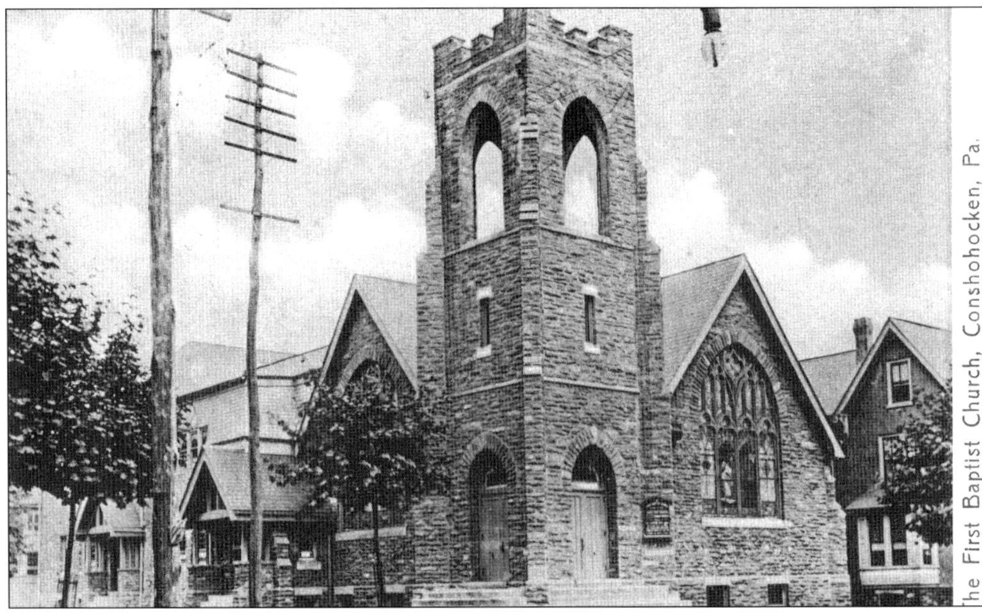

The First Baptist Church, on Fourth Avenue and Harry Street, had its beginnings from the Balligomingo Baptist Church in West Conshohocken. In 1865, a small group of members from Balligomingo Baptist Church formed a Sunday school in Conshohocken. The first meeting was held in Stemple Hall on Fayette Street. Later, meetings were conducted at Rose Hall. In 1869, a chapel was under construction at Fourth Avenue and Fayette Street for Conshohocken Baptist Sunday School and Missionary Association.

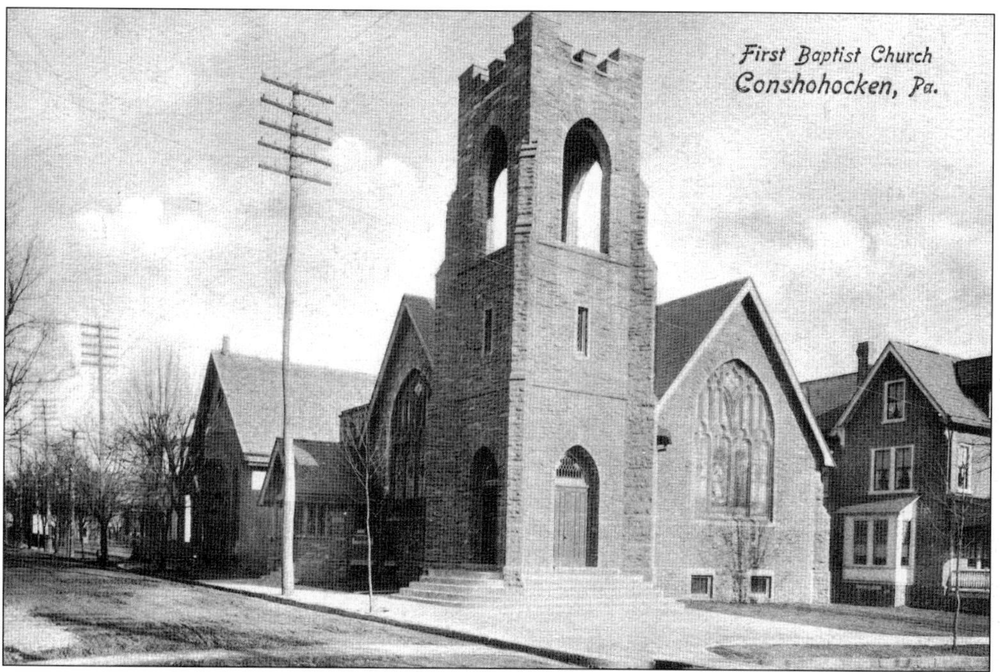

In the early 1900s, the First Baptist Church, also known as Conshohocken Baptist Church, underwent an expansion with the addition of an auditorium and Sunday school. In 1917, the church's social building was used for a short time as a hospital during the influenza epidemic.

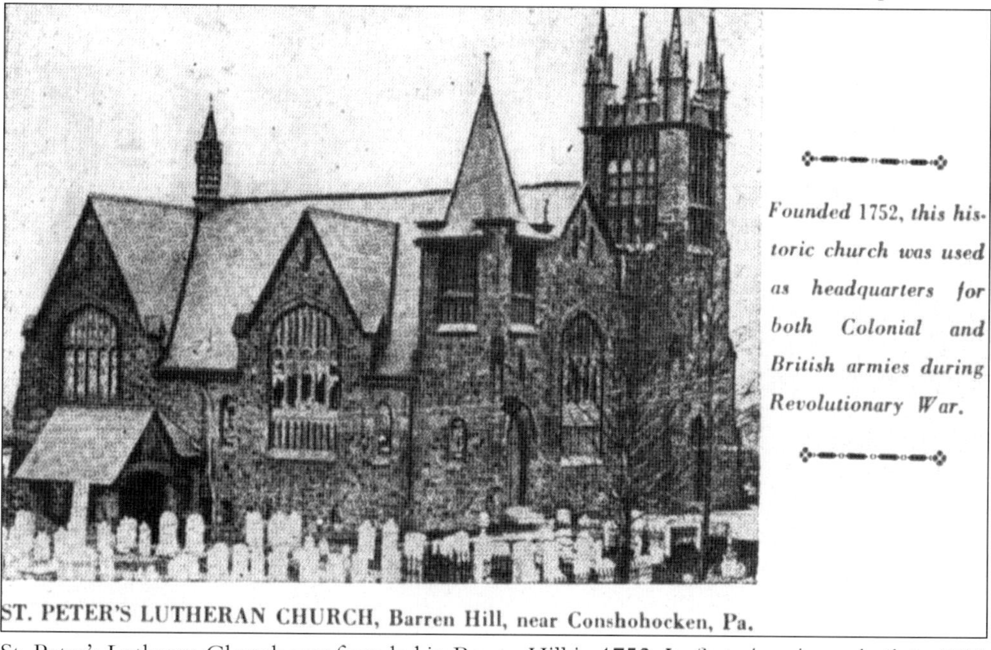

St. Peter's Lutheran Church was founded in Barren Hill in 1752. Its first church was built in 1760 on Church Road in what now is called Lafayette Hill. The British almost destroyed it during the Revolutionary War in 1778, when General Lafayette quartered there and used it as an observation point. The church was restored in 1809 but was destroyed in 1899 by fire. The present stone structure was constructed in 1901 and enlarged in 1958.

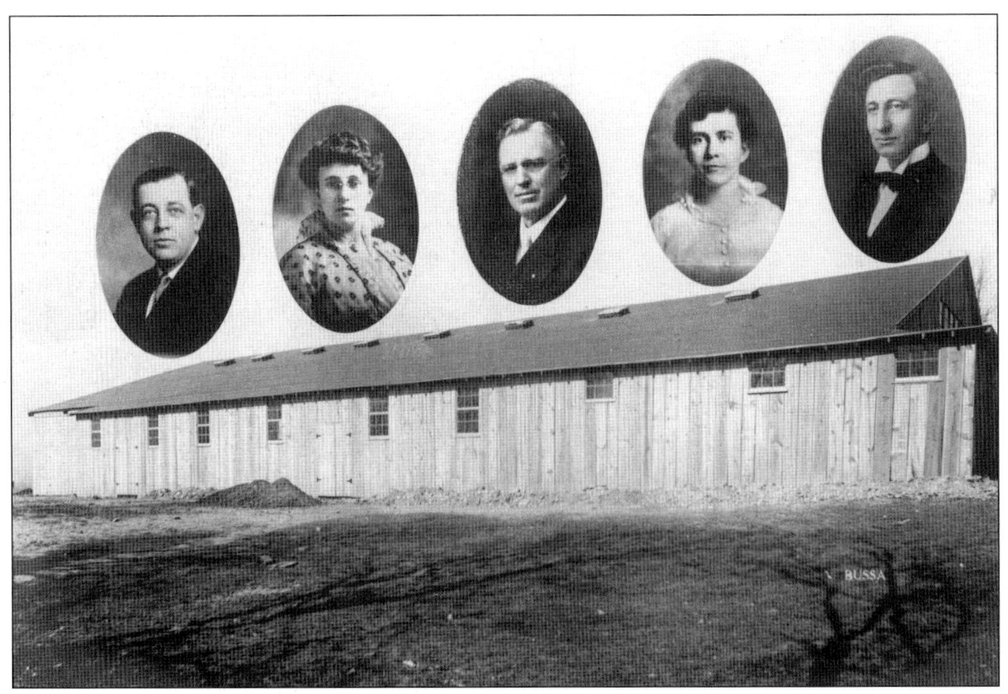

The people of Conshohocken closely identify with the their churches. Most started with humble beginnings, usually renting space in existing social halls or temporary structures. Conshohocken also saw its share of traveling church revivals, which did not set up permanent roots in the community. These two photograph cards are great views of a church in its infancy. The building appears to be a long barn. The interior view has a banner that reads, " Conshohocken for Christ."

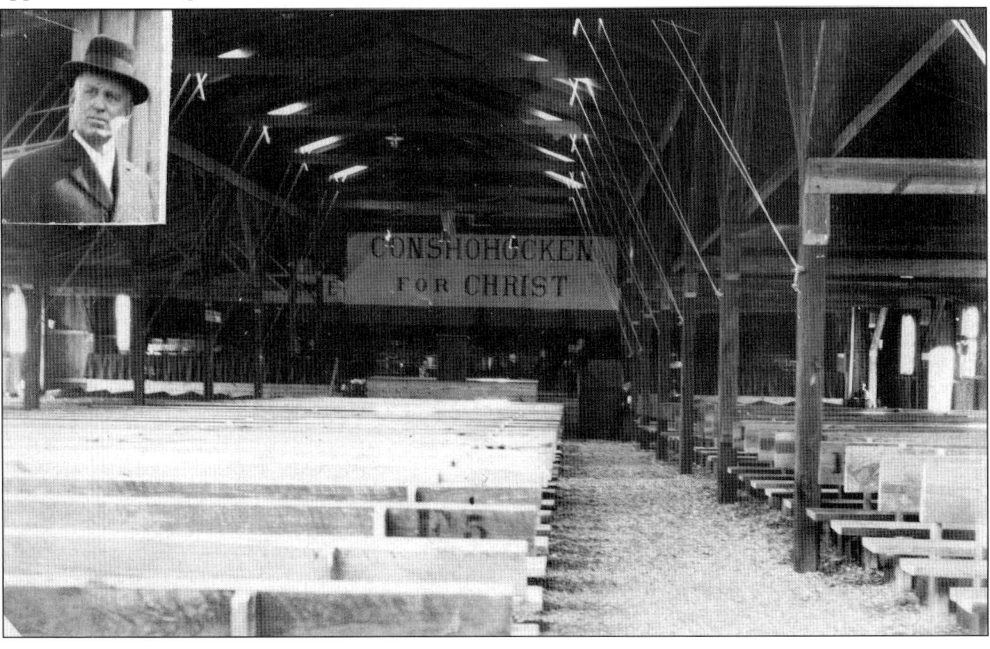

The first religious meetings of the Society of Friends in Plymouth were held *c.* 1686. The deed to the present meetinghouse land at the corner of Germantown and Butler Pikes dates from October 6, 1704. During the Revolutionary War, the meetinghouse served as a hospital after the Battle of Germantown. In 1827, the Society of Friends (known as Quaker) split into two groups, Orthodox and Hicksite. The main body of the Plymouth Friends adhered to the practices of the Hicksite Friends, and the Orthodox group built a meetinghouse next door on Butler Pike in 1828. In 1955, the split was resolved, and there is now only one Society of Friends. This is the oldest church in the area.

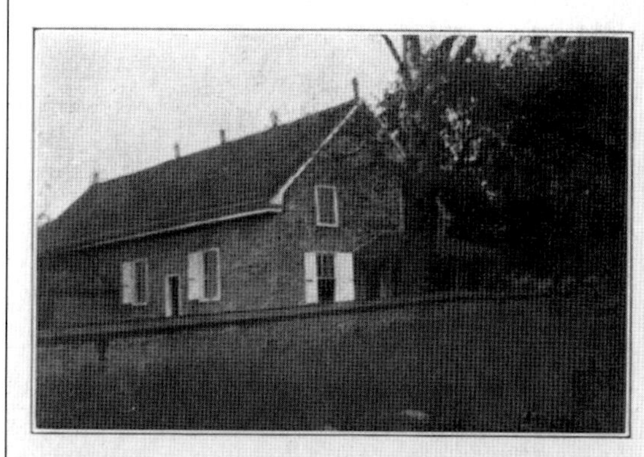

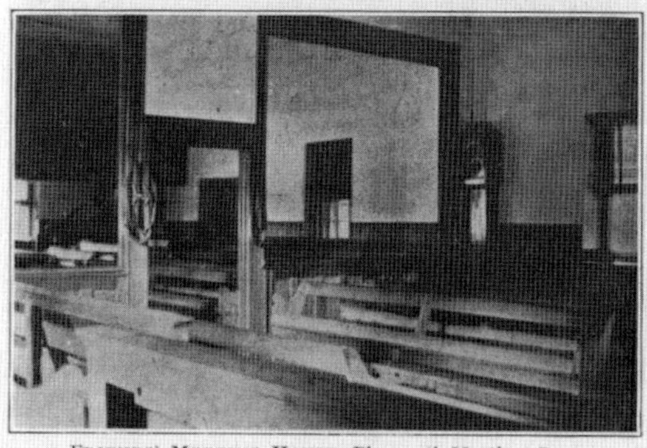

FRIENDS' MEETING HOUSE, Plymouth Meeting, Pa.

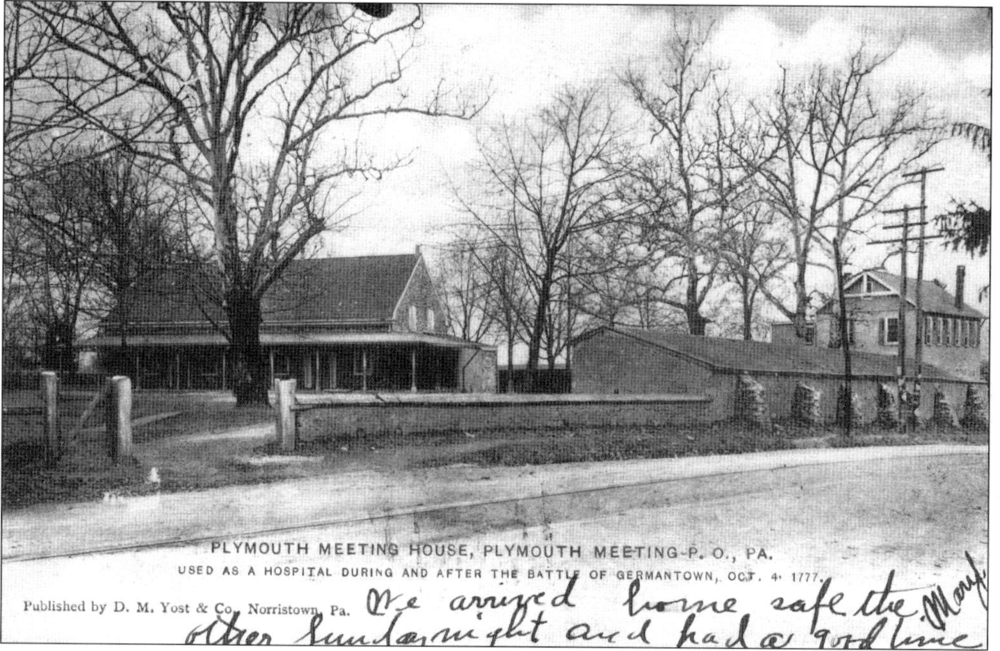

PLYMOUTH MEETING HOUSE, PLYMOUTH MEETING-P. O., PA.
USED AS A HOSPITAL DURING AND AFTER THE BATTLE OF GERMANTOWN, OCT. 4, 1777.

Published by D. M. Yost & Co., Norristown, Pa.

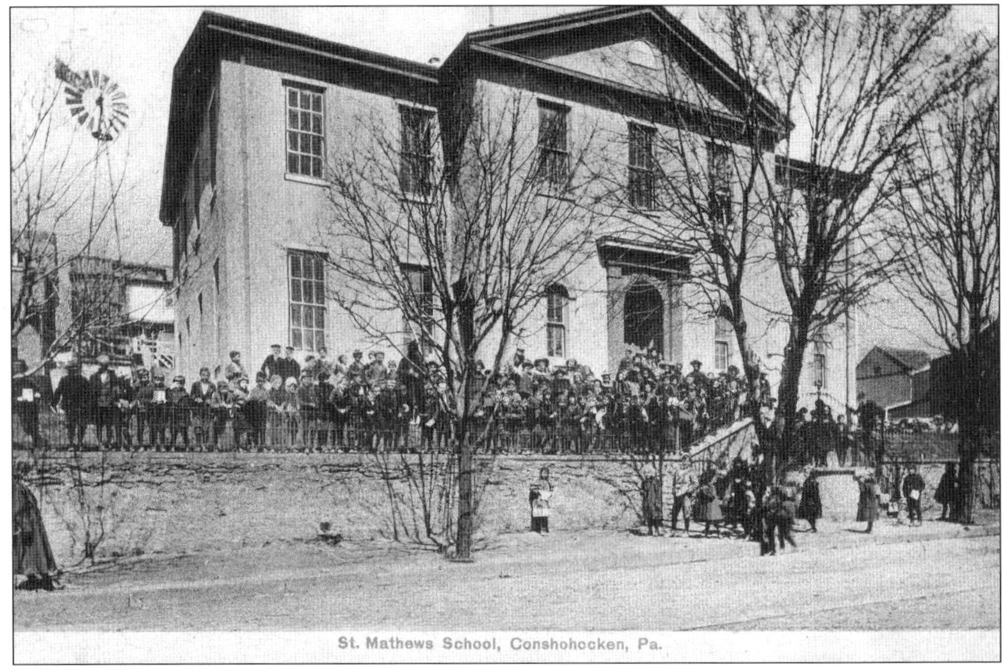

Rev. Richard Kinahan opened St. Matthews School on September 21, 1863, in the church basement at Hector and Harry Streets. Soon, the number of students overwhelmed the basement school, and a new school was built on Hector Street below Ash Street at the cost of $15,000.

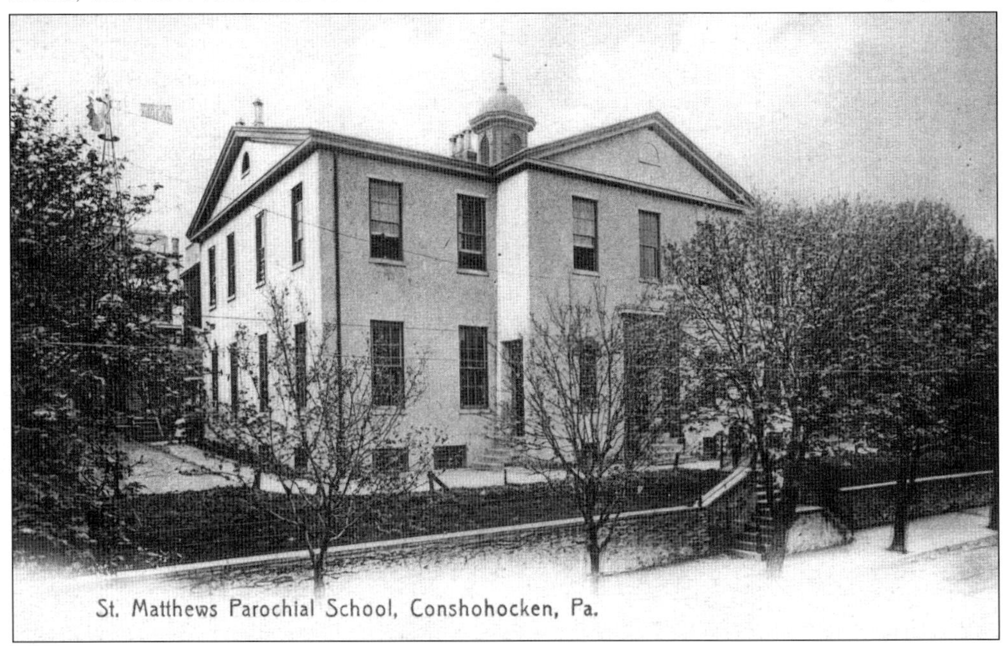

St. Matthews Parochial School was established to address the educational needs of the children of Irish immigrants. Of the 727 people living in the borough at the time of incorporation, 658 were Irish. The building on Hector Street served as a grade school and high school until *c.* 1930. At that time, the grade school moved to adjoin the rectory at Third Avenue and Fayette Street. In 1956, the new high school opened on St. Matthews Avenue in Plymouth Township.

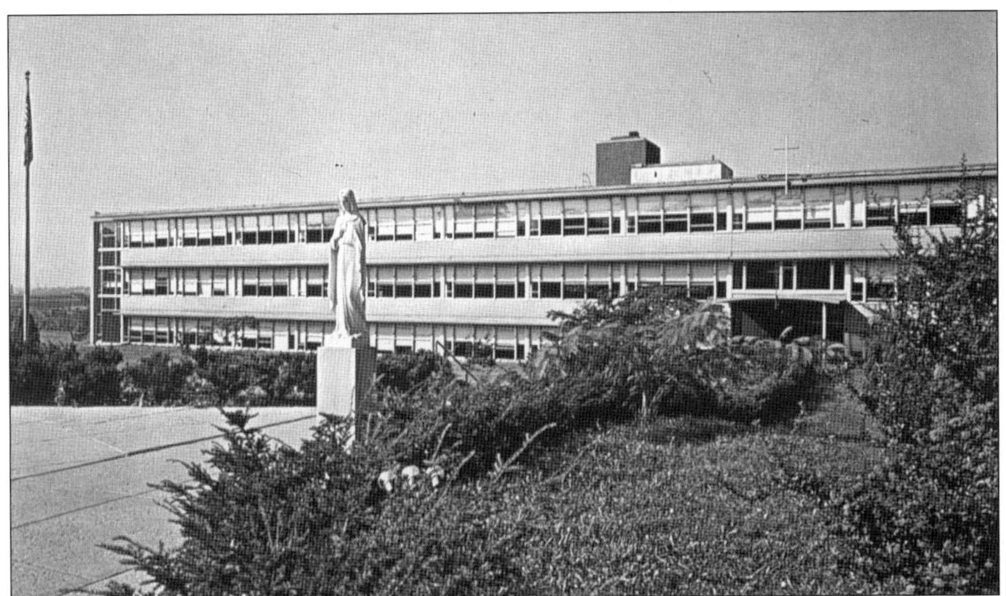

St. Matthews High School was the first free Catholic high school in the United States. This is a view of the school when it was located on St. Matthews Avenue in Plymouth Township. In 1966, the school was renamed Archbishop Kennedy in honor of Thomas F. Kennedy, a member of the first graduating class of St. Matthews and its principal from 1878 to 1879. In 1993, Archbishop Kennedy merged with Bishop Kendrick in Norristown, and the new high school became Kennedy-Kendrick in Norristown.

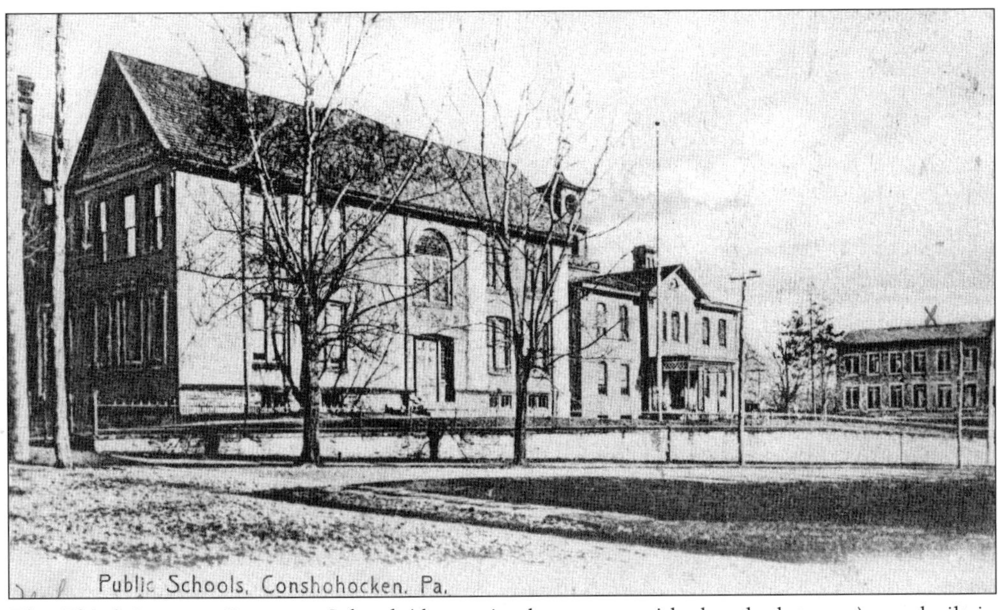

Public Schools, Conshohocken, Pa.

The Third Avenue Grammar School (shown in the center with the clock tower) was built in 1867 on Third Avenue below Harry Street. The school was later renamed the Hoffecker School after Reuben F. Hoffecker, the school's former principal. Another schoolhouse, the Harry Street School (left) was added to the grounds in 1885. Later, a third building was added. In 1898, the district built a manual training school (building on the far right) in the same complex of schools.

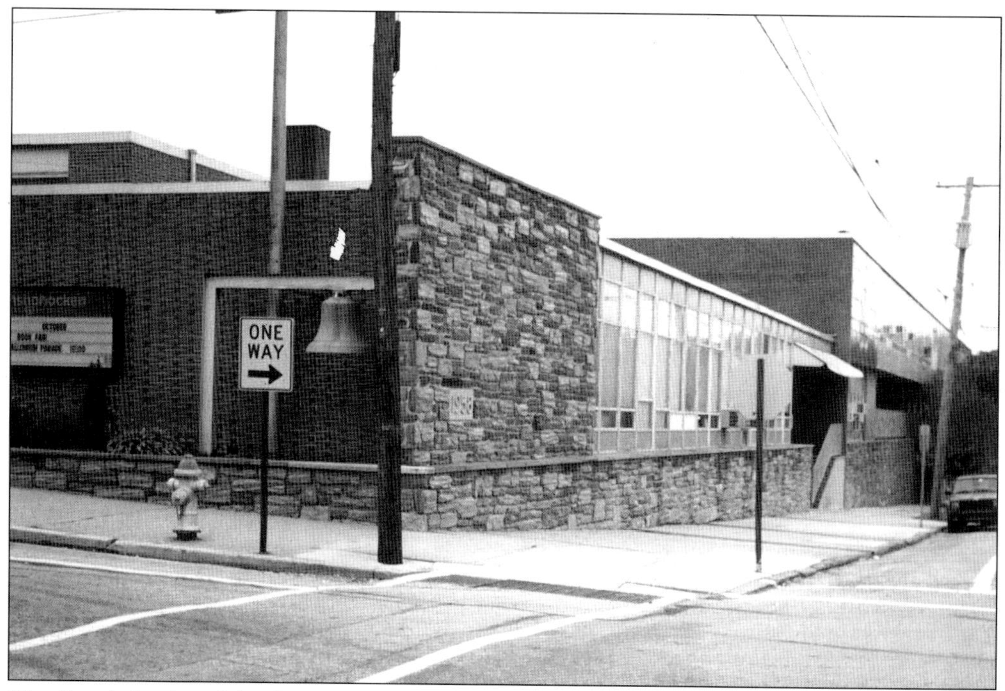

The Conshohocken School District was established in 1850 at the time of the town's incorporation. Classes were held in Stemple Hall until the first school building was erected in 1855 between First and Second Avenues, bordered by Fayette and Forrest Streets. Today, Conshohocken's public elementary school is Harvey S. Walker, located on Third Avenue and Harry Street.

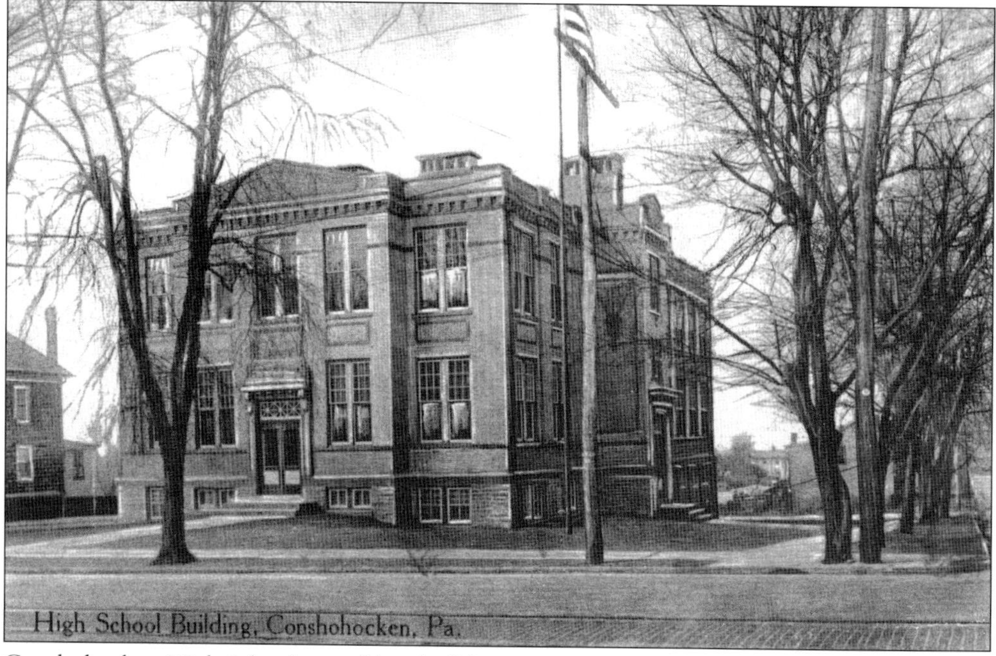

Conshohocken High School started in a building next to the grade school on Third Avenue. Its first graduating class was in 1872. This is a view of the new high school that was erected in 1913 on the west side of Fayette Street at Seventh Avenue.

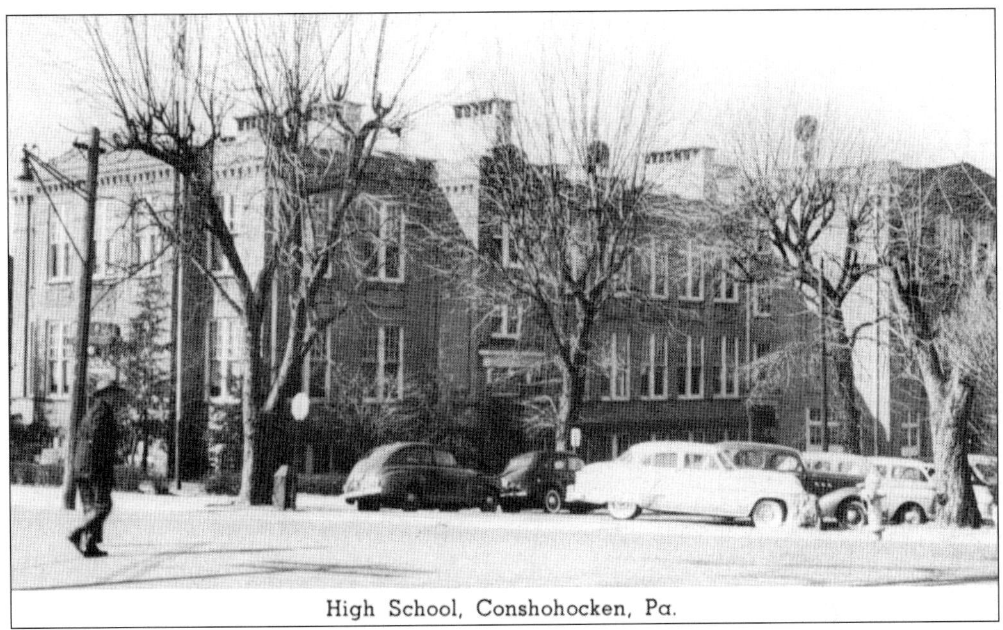
High School, Conshohocken, Pa.

This Seventh Avenue view of Conshohocken High School shows the auditorium and gymnasium that was added to the original building in 1922. This institution served the community for 53 years. In 1966, the school was vacated, and the district joined with Plymouth and Whitemarsh school districts to form the Colonial School District. The school building on Seventh Avenue and Fayette was then used by the Montgomery County Community College until 1972, when the college moved to Blue Bell. Eventually the building was demolished.

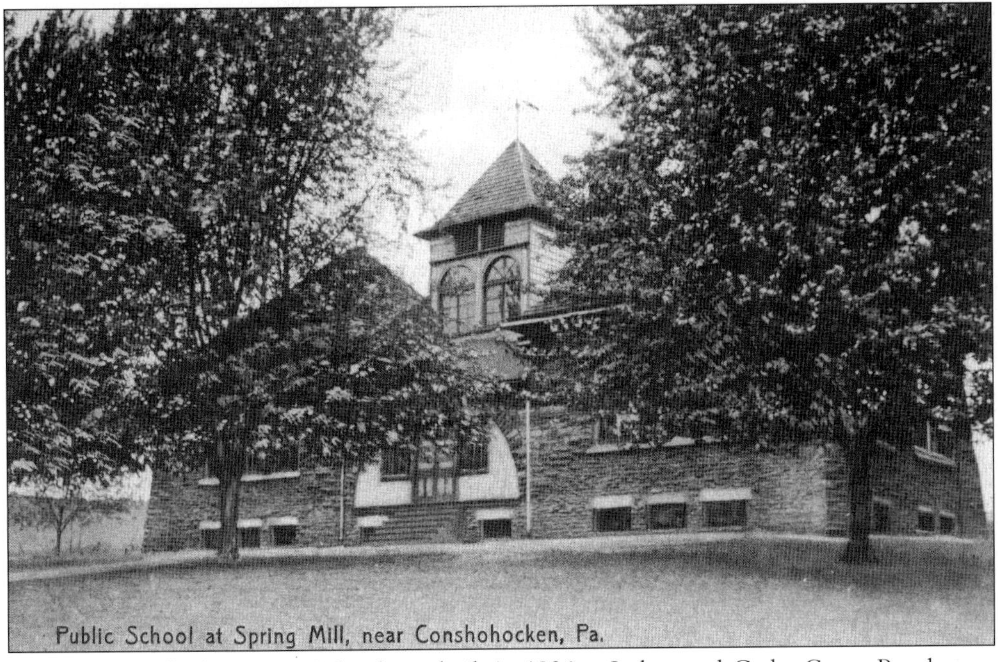
Public School at Spring Mill, near Conshohocken, Pa.

The Spring Mill Elementary School was built in 1926 at Joshua and Cedar Grove Roads on a 12.7-acre site. Additions to the school were made in 1956, 1959, and 1967, for a total of 24 classrooms. The school was closed in 1982.

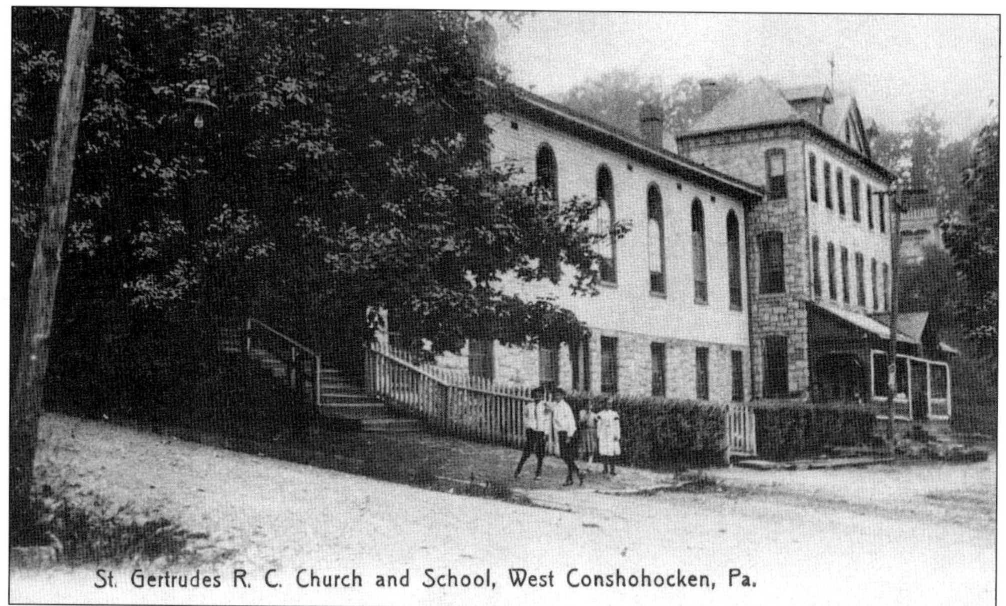

St. Gertrude's Roman Catholic Church was founded in 1888, and a church building was erected on the corner of Merion and Bullock Avenues in West Conshohocken. About the same time, the school was started in the basement of the church. Soon afterward, the parish bought the Moir homestead on Merion Avenue for its convent and schoolhouse. School was held in this building until a new grade school was built in 1954. In 1977, St. Gertrude's school closed.

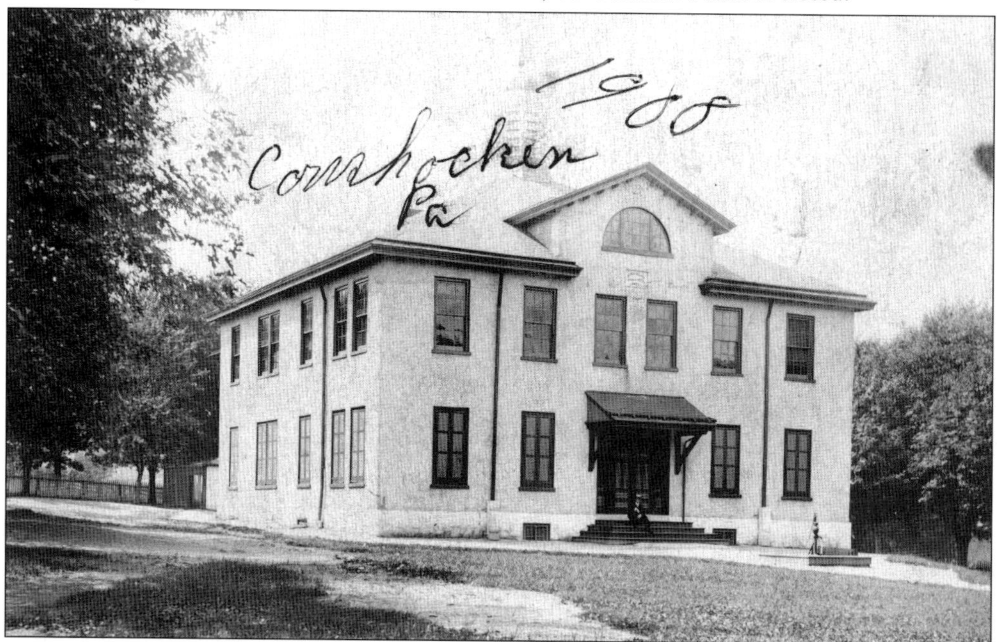

This is a rare photograph card of the Bullock School in West Conshohocken. The borough acquired a lot from George Bullock and built the school in 1875. The Bullock School was a high school for residents of the boroughs of Upper Merion, Rebel Hill, and Gulph Mills. In 1903, fire forced the closing of the school until repairs and remodeling were completed. The school reopened in September 1903 and functioned as a high school until the mid-1920s.

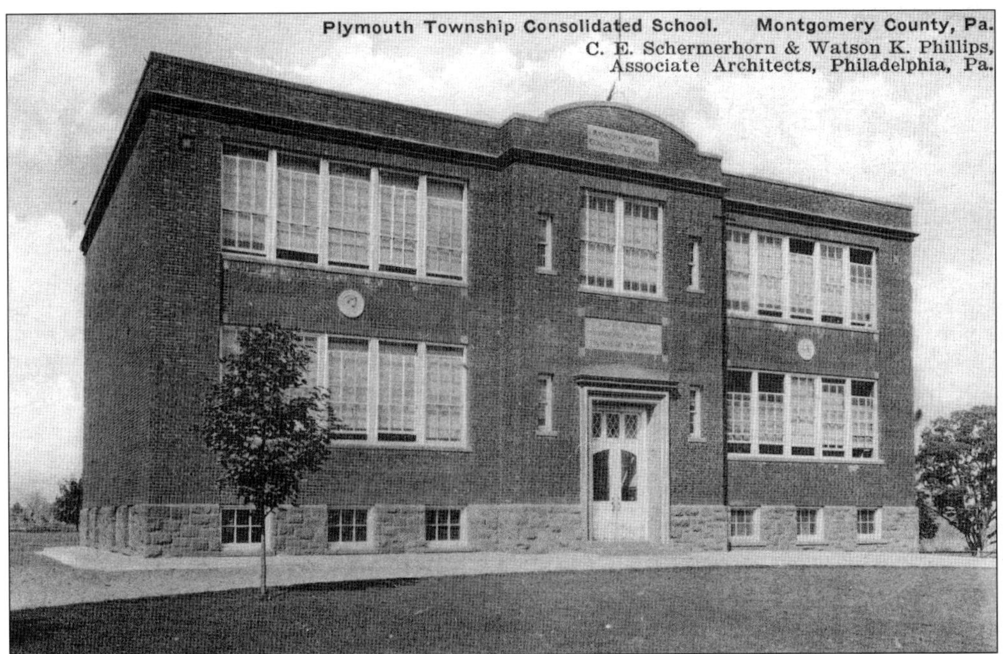

The Plymouth Township Consolidated School opened in 1915 on Butler Pike between Ridge and Germantown Pikes. The school served the community until the mid-1970s, when it was closed and used as a storage facility by the Colonial School District. In 1981, the property was sold to the Harmonville Fire Company. Later, the building was demolished and a new firehouse was erected.

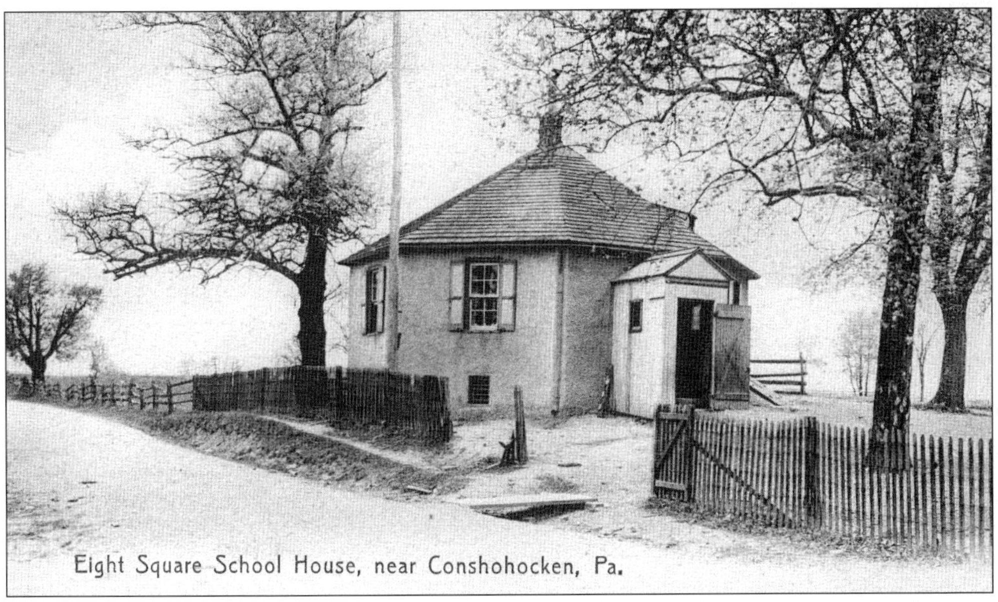

This single-room octagonal schoolhouse, which is now the site of an apartment complex, was located on North Lane between Fayette Street and Ridge Pike. This schoolhouse was in operation from the 1800s until 1915, when the Plymouth Consolidated School was opened.

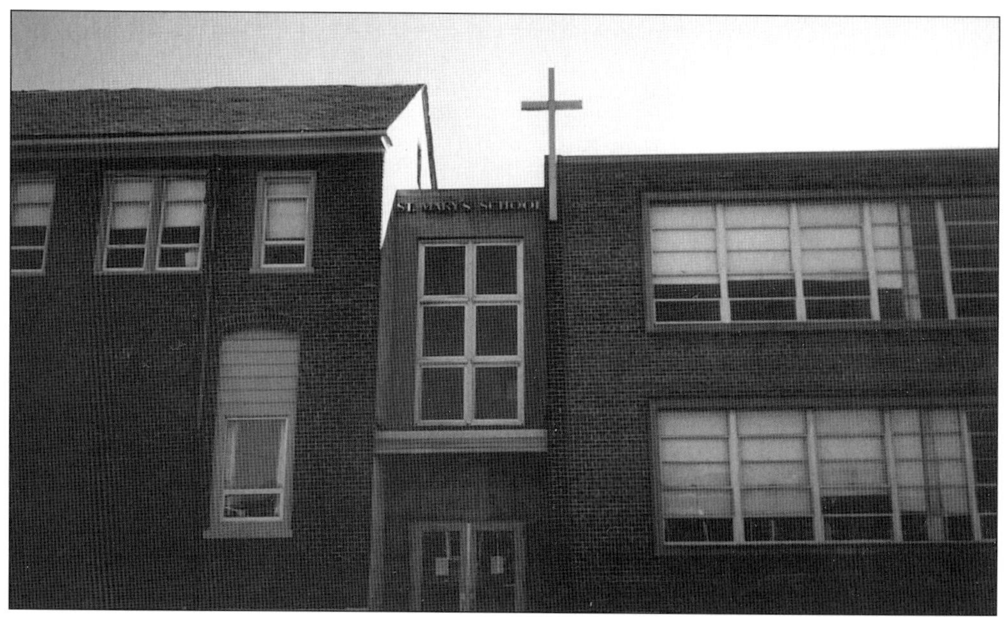

St. Mary's School began in 1908 in the brick church building, which the congregation has outgrown. The school opened with 87 children and two teaching sisters. By the time a new school was built in 1928, attendance had grown to 327 children. In the late 1990s, enrollment was not high enough to continue the school. The building has been used as a temporary police station during renovations of the current police station.

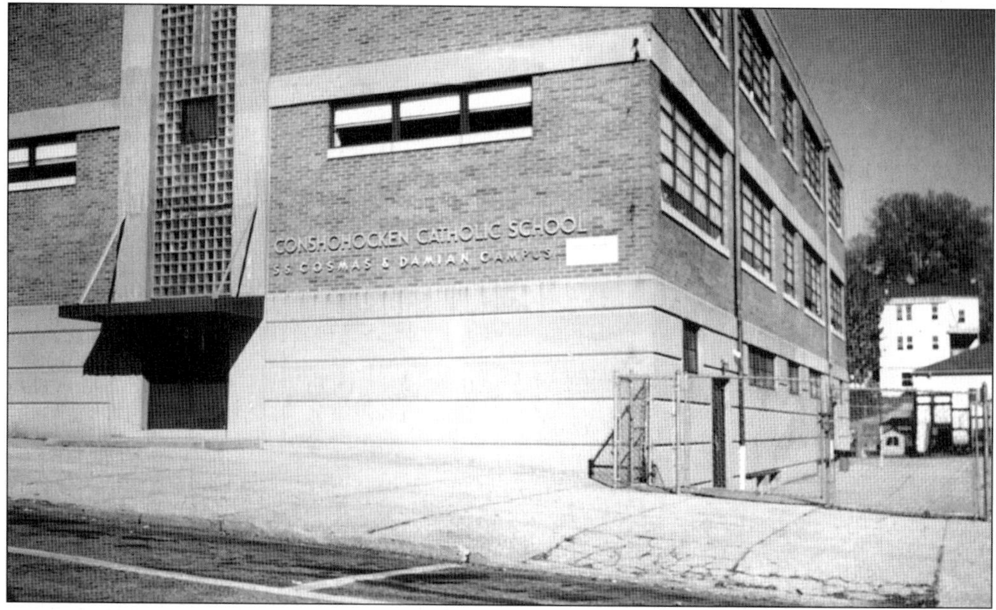

SS. Cosmas and Damian School began in 1953 on the auditorium stage of the newly constructed church on Fifth Avenue. Ground was broken for construction of a school building on Fifth Avenue between Forrest and Maple Streets in the fall of 1953. By the time the new school year began in 1954, construction of the school was complete and ready for students in grades one through eight. A kindergarten was added in 1955. In the late 1990s, the school merged with St. Matthews and formed the Colonial Catholic School.

Ten
General Views

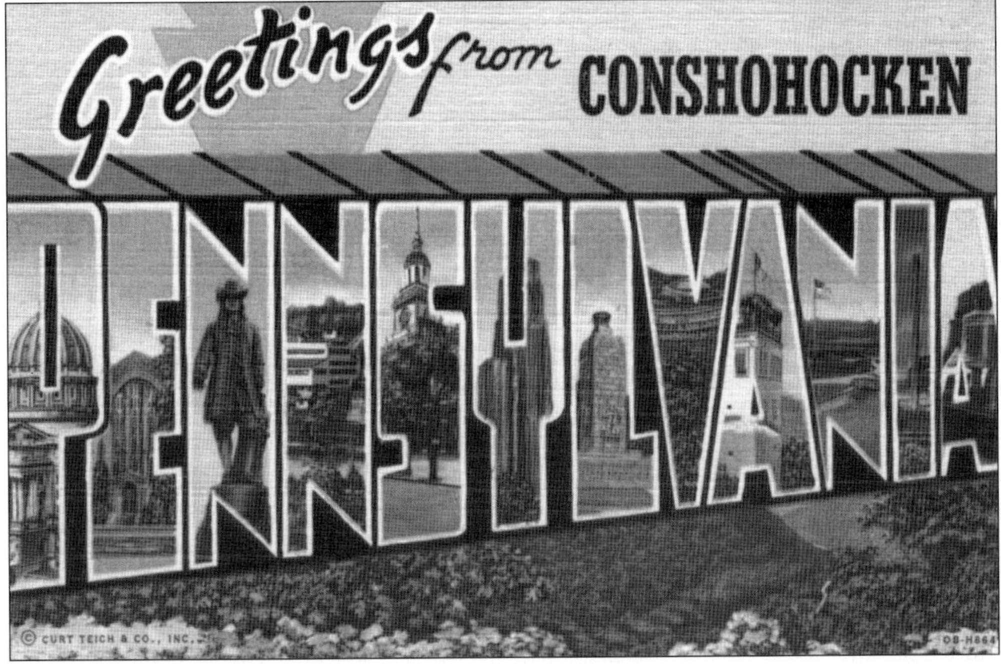

Generic greeting cards were very popular and easily found in the local grocery stores or drugstores. The scenes were not significant to any particular town. These postcards were mostly a way for loved ones to keep in touch. In this chapter is variety of "greetings from Conshohocken" cards. This is considered a large-letter greeting card.

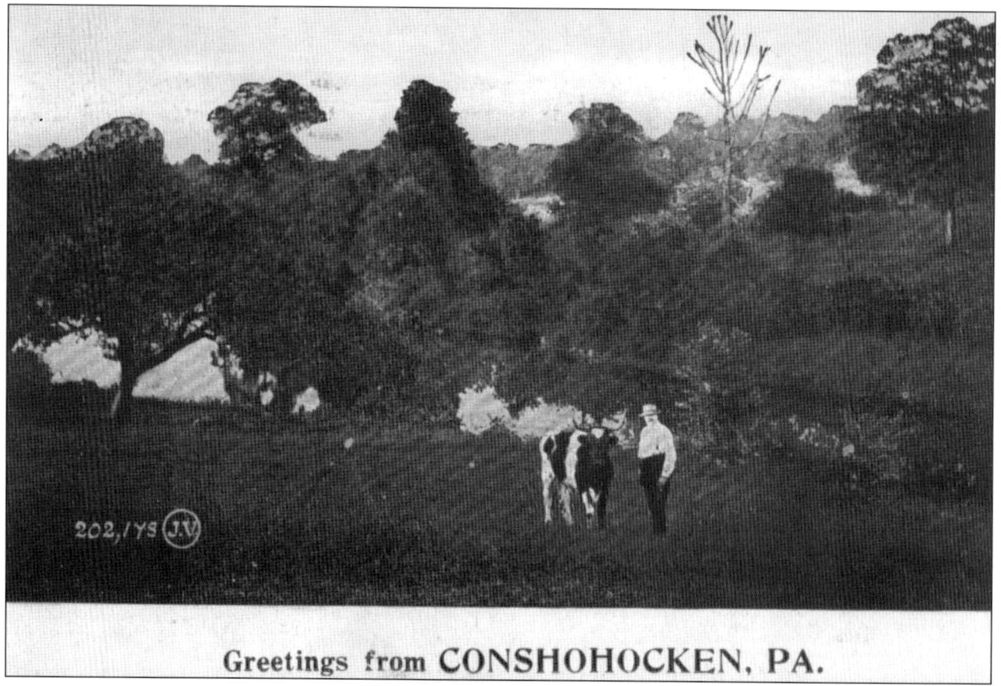

On June 11, 1931, May from Conshohocken writes her friend Ruth in Kutztown, "Dear Ruth, Well how do you like the rain? I do hope it will be nice over the weekend. Indeed I am glad school is so near over. Guess you are busy working. Just do not work to hard. Well I guess that is all. See you next week."

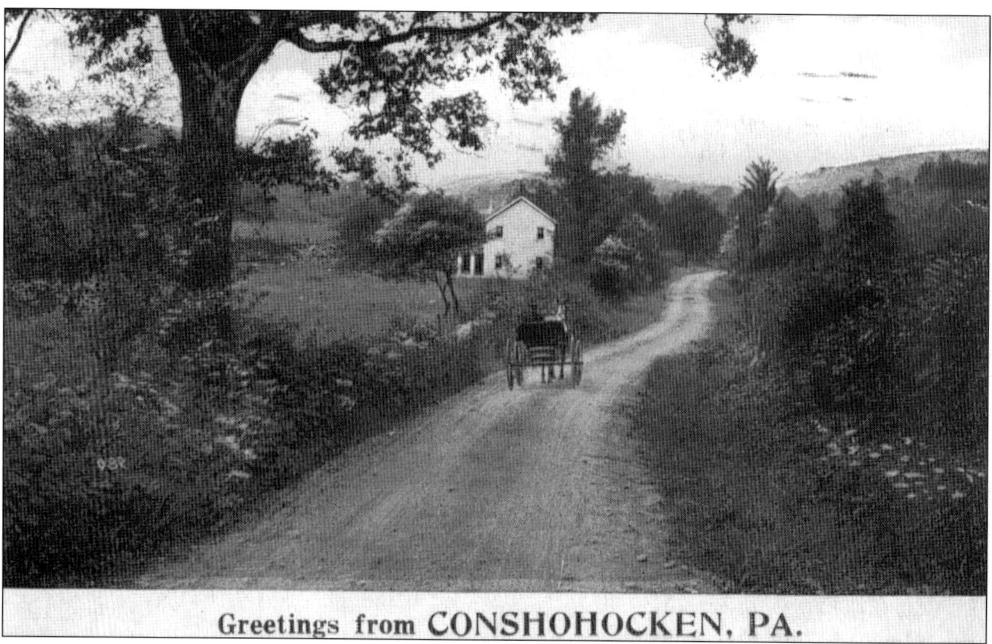

Although this is a generic card, a scene like this would have been very common for Conshohocken in the early 1900s. The cart looks like it could be traveling down Spring Mill Avenue to the gristmill.

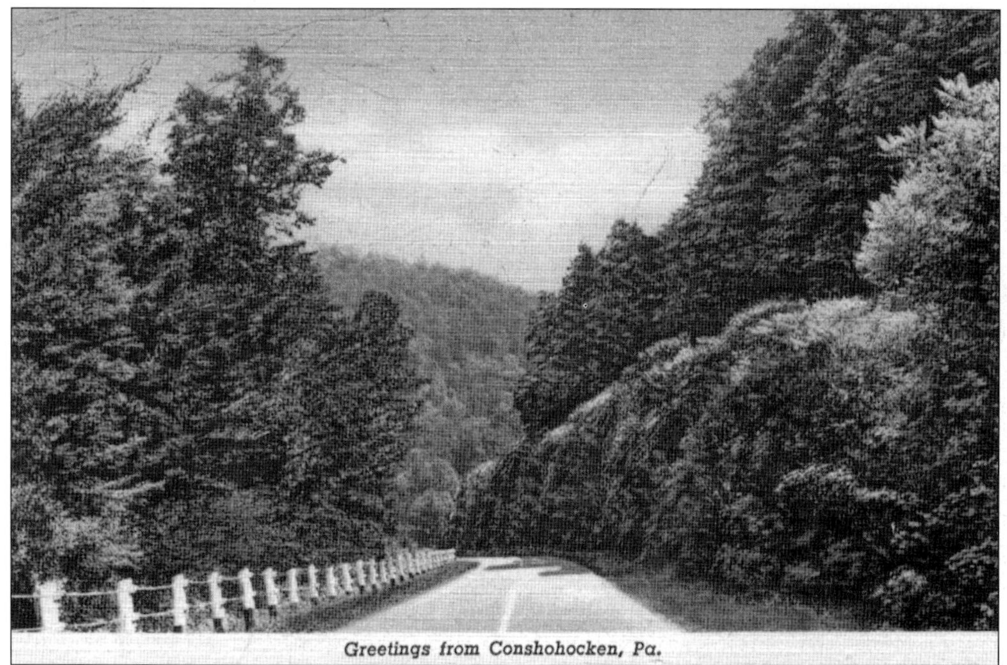
Greetings from Conshohocken, Pa.

Although some postcards do not contain handwritten messages, the photographs on them still reveal or evoke historical facts. Conshohocken Council appointed the town's first policeman, John A. Harold, in 1873 for a salary of $40 a month.

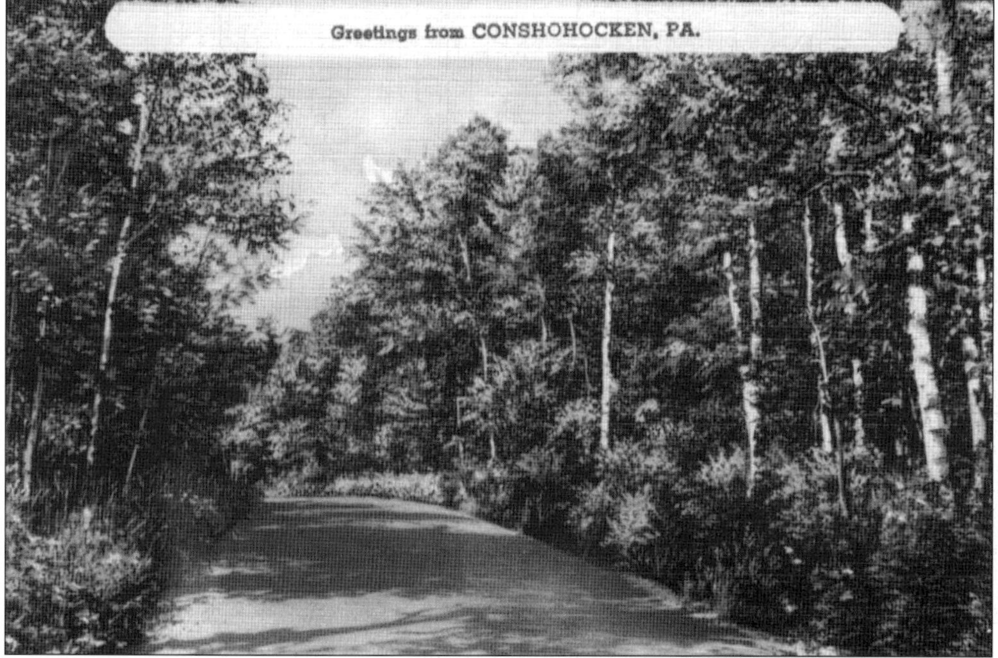
Greetings from CONSHOHOCKEN, PA.

Some of the borough's older streets bear names of early settlers of the region. Included is Hector Street, named for Edward Hector, a black wagon master in Washington's army. He led an escape that brought him stature as a local hero. Edward Hector died at age 90 in 1834 in a cabin where Hector joins Fayette Street.

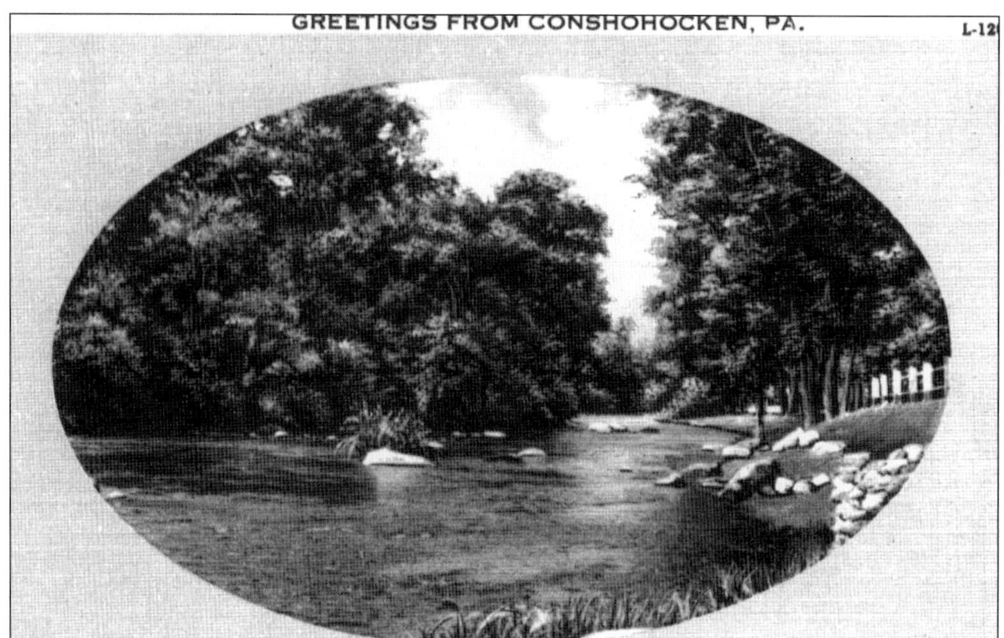

In 1848, ironmaster James Wood, Matson Ford Bridge Company president Isaac Jones, Ford Hotel proprietor James Wells, farmer Cadwallader Foulke, and gristmill operator David Harry met at the Norristown Montgomery Hotel to apply for a charter to make their riverside community a borough and to give it a name. The suggested names for the town (Riverside, Wooddale, and Conshohocken) were placed in Jones's hat, and Wells selected the name from the hat.

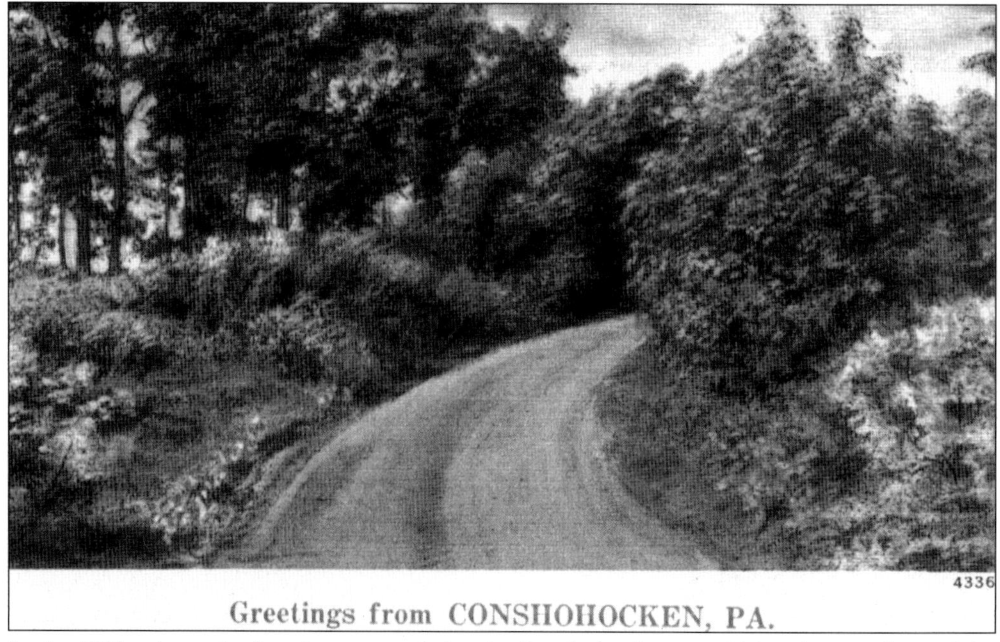

In the 1900s, the major immigrant population in Conshohocken was Irish. The members of the Irish community lived in neighborhoods in the area of West Elm and Colwell Lane, along Maple Street from Elm to Third Streets, around Fifth and Wood Streets, and along Elm Street west of Plymouth Creek.

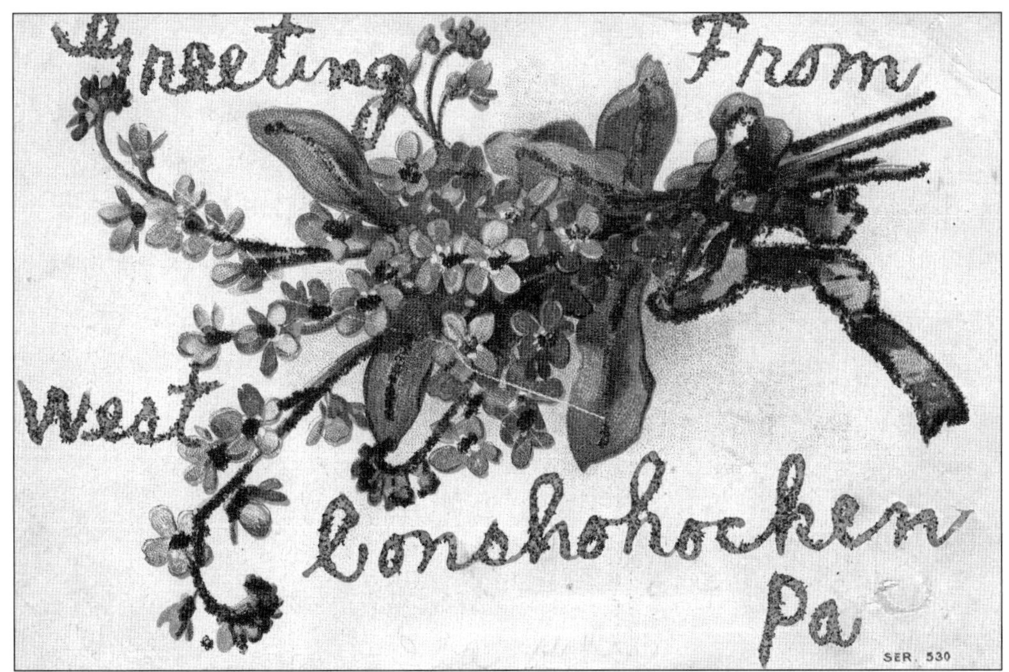

In 1833, Conshohocken had one store, one tavern, one rolling mill, one gristmill, and six houses. Those homes, according to a census at the time, belonged to David Harry, Cadwallader Foulke, Isaac Jones, Dan Freedley, and C. Jacoby. Historians have speculated that Edward Hector was the owner of the sixth house.

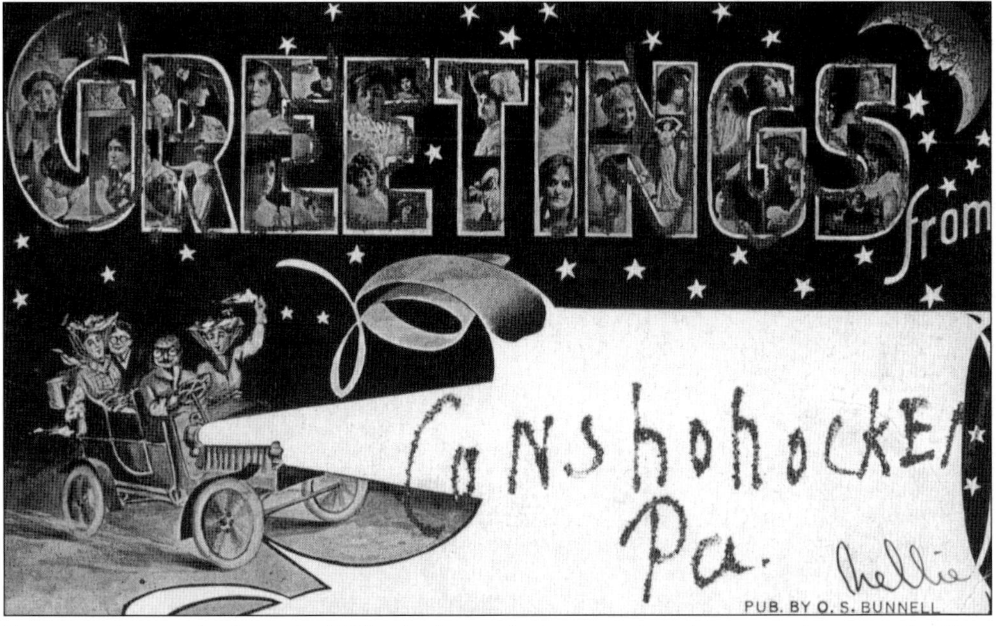

For entertainment in the early 1900s, the borough citizens enjoyed moving pictures at the Gem and Bijou Theaters, playing pool at the Subway Pool Parlor or Hart's Pool Parlor, and going to the Meadows for an exciting game of football. Life was anything but boring in this small town. There were also church socials, civic fundraisers, and parades to enjoy.

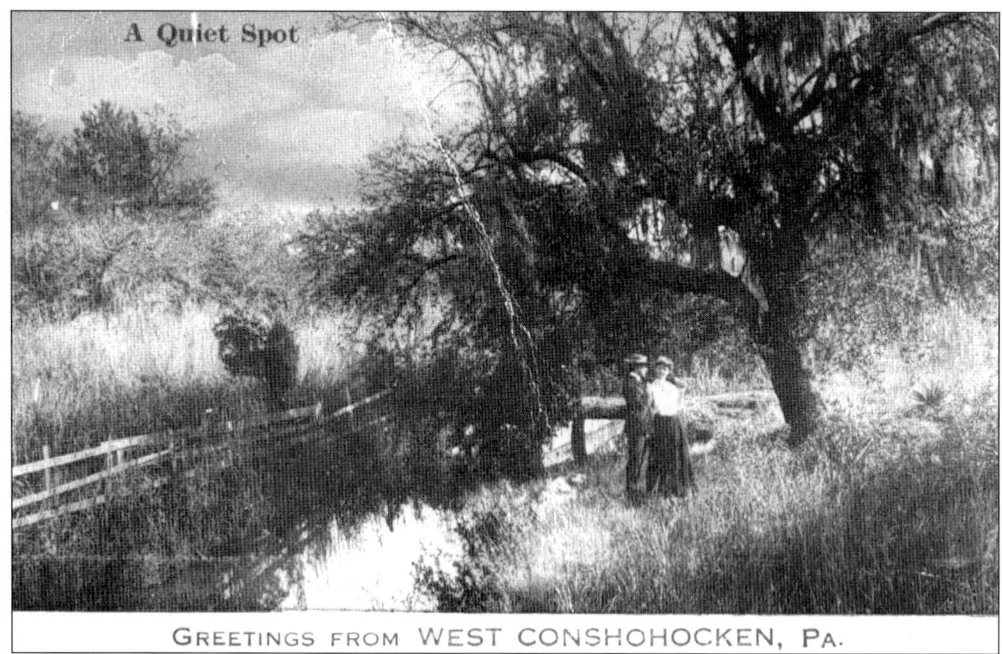

GREETINGS FROM WEST CONSHOHOCKEN, PA.

West Conshohocken was incorporated on October 6, 1874. Numerous mills and quarries once lined the Gulph Creek, which empties into the Schuylkill River at West Conshohocken. Today, industrial parks and professional buildings have replaced the old mills, but with growth comes a traffic nightmare. The community has lost a significant amount of real estate over the years to the Schuylkill Expressway and the Blue Route.

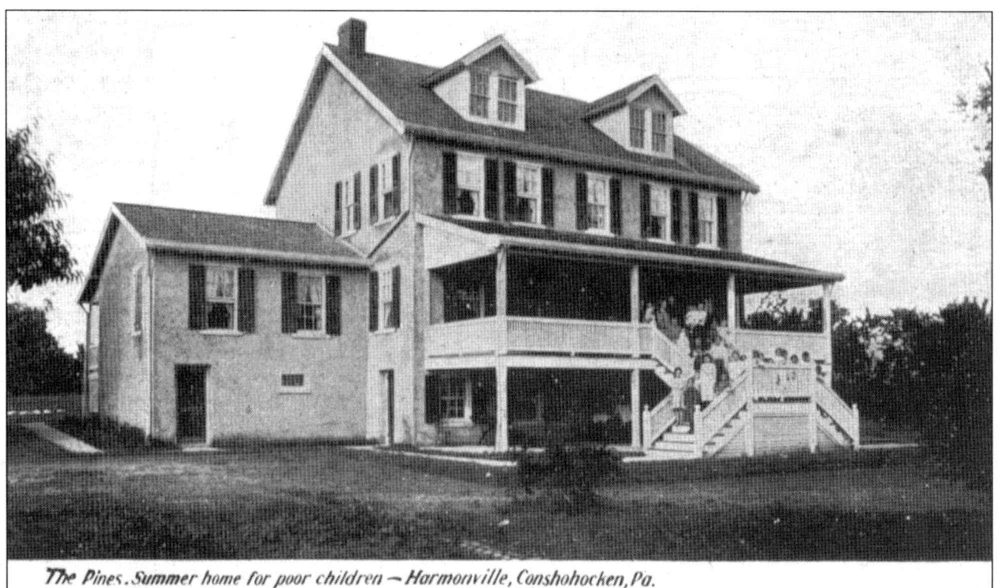

The Pines. Summer home for poor children — Harmonville, Conshohocken, Pa.

This summer getaway was located on Ridge Pike near Butler Pike in Harmonville. The Pines was a summer retreat for mothers and children of economically depressed families. Most of the children who stayed at the home were from the Philadelphia area. While staying at the Pines, the children had ample room to play and swim, while their mothers got a well-deserved rest on the porch.

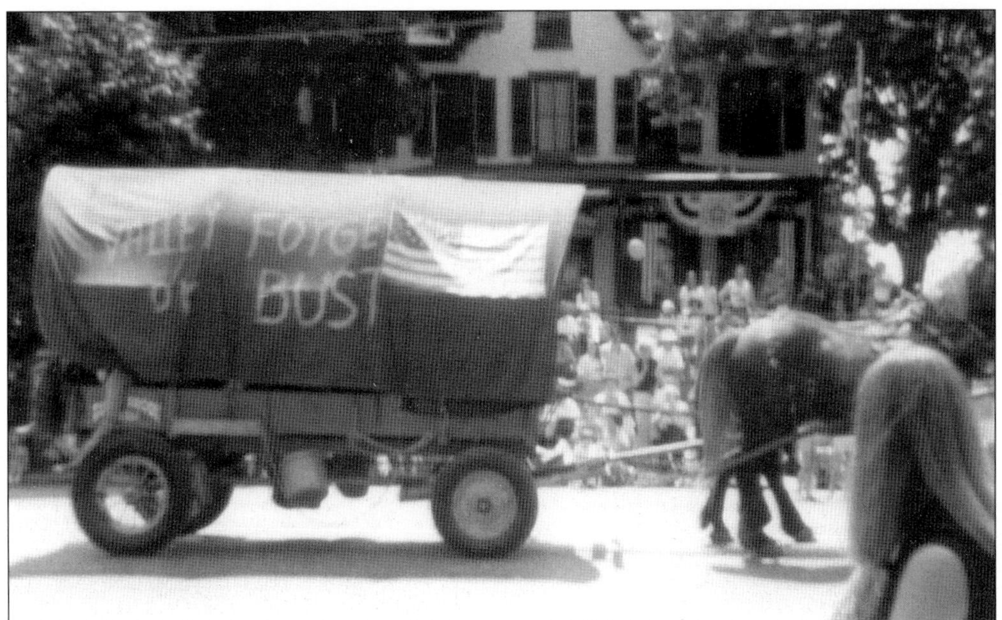

Conshohocken played an important role in the Wagon Train Bicentennial celebration. In July 1976, the town hosted two wagon trains on their way to Valley Forge. One was from the Northern Great Lakes region, and the other, the Colonial wagon train, from New York and New Jersey. Two encampments were used: the grounds at Archbishop Kennedy High School and the "B" Field. The train participants cooked over campfires and entertained the townspeople with music and square dances. Above is one of the many wagon trains that parade down Fayette Street past the library. The sign on the train reads, "Valley Forge or Bust." Below is the New Jersey wagon train.

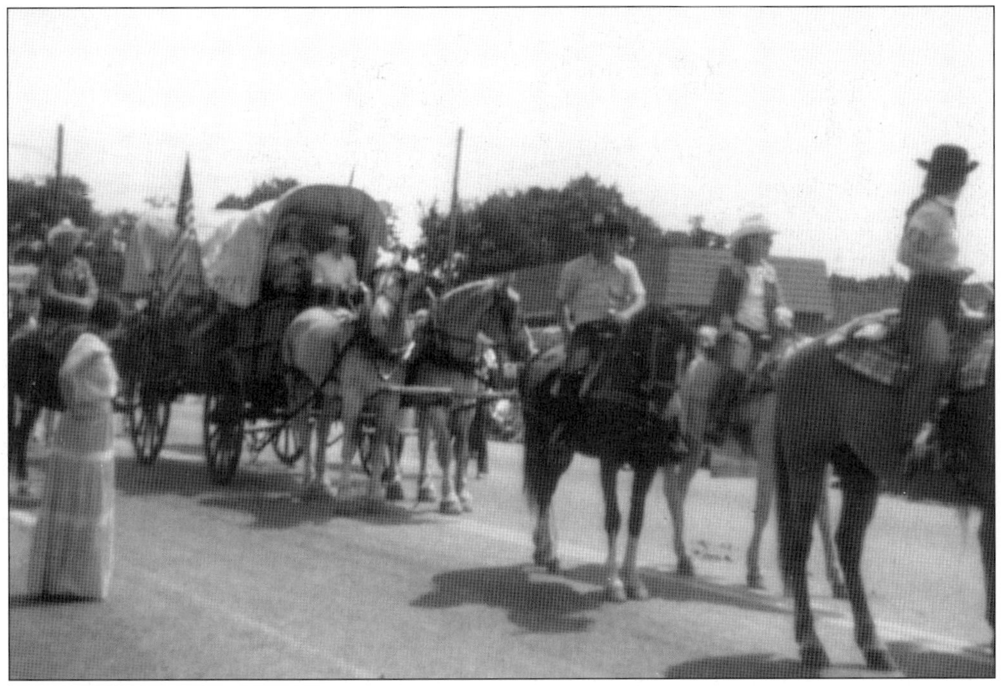

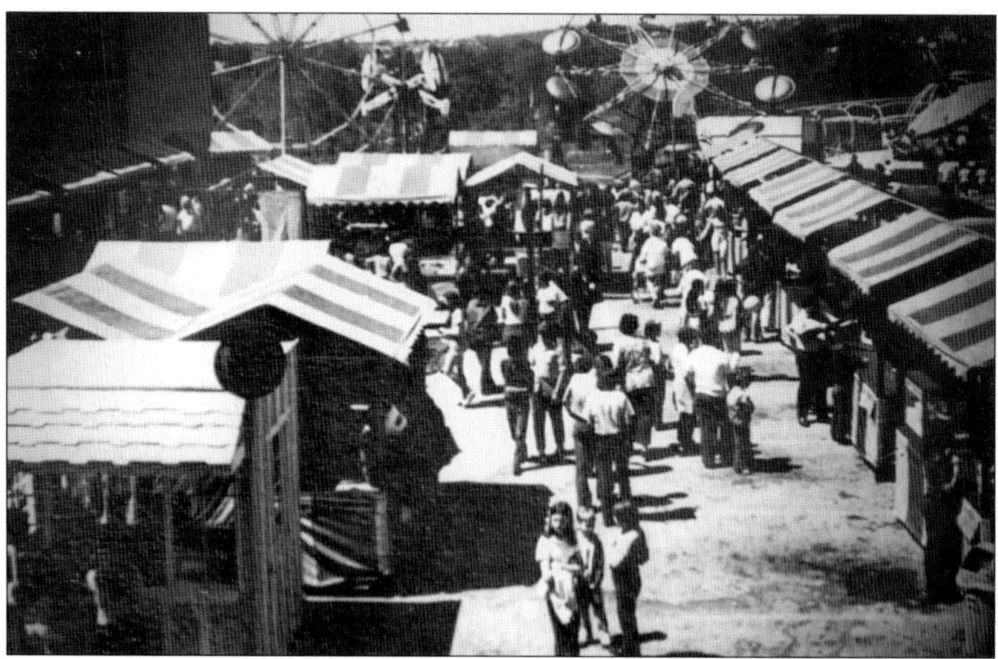

Throughout the years, the Conshohocken community has sponsored many carnivals, parades, fairs, races, concerts, fireworks displays, and hosts of other community activities and fundraisers. This is the Kennedy Carnival in the parking lot of Archbishop Kennedy High School. This fundraiser attracted thousands of local residents and their families to the great hair-raising rides and the booths of chance.

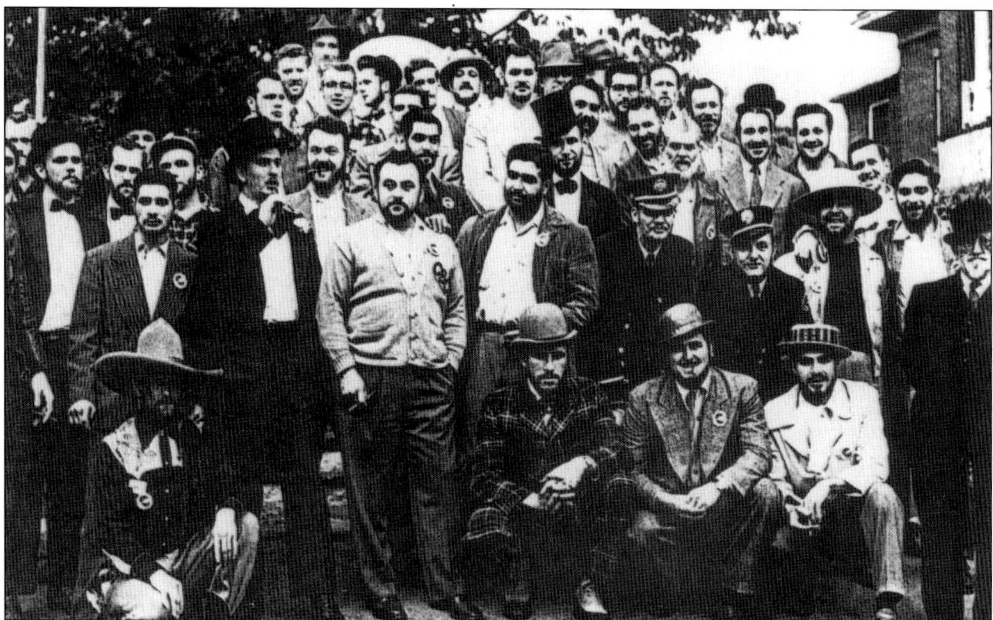

In 1950, Conshohocken was celebrating its 100th anniversary. Some of the town's men prepared for the centennial parade celebration by growing beards. They were known as the Brothers of the Bush. There are a lot of familiar faces in the crowd, many complemented by unique hats. (Courtesy of Jack Coll.)

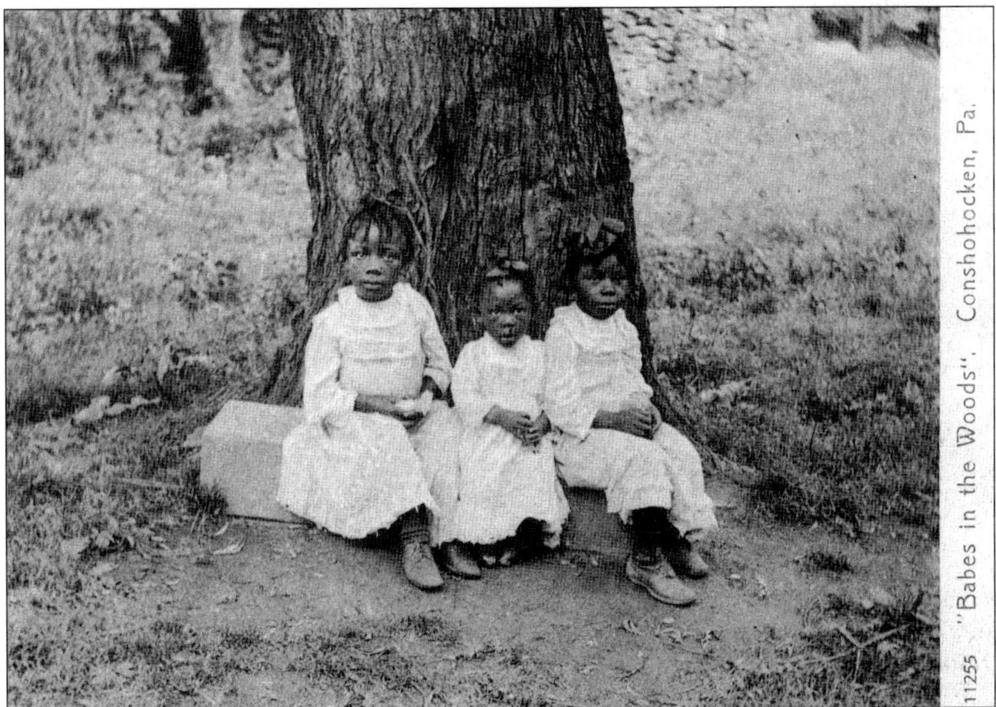

This postcard is titled "Babes in the Woods." The unique 1906 view was taken at Bubbling Springs, probably during a church outing or picnic. These three little girls are on their best behavior while sitting for a picture beneath the towering oak.

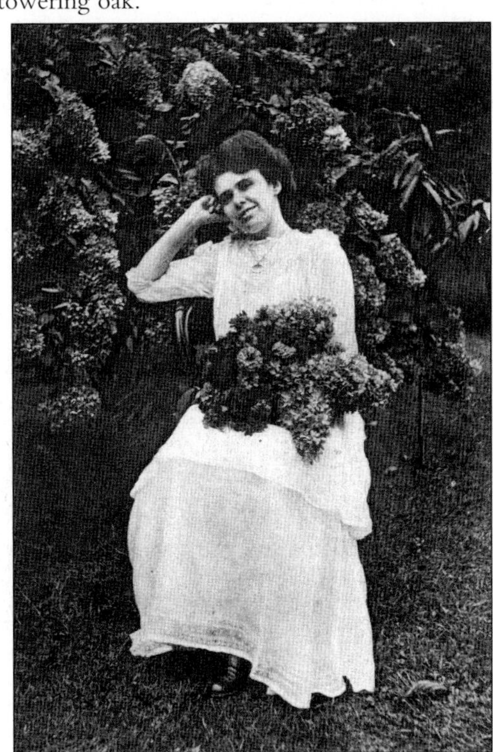

This precious photograph of a young lady being honored with a lovely bouquet of flowers depicts the crowning of a 1920s Miss Conshohocken. In the early 20th century, it was traditional to elect parade queens, playground queens, and homecoming queens.

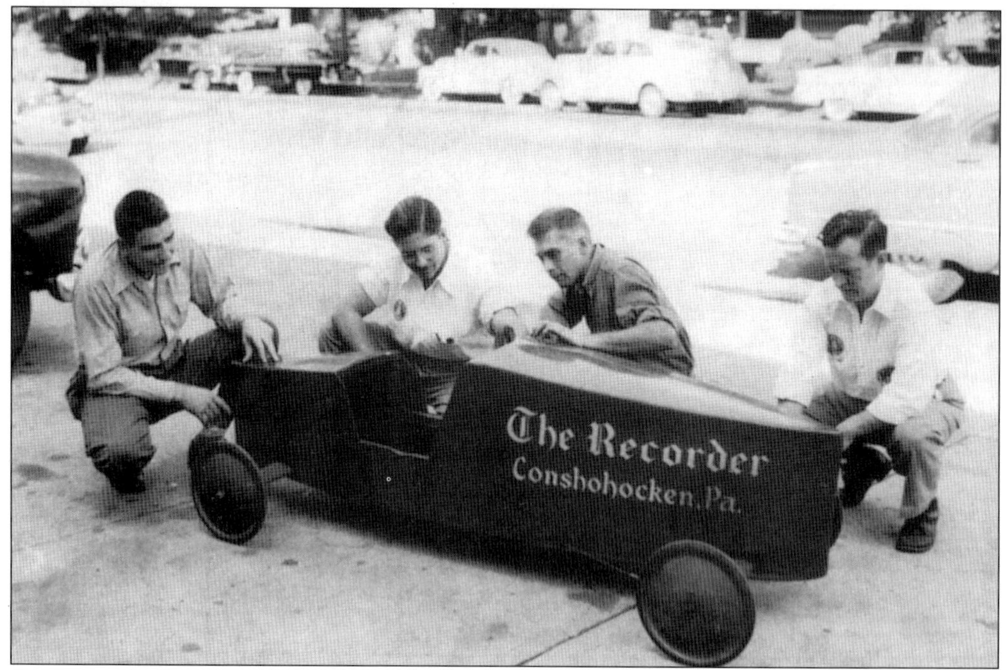

The soapbox derby has kicked off the Independence Day celebration in Conshohocken since 1938. Originally, the race was held along Spring Mill Avenue but was later moved to Fayette Street. Thousands of spectators line the street every year to watch the racers compete. Conshohocken is sanctioned with the national derby in Akron, Ohio.

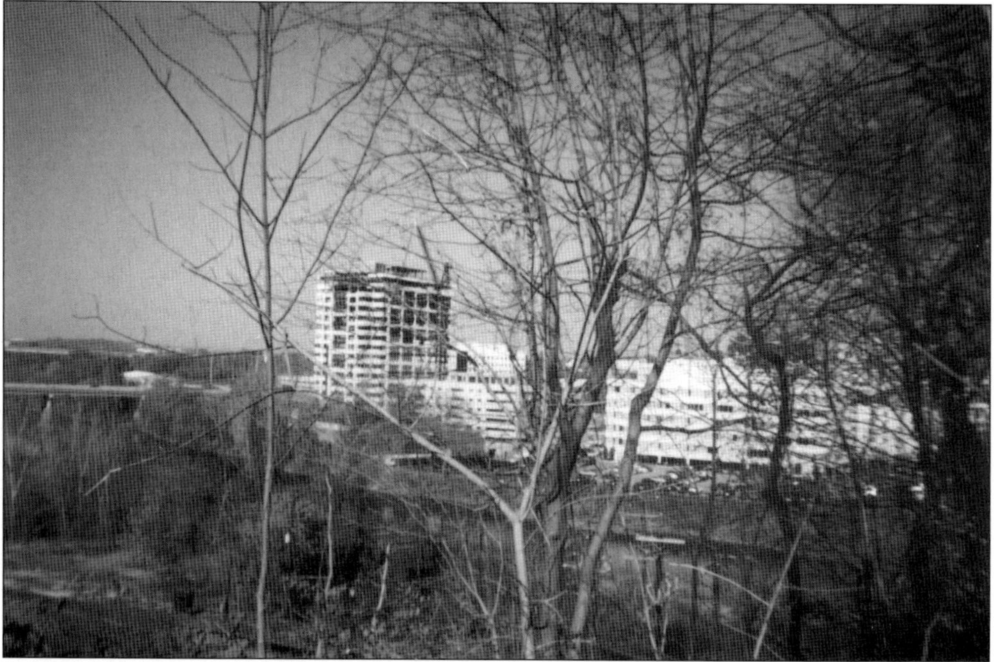

The face of Conshohocken has changed dramatically within the last quarter century. Where once stood the large industrial center and rolling mills now stand high-rise professional buildings and hotels. Development along the riverfront is occurring rapidly.